Praise for

COLLISION

"Rock-solid...Abbott keeps the action zipping along as the body count mounts, and Ben becomes far wiser and far tougher as he learns the harsh realities of kill or be killed."

—*Publishers Weekly*

"COLLISION is the best evidence yet that Jeff Abbott is one of the finest thriller writers working today. Electric with action and lightning-paced, I literally could not put it down. Don't miss it." —Harlan Coben

"COLLISION is a powerhouse tale of good bad guys, bad good guys, and every shade in between. Jeff Abbott delivers a frenzy of action in this race-against-the-clock thriller about an ordinary guy arrested for murder whose only hope lies in trusting the very man who framed him." —Lisa Gardner

"Riveting...the action never lets up...The twists are shocking, and the characters are all too real."

—*Library Journal* (starred review)

Acclaim for Jeff Abbott's Sam Capra Thrillers

THE LAST MINUTE

"An explosive cocktail." —*Washington Post*

"[An] adrenaline rush that won't stop."

—*San Antonio Express–News*

"Deliciously crafty...heart-pounding thrills...a stunner...*Adrenaline* has all the hallmarks of a career-changer. It should launch him into the Michael Connelly or Dennis Lehane stratosphere...Abbott sets a merciless pace, but he never lets speed hinder his writing...glorious sensory acumen...with just the right amount of snarky wit."

—*Dallas Morning News*

"Extremely compelling...a thriller that will get even the most jaded reader's pulse racing...a grand slam home run...*Adrenaline* rivets the reader from the very first paragraph, and Capra proves to be a character with enough skills and depth to be extremely compelling...Everyone will want to see what Abbott, and Capra, have up their sleeve next."   —Associated Press

"Thrilling."   —*New York Daily News*

"Exhilarating...Confirms Abbott as one of the best thriller writers of our time...This is a book that's getting a tremendous amount of buzz; everyone's talking about it. I think Jeff Abbott's the next Robert Ludlum. And I think Sam Capra is the heir apparent to Jason Bourne...The most gripping spy story I've read in years...It just grabs you. Great read!"   —Harlan Coben

"Exhilarating...keeps the intensity at a peak level...*Adrenaline* proves worthy of its title."   —*Columbus Dispatch*

"[A] complex, mind-bending plot...If Sam improves on his parkour skills, the future thrillers will spill over with nonstop action, just as *Adrenaline* does."

—*San Antonio Express-News*

"This is a wonderful book and the start of one of the most exciting new series I've had the privilege to read...Sam Capra is now on my short list of characters I would follow anywhere. *Adrenaline* provides the high-octane pace one expects from a spy thriller, while grounding the action with a protagonist that anyone can root for."　　—Laura Lippman

"This one hooked me and didn't let go...Abbott does a great job with pacing and switching perspectives."
　　　　　　　　　　　　　　　—*Seattle Post-Intelligencer*

"*Adrenaline* lives up to its name. It's pure thriller in pace, but Abbott manages to keep the book's heart anchored in the right place. The characters aren't cardboard action figures, but people under incredible stresses and strains. I read it in a big gulp."　　　　　—Charlaine Harris

"A white-knuckle opening leads into undoubtedly the best thriller I've read so far this year...*Adrenaline* will surely vault Abbott to the top of must-read authors. The relentless action will hook you from the heart-stopping opening to a conclusion that was as shocking as it was heart-rending."
　　　　　　　　　　　　　　　—*Ventura County Star* (CA)

"Nail-biting."　　　　　　　　　　—*Austin Chronicle*

"*Adrenaline*, like its namesake hormone, is all about pace, and a high-speed pace at that. A word of caution: Don't start reading [it] just before bedtime!"　　　—*BookPage*

"Engaging from the first paragraph, terrifying from the second page, *Adrenaline* accomplishes what most modern thrillers can't. It makes us care about its characters even while we're speeding headlong down the ingenious rabbit hole of its plot. Well done!"　　　—Eric Van Lustbader

COLLISION

JEFF ABBOTT

GCP

GRAND CENTRAL
PUBLISHING

NEW YORK   BOSTON

Copyright © 2008 by Jeff Abbott

All rights reserved. In accordance with the U.S. Copyright Act of 1976, the scanning, uploading, and electronic sharing of any part of this book without the permission of the publisher is unlawful piracy and theft of the author's intellectual property. If you would like to use material from the book (other than for review purposes), prior written permission must be obtained by contacting the publisher at permissions@hbgusa.com. Thank you for your support of the author's rights.

Grand Central Publishing
Hachette Book Group
237 Park Avenue
New York, NY 10017

www.HachetteBookGroup.com

Printed in the United States of America

OPM

Originally published simultaneously in the US by Dutton and in the UK by Sphere in 2008.

First Grand Central Publishing Edition: June 2013

10 9 8 7 6 5 4 3 2 1

Grand Central Publishing is a division of Hachette Book Group, Inc. The Grand Central Publishing name and logo is a trademark of Hachette Book Group, Inc.

The Hachette Speakers Bureau provides a wide range of authors for speaking events. To find out more, go to www.hachettespeakersbureau.com or call (866) 376-6591.

The publisher is not responsible for websites (or their content) that are not owned by the publisher.

For Bill and Mildred Groth,
My uncle and aunt,
thanks for a million laughs

*Men die because they cannot join
the beginning to the end.*
—ALCMAEON

TWO YEARS AGO

END OF THE HONEYMOON," Emily said. "You tired of me yet?"

"Absolutely." Ben Forsberg watched her standing at the sink at the rental house's kitchen, smiled as the light from the Maui sun played across her face. "I've already called several divorce lawyers. Probably be best if we didn't sit together on the flight home."

"And I thought it was just me." She gave him a glance over her shoulder, bit at her lip, fought down the grin. "This marriage was a huge mistake."

"I'm consumed with regret."

She flicked water at him and came to the kitchen table where he sat. She slid into his lap and he took her in his arms. He gave her a long, slow, unhurried kiss. She kissed him back, ran her foot along his calf, and then stood.

"I was kidding," he said.

"I know, Einstein. Go shower. You smell like golf."

"What does golf smell like?"

"Sweat, grass, sunshine, and frustration. Usually in that order."

"What's the smell of frustration?" he asked, starting to laugh.

"You'll soon know," Emily said, "if you don't go shower. You'll be one highly frustrated new husband." She gave him a small, chaste kiss and a light pat on his rump as he stood.

"I love it when you threaten me," Ben said, kissing her again.

"Not a threat, sweetie, go get cleaned up. It's my turn to fix us lunch. Then we'll have dessert before we have to go to the airport." She touched his lips with her finger and smiled.

"I don't want to go home," he said. "I'm not ready for you to turn back into the Queen of Spreadsheets."

"Or you to be the King of Contracts," she said. "We could just stay here and never go back to work."

"Be poor and homeless in Maui. Brilliant idea." He leaned back from her. "Work is overrated."

"Except for bringing us together. Speaking of which, I need to call Sam before we leave for the airport."

"Remember? No work calls. I've kept my side of the deal."

"Yes, well, I'll keep my marriage vows to you but everything else is negotiable. Go shower." She kissed his finger with its new band of gold. "I like you in nothing but your wedding ring."

He headed for the shower, glancing back at her as she finished washing her hands. His wife. He smiled big but he turned his head so she wouldn't see his grin. She'd think he was being silly.

He showered fast, trying not to think of the real world that awaited back in Dallas. He toweled off, hearing her wrap up a conversation with their boss, laughter in her tone. He heard her hang up, then water jet into the kitchen sink. He slipped on his simple gold wedding ring, its slight weight welcome on his finger, and pulled the towel around his waist. She'd mentioned dessert with a twinkle in her eye. Maybe they'd have a treat before lunch, make love in the kitchen, the sort of crazy out-of-bounds thing two normally proper workaholics did in their honeymoon's last hours.

He smoothed his hair flat in the mirror. He heard the glass shatter, a loud tinkle. "Babe?" He remembered her toes tickling his calf when they kissed. If she'd dropped a glass, she'd be risking those bare feet. "Babe? You drop something?" He slid his feet into his sandals.

Ben hurried into the kitchen. Emily lay sprawled on the tiles, as though a hand had slammed through the window and shoved her to the floor, leaving a wet, red, huge fingerprint on her forehead.

"Emily." Ben knelt by her, his voice soft as prayer. Calm, not screaming, because this couldn't be. They had to make love, eat lunch, get to the airport. "Emily. Please. Wake up—"

1

NICKY LYNCH LAY LOW on the building's roof, steadying the sniper's rifle, watching the two targets arguing out the last moments of their lives. He stared through the crosshairs, waiting for the shot when he could take both the geek and the big guy in rapid fire. Rush jobs made him nervous; he hadn't had enough time to prepare. His body was still on Belfast time, six hours ahead of Austin, Texas. He blinked. *Stay focused,* he told himself.

"You going to shoot today?" Jackie's voice whispered into his earpiece. His brother waited in the lobby of the office building across the street, anxious for Nicky to work his double-shot magic so Jackie could go inside Adam Reynolds's office and finish the job.

"Radio silence," Nicky said into his mouthpiece.

"Any day now." Jackie's impatient sigh made an electronic crackle in Nicky's ear.

"Silence," Nicky repeated into his microphone, keeping his annoyance in check. Killing took only a second, but precautions, so that the job went cleanly, took time. Jackie was too restless; he had the impatience of a fever.

Nicky put his mind back to the kills. The angle into the office where the two men argued wasn't ideal, but the client had been quite specific in how he wanted the job done. The big guy, standing near the window, wasn't quite close enough… and Nicky had to complete the hit with the first shot. Jackie would be in the office less than a minute after the two men were dead, and he did not want either man breathing when his brother stepped inside to plant the goods. Especially the big guy. Nicky didn't want Jackie within ten meters of that man.

If the two would just stop moving. The honking, stop-and-start traffic of downtown Austin jerked on the street nine stories below him. A distant rumble touched the sky; a spring storm deciding whether to grant a cooling rain. He tuned out the noise, because the prime chance for the kill shot might come at any second. The office was large, its narrow windows divided by white limestone. He was at the same height as the targets, but he had to hide close to a roof air-conditioning unit and the angle was awkward.

He frowned. Best if the two stood in the same slender window frame, close together, but the pair stood off from each other like wary lions. The geek wore a scared frown, as though he were shoving aside all the numbers and facts in his oversized brain and searching for unused courage. The geek should be scared, Nicky thought. He had read the notes about the big guy with a mix of admiration and shock. It wasn't every day you got to kill such an interesting man. Nicky had killed thirty-six people but none so…accomplished. He almost wished he could have bought the big guy a pint, chatted with him, learned from him, soaked in his exploits. But the very best ones, he thought, always kept their secrets.

Now the big guy laughed—Nicky wondered what was so funny—and he moved halfway into one window's frame. But not far enough for a certain shot.

And then the geek pulled a gun from his desk and aimed

it at the big guy. Nicky held his breath. Maybe they'd do his job for him, kill each other, and he could just watch.

"Stay back," Adam Reynolds said. The gun made for an unfamiliar weight in his hand—he had purchased it only three days before, a necessary precaution. He had spent five hours on the Internet researching the right pistol. But he hadn't spent nearly enough time practicing how to shoot. Adam's lungs tightened with fear, his back prickled with heat, his tongue seemed coated with sand.

This was what happened when you went hunting for dangerous people. Sometimes they found you instead. Just keep him at bay, Adam thought. Help was on its way.

The gun did not seem to make the big man standing near the window nervous. "Give me that before you shoot off a toe or finger or something even more valuable, Adam."

"No," Adam said. He flicked the man's business card off his desk and tossed a bound proposal at the man's feet. "Take back your stage props. You're nothing but a con man."

The big man shrugged. "So I lied to you. You're a liar, too. Let's stop lying."

"You first. What's your real name?"

The big man laughed. "I'm nobody."

"No, the problem is you're too many different people, mister." Adam straightened the gun, steadied his grip. "You've got more names than a cat's got fleas. I found them all. Every alias you've used in the past few months. I want to know who you really are."

The big man's gaze narrowed. He took a step away from the window, a step toward Adam. He kept his hands at his side. "Deal, Adam. I'll tell you who I really am and who I work for, if you tell me who hired you to hunt me down."

"I have the gun, so I will ask the questions and you will answer them."

"Yes, Adam, you do indeed have the gun," the big man said, as though that fact didn't really matter to him.

Adam swallowed. "What's your real name?"

"My name's unimportant. What matters is why you're searching for me, who paid you to look for me. That's the only reason I arrived on your doorstep, Adam, because you were looking for me." He crossed his arms. "Did it occur to you that maybe I'm one of the good guys?"

"I...I know what you are." Adam's voice broke. "You're a terrorist. Or you're connected to a terror group."

"You could not be more mistaken," the big man said. He laughed. "You're kind of book smart and street dumb all at once, aren't you?"

Adam shook his head. Put both hands on the pistol's grip to fix his aim.

"Adam, this is why you're in trouble. You had to break a number of laws to find me and all my aliases: banking laws, privacy laws, federal statutes protecting classified material. All that data you used to find me scattered among databases where you have no clearance or access. Someone gave you that access. Tell me who, and I promise you'll be safe and protected."

"Sit on the floor, put your hands on your head," Adam said. "I've already called a friend of mine in Homeland Security. They're on their way here, so if you hurt me—"

"Hurt you?" The big man frowned. "Doubtful. You have the gun." He took a step forward. "Brilliant computer programmers don't just suddenly start finding people who never want to be found. Who do you work for?"

"I'll shoot. Please. Stop." Adam didn't sound convincing, even to himself. "Please."

The big man risked another step toward Adam. "You're way too nice a guy to shoot me, and I'm not going to hurt you. So give me the gun, genius, and let's talk."

Nicky watched through the crosshairs. The big guy was moving forward, slowly, and the geek was suffering the tortures of the weak, not wanting to shoot a fellow human being. Then a thought occurred to Nicky: What if the geek did shoot the big guy? *Will I get paid if I don't shoot them and one kills the other?*

The thought panicked him. He glued his eye to the scope. Take the shot, leave no wiggle room for the client to argue the fee or debate whether or not services were rendered. He needed the money.

The big guy came forward, moving toward the geek, calm. The geek lowered the gun a fraction of an inch.

Both men in the same window now. The big man reaching for the wobbling gun. *Don't wait.*

In two seconds, Nicky Lynch calculated the ramifications of the choppy wind gusting hard from the bend of Lady Bird Lake that hugged Austin's downtown, did the math for the deflection of the glass, touched his tongue to the roof of his mouth, and fired.

The big guy dropped. Nicky pivoted the barrel a fraction, fired, saw the geek jerk and fall. Stillness in the room, twin holes in the window. He watched for ten seconds, then pulled back from the lip of the office building's roof. Below him people hurried on their late afternoon errands, unaware of death in their midst: suited men and women walking toward the Texas state capitol, most with cell phones grafted to their ears; a street musician braying a Bob Dylan song, strumming a guitar in front of a case dotted with spare change; a huddle of workers awaiting a bus. No one looked up at the muffled sounds of the shots.

It had gone all right, for two such difficult shots. He ducked behind the air-conditioning unit, wiped his hands on the maintenance uniform he wore. He dismantled the rifle with practiced grace. He tucked the rifle's parts into a duffel bag and headed for the roof stairs. "You're clear," he said into the mouthpiece to Jackie.

"Heading in," Jackie said. "Going silent."

"Silent." Nicky signed off. Jackie tended to chatter, and Nicky didn't want him distracted.

A boom of thunder crackled, the waiting storm starting to rise, the breeze electric with the sudden shift.

Bizarre requirements, Nicky thought, but the client specifically wanted the job done this way: murder the targets from a safe distance and then leave a manila envelope on the geek's desk. The money was caviar-and-champagne good, enough to keep him in liquor and books for a stretch of several months in St. Bart's. He needed a vacation. Jackie would use his share of the money for hunting down rare Johnny Cash vinyl recordings and spend time scribbling more bad songs. Jackie and his music. Waste of time. Maybe Nicky'd talk his brother out of frittering away his cash, get him to come drink in the Caribbean sun. You wanted warmth after you killed, Nicky thought as he reached the street.

In his earpiece, Jackie got the all-clear from Nicky and summoned the elevator. A crowd of pinstriped lawyers walked in from the street, pooling around him, chatting, waiting for the elevator doors to open.

He didn't want to be remembered, so he let the lawyers crowd the first elevator that came. He thumbed the Up button again and waited an extra ninety seconds for an empty elevator. He rose to the top floor alone. The hallway was empty. No one had heard the silenced shots—no one, at least, had emerged from the neighboring offices in panic to crowd the hallways. Good—no one would remember his face as he completed his errand. This assignment, although a rush job, was big; the targets were important. *Do it right,* he thought, *and you'll shut up Nicky's carping.*

Jackie approached the suite; the sign read Reynolds Data Consulting. The office door was locked, and he opened it with a lockpick in under ten seconds. He pulled his steel blade free from his coat, just in case either man was spasming out the last of his life. But he wasn't going to stab unless necessary. Not even for fun. A knife wound would confuse the police.

He stepped inside and closed the door behind him. The office was silent. Jackie put the large envelope under his arm. The geek lay in sprawled surprise beside the desk, blood spreading from his head, mouth slack, eyes finally vacant of brainstorms.

Orders were to leave the sealed envelope on the desk. But first Jackie stepped around the desk to take a peek at the big guy.

Across the street, Nicky Lynch shouldered past a crowd of techies spilling out from the parking garage ramp, heading for early drinks in the Warehouse District. He walked up the ramp and took a left. He pressed the remote for his Mercedes, beeped open the trunk. He put the rifle case inside and slammed the trunk closed. As he slid behind the wheel and started the engine his earpiece crackled, Jackie yelling, not making sense. "He's gone!"

Nicky glanced into the rearview just in time to see the big guy running up behind the car, drawing a gun from underneath a jacket. For a half second, shock seized him. Then he ducked for the loaded Glock he kept under the seat and closed his fingers around it. The driver's window exploded; agony lanced his shoulder.

This was not happening. Impossible. The shot had been true...

"Who sent you?" the big guy asked.

Nicky's mouth worked; his arm didn't. He fumbled for the gun with his good hand.

"Last chance. Answer me," the big guy said.

Nicky lifted the gun with an angry grunt. The answering barrage sprayed his life's blood across the dashboard and the front windshield.

Jackie, run, Nicky thought, staring at the red mist, then died.

The big guy stood at the shattered window and fired four neat, tidy shots for insurance into Nicky Lynch's chest and head. Adam Reynolds's gun went warm in his hand.

"Always make sure, mister," the big guy said. He swallowed the bile in his throat. Today had gone all wrong. Time to walk away from the whole mess. Wrap up the package for the cops.

Let the police chase a nobody. He took a business card from his pocket and tucked it into Nicky Lynch's bloodied jacket. He wouldn't need it anymore. He hurried away from the car, hiding his gun under his light jacket, taking the staircase. Someone would spot the bullet-riddled car within minutes.

He walked out onto the sidewalk as a light, gentle rain began to drop from the marble-gray sky.

One street over, Jackie ran in a panicked pell-mell from the building, sprinted hard toward the garage, dodging traffic and old-lady shoppers and coffee-swilling lobbyists. Cars slammed on brakes, honks jeered him as he sprinted into the street. He slipped his knife into his jacket pocket, his hand closing hard around the Glock under his windbreaker, scanning the faces behind him, scared. He kept the folder of photographs clutched under his arm. He heard a woman shriek as he hurried up the ramp. He braked on his heels and peered around the concrete pillar. A woman and two men huddled around the Mercedes, a smear of red on the windshield. One of the men was on his cell phone, calling 911. The woman had her hand clamped over her mouth as though repressing a scream.

Jackie stepped close enough to see there was nothing he could do.

Nicky was dead.

Jackie's throat closed on itself. He remembered to breathe. He turned away, stumbled down the ramp. The police would be here within moments. He fought every urge to go to his brother and fold him into his arms, swallowed the need to drop to his knees and cry.

The big guy wasn't dead.

But, Jackie thought with a hot rage in his heart and tears crowding his eyes, he soon would be.

2

WE'RE IN DEEP TROUBLE," Sam Hector said. "Ten-million-dollar contract choked this morning."

"I'm sorry, Sam," Ben Forsberg said into his cell phone.

"It's a deal with the UK government to provide additional security for their embassies in four east African countries," Hector said. "I can't lose another big contract, Ben. I've sent you the details and I want you to go through the information tonight. All vacations must end."

"Sure." Ben was close to home, the top up on his BMW, because as he approached Austin the spring sky clouded with rain. He wished that Sam hadn't called it a *vacation*. Ben no longer took vacations; he had alone time, away time. He'd been away for only six days. "I'm ready to go back to work."

"Good, because the deals are drying up," Hector said. "I wish you would come back to work for me full-time. I need you."

"How's the negotiation with the State Department coming?" Ben wasn't interested in rehashing that conversation; he liked working freelance now and living in Austin. The Dallas office reminded him too much of Emily.

"Another precarious situation. We're in disagreement on

five or six points. Undersecretary Smith is being intractable on the level of training that our security personnel have to have for the next Congo assignment, while not wanting to pay a commensurate price. Which is ridiculous. Congo is amazingly dangerous right now. They need us and she's being obstinate, thinking she can handle it with regular government personnel."

"I'll talk to her." Ben didn't expect the negotiations to be prolonged; the security situation in Congo was deteriorating, terrorism on the rise; the State Department personnel stationed there needed a greater level of protection, and a contract with the professional soldiers of Hector Global was the cheap and fast answer. Hector Global did several million dollars' worth of business with the State Department each year, providing armed security for its employees; a new rising conflict in Congo was a tragedy, but an opportunity as well. Someone had to protect the diplomats, and no one could do a better job than Hector Global. "If the situation there deteriorates, it might help us close the deal—she'll get scared."

"I like scared people, because we're in the business of making fear go away," Hector said.

"You still want to use that as a motto," Ben laughed. "Fear is not a good slogan."

"Whatever. I also suspect she's stalling so she can get you back up to Washington again."

Ben moved into another lane, headed north on MoPac, the major north-south artery for west Austin. He exited into the suburb of West Lake Hills so that he could take back roads home to central Austin; the infamously slow Austin traffic had already begun its daily dragging shuffle.

"Ben? Did you hear me?"

"Sam. Don't kid, you know I'm not ready for—"

"You cannot live in this bubble you've created for yourself." Now Sam Hector sounded less like a client and more like a chiding father. "You just spent five days alone, Ben, at a resort known for catering to people twice your age. Emily would not want you isolating yourself."

Ben said nothing. He had found it best to endure this kind of advice in polite silence.

"Ms. Smith has asked me about your interests, how often you come to Washington, what food you like to eat. As soon as our negotiations are done, I suspect she'll ask you out the next time you're in D.C."

"Does she know I'm a widower?"

"I told her. But not every detail. That's up to you."

"E-mail me Smith's concerns on the contract and I'll craft our response."

Sam Hector was silent for a moment on the other end of the line. "Forgive me. I'm only trying to be helpful. We all worry about you..."

"Sam, I'm really fine. And I'll talk to you tomorrow morning."

"Take care, Ben." Sam clicked off the phone.

No woman had asked him out in the two years since Emily died, and he had no plans to ask out any woman. He tried to imagine how he'd react to an invitation. He had nothing to give, nothing to share, nothing to say. A slight cold terror touched his skin. He lowered the car's window, let fresh air wash over his face as he turned off the highway toward home. He clicked on the radio: "A bizarre shooting in downtown Austin today left two dead..." the announcer said, and Ben switched off the radio. He did not like to hear about shootings. Two years after his wife's death, the very word twisted a knife in his spine, brought back the horrible memory of Emily sprawled dead on the kitchen floor, a bullet hole marring her forehead.

Random, pointless, for no reason, some unknown idiot firing rounds at empty houses. He eased his grip on the steering wheel, tried not to remember.

Ben lived in Tarrytown, an older and expensive neighborhood on the west side of Austin. His house was small by the neighborhood's increasingly grandiose standards—Tarrytown had been invaded by megamansions, towering over the original houses on the cramped lots—but the limestone bungalow suited him. He pulled into his garage just as the simmering storm broke into soft rain. His flower beds needed springtime tending and the yard could use a mowing.

Ben went inside his house and set his duffel bag on the kitchen floor. He grabbed a soda from the refrigerator and headed back into his office. He cracked open the laptop and downloaded five days' worth of e-mail. Most of his clients knew he was gone this week, so there was less than normal. He saw an encrypted note containing the specifics of Sam's hot UK deal. He frowned at a couple of messages: a request from a business magazine reporter to respond to allegations of security contractor malfeasance involving a company he'd never worked with; three e-mails from people he didn't know, protesting the use of private security forces in Iraq and Afghanistan; and e-mails from six people with military and security backgrounds, looking for work with Hector, asking him for advice and help.

Where there were millions at stake, and guns involved, controversy always loomed. He understood people's concerns about private contractors being used in war, but the reality was that the government was offering big-dollar contracts, and people of both dubious and high integrity went after them. Hector Global was one of three hundred private companies offering security and training services in Iraq alone. Ben was careful to work only with the contractors with good records and highly professional staffs. Many of them, other than his biggest client, were new, staffed by former soldiers and unused to navigating government deals. His guidance made it easier for them to win favorable terms.

There were well over a hundred thousand private security contractors on the ground in Iraq, training security forces and police, protecting facilities and dignitaries. The money was excellent. Ben had helped Sam Hector grow his company into a three-thousand-employee behemoth in the security world, with thousands more independent contractors on call, to provide everything from security to computer expertise to food services.

A soft red 6 glowed on his answering machine's readout. He decided to deal with the rest of the real world after he took a shower. Technically, he was still on his alone time, he told himself.

Ben showered and rubbed a towel hard across his skin. The mirror showed a bit of early spring sunburn on his nose and cheeks from his lake walks; he was of Swedish descent, and the sun wasn't always gentle on his pale, slightly freckled skin. He smoothed out his thick thatch of blond hair with a comb of his fingers, brushed his teeth, and decided not to shave over the sunburn. He dressed in jeans, tennis shoes, and a long-sleeved polo shirt. He reached for the soda he'd left on the counter and then the doorbell rang, a low, long, almost mournful chime.

Two people stood on his bricked porch. Ben had been around enough government agents in his work to recognize them as such—the stance, the careful neutral expressions. One was a petite, dark-haired woman in her early thirties, wearing an expensive, tailored gray suit. She had brown eyes and a mouth set in a frown, and when Ben opened the door, her gaze was so fierce that he nearly took a step backward. The man next to her was thin and silver-haired, expressionless.

Behind them, Ben saw a car, with two thick-necked men in suits and sunglasses standing at attention near the passenger door.

"Mr. Forsberg?" the man said.

"Yes."

Both showed photo IDs. Department of Homeland Security, Office of Strategic Initiatives. It wasn't a division at Homeland Ben recognized from his consulting work, like FEMA or the Secret Service. "I'm Agent Norman Kidwell. This is Agent Joanna Vochek. We'd like to speak with you."

Ben blinked at the badges. Kidwell was in his forties, with a hardscrabble face that was alien territory for a smile, dark eyes that gave a glance more calculated than kind, a suggestion of granite under the skin of his jaw.

"Okay. About what?" Ben asked.

"It would be better if we could talk inside, sir," Kidwell said.

"Uh, sure." He wondered if one of his clients had messed up, gotten cute with a contract with Homeland. But they couldn't just call him? He opened the door wider. The two agents stepped inside.

"How can I help you?" Ben shut the door.

"Let's sit down," Kidwell said.

"Sure." He went into the kitchen and they followed him, Vochek staying very close to him. He noticed her glance surveying the room, as if mapping every exit. "Would you like a soda or water?"

"No," Kidwell said.

"Heading on a trip, Mr. Forsberg?" Vochek pointed at his duffel bag.

"No, I've just gotten home." He sat at the kitchen table. Kidwell sat across from him. Vochek stayed standing, planting herself between him and the back door.

"Where have you been?" she asked.

"Marble Falls." It was a small town an hour west of Austin. "My parents' condo."

"Were your parents with you?" Kidwell asked.

"No. They've both passed away."

"Were you alone?" She crossed her arms.

"Yes. Are you going to tell me what this is about?"

Kidwell opened a notebook and rattled off Ben's full name, his birth date, his Social Security number, address, and home phone. "All correct?"

Ben nodded.

"You have an office phone?"

"I work out of my home; my cell serves as my office number."

Kidwell kept his gaze unwavering, as if a thread connected his eyes to Ben's. "Do you have any other cell phone accounts?"

"No." He suspected he was about to be dragged into a bureaucratic mud hole; clearly a client had screwed up in a contract with Homeland and he was going to have to endure endless protocol before these two got to the point.

"You advise government contractors," Kidwell said.

Ben nodded and tried a cautious smile. "Is one of my clients in trouble?"

"No. You are." Kidwell tucked his chin into the V of his hand, between thumb and forefinger.

"Because?"

Vochek leaned against the wall. "Do you have a client named Adam Reynolds?"

"No."

"Do you know him?" Vochek asked.

Her insistence on the word *know* made him more cautious. "If I've met Mr. Reynolds, I don't recall it."

"He designs software for the government. A one-man shop, but highly effective," Vochek said. "He's a very smart guy."

"Then I'm sorry I don't know him." Sweat broke out along Ben's legs, on his back, in the cups of his palms. He tried another awkward smile. "Listen, I sincerely want to help you, but unless you tell me why I'm in trouble, I'm phoning my lawyer."

Kidwell pulled a photo from his jacket pocket and slid it across the table to Ben. "Do you recognize this man, Mr. Forsberg?"

Ben guessed the photo had been taken at a distance and then computer-enhanced, colors sharpened, details made clear. It showed a man, short and stocky, glancing over his shoulder as he walked down a busy street. He wore a hat pulled low on his head, its brim dripping rain. He was adjusting his collar against the wet and the wind, and his fingers were surprisingly delicate and long.

Ben pulled the picture close again, inspected the man's face, racked his memories. "I don't recognize him, I'm sorry."

Kidwell said, "Nicky Lynch."

"I don't know him."

Kidwell scratched his lip. "He looks meek. He's not. His father was a torturer and gunman for the IRA before he died, and Nicky took over the business. When Northern Ireland got boring after the disarmament, Nicky went for hire. He's one of the most feared freelance assassins in the world. We believe he's done all sorts of nasty work for hire: training al-Qaeda snipers in Syria, eliminating political resistance leaders in Tajikistan and Pakistan, killing judges and witnesses in Mexico and Colombia for drug cartels."

"Now I definitely don't know him," Ben said.

"Are you sure?" Vochek asked with a doubtful tone.

"Yes, I'm sure. What is this?"

"This afternoon we believe Nicky Lynch killed Adam Reynolds, here in Austin. Mr. Reynolds had called me in Houston at noon, asked me to come immediately to Austin, on a matter of national security," Kidwell said.

Ben looked up from the unassuming face of the killer in the photo and shook his head. "What does this guy have to do with me—"

"You tell us, Mr. Forsberg," Vochek interrupted. Now she leaned forward, put her hands on the table, her face close to his. "Because Nicky Lynch was shot to death and your business card was in his pocket."

3

Your business card was in his pocket. The sudden hush in the room took on a weight.

"Explain why Nicky Lynch had your business card, Mr. Forsberg," Kidwell said.

Ben found his voice. His lungs felt filled with lead. "It has to be a mistake..."

"I can think of two possibilities. One, you are associated with Lynch. Two, you are being targeted by him." Vochek shrugged. "Which is it?"

"This is a sick joke, right? Please, because it is seriously not funny."

"Not a joke," Kidwell said. "We believe Lynch shot Reynolds through his office window with a high-powered sniper rifle from across Colorado Street."

Through a window. Sniper rifle. Emily lying on a floor. The words, the memory, made the world swim before his eyes. He squinched his eyes shut, took a deep breath. "No...this has nothing to do with me..."

"We found a proposal with your letterhead on the floor of Reynolds's office," Vochek said. "Help yourself, Ben. Cooperate with us."

"But I didn't know him." Ben sank back to the chair.

"Give me your phone," Kidwell said. Ben slid the smart-phone to him and Kidwell handed it to Vochek. "Find out his recent calls." She started clicking through the menus.

Ben rubbed at his forehead with his fingertips. A slow burn of anger lit in his chest, piercing the haze of shock. "If I don't know him, then your second option...is some-one wants me dead. There's just no reason." He suddenly wanted Kidwell to nod, to agree, but the poker face stayed in place.

"Do you have any enemies?" Kidwell asked.

"*Enemies?* No." It was the kind of grab-your-guts ques-tion the police asked him after Emily died, and when he looked up at their faces he saw the familiar stain: suspi-cion. The same poisonous frowns the police in Maui and later Dallas had worn while talking to him after Emily's murder. Suspicion had already doused his life once with acid. Not again. *Not again.* "Who killed Lynch?"

"We don't have a suspect." Vochek glanced up from studying the list of recent calls on Ben's phone. She held his gaze with her own piercing stare, then went back to study-ing his call log.

I'm the suspect, he realized.

Kidwell slid another picture to Ben—a snapshot of Ben's business card. Blood smeared the edges. The listed busi-ness number wasn't his cell number, but his home number had been jotted in pencil.

He tapped a finger on the picture; hope rose in his chest. "That's not my business phone."

"According to the cellular company, you opened a cell phone account with that number last week," Vochek said.

Ben shook his head. "I sure didn't. What about this pro-posal you claim I wrote?"

"It outlined getting government contractors, including several of your clients, to finance Reynolds's ideas for new software products."

"I never wrote it." Ben shoved the photo back at Kidwell. "Anyone could copy my logo off my website. Forge a proposal to make it appear it came from me, print a fake business card."

"They could. But why?"

He had no answer, and as his shock morphed into anger, he decided to turn the questions back on them. "If this is an investigation, why aren't the Austin police or the FBI here to talk to me?"

Ben saw a glance he couldn't read pass between Vochek and Kidwell. "Due to the highly sensitive nature of this case and how it could impact on national security, we have jurisdiction over your questioning," Kidwell said.

"How exactly does this impact national security? I think I better—"

But Vochek cut him off. "This week you were scheduled on Adam Reynolds's Outlook calendar, three times. Explain."

Ben shook his head. "I told you, I was in Marble Falls."

"Just an hour away." Kidwell said. "You could drive back and forth with ease."

"Could have but I didn't."

"So Reynolds's calendar is complete fiction?"

"As far as me being scheduled, yes."

Silence for ten long seconds. "I'm going to give you a single chance to come clean, Mr. Forsberg. Do you know of any terrorist threat that Adam Reynolds uncovered?" Kidwell asked.

"No. None. I swear I don't."

"You see my problem." Kidwell stood. "Adam Reynolds did significant work for our government, and he was murdered today by a man with known terrorist ties. Your name is the only name tied to the killer and the only name that's all over Reynolds's office and calendar. Now, by our simple but effective geometry, that means you have a suspected terrorist tie."

Ben's breath stopped, as if a noose had closed around his throat. "You're wrong."

"I'd like to search your house."

Ben shook his head. "What Homeland office are you with—Strategic Initiatives?" He remembered the notation on their badges. "I never heard of your group, or any of these people you're trying to connect me with. I want my lawyer here, and I want you to get a warrant."

"Neither is necessary," Kidwell said.

Vochek knelt close to Ben's chair. "Cooperate with us, Ben, and I'll do everything I can to help you."

"The only help I want is from my lawyer." He stood and reached for the phone. Kidwell wrenched it from his hands, drew a gun, aimed it at Ben's forehead.

Ben stepped back, nearly stumbled over his chair. "Oh, please...are you crazy?" He raised his hands, palms high in surrender, suddenly afraid to move. This could not be happening to him.

"You're not calling anyone." Kidwell noticed the blinking answering machine and hit the Play key. Six messages. The first three were from various friends, inviting Ben to dinner and to a UT baseball game and to go to the movies this weekend; then there was a message from a telemarketer about a survey about the automotive market; a reminder from the library that Ben had an overdue book; and then the sixth message, spoken by the slightly nasal, tense voice of a stranger:

"Hi, Ben, it's Adam Reynolds. Just confirming our meeting at four this afternoon. I'll see you in my office. Call me at 555-3998 if you need to reschedule."

Silence in the room, just the beep and the computerized voice on the recorder saying, *End of messages.*

"Ben." Kidwell looked past his gun at Ben. "You're a deal maker. I strongly urge you to make a deal with us."

Panic hummed in Ben's skin. "I swear I'm telling you the truth. I don't know anything. I don't."

"Let's get him to the office, Agent Vochek. And get a computer forensics team from Houston to search every square inch of this house. I want it all—papers, computer files, phone records, everything he's touched."

Ben took a step back from the gun. "I'm not going anywhere with you."

Kidwell lowered the gun toward Ben's legs. "I'll shoot you in the kneecaps and we'll take you out on a stretcher." He gestured with the gun. "Your choice."

Ben stared at the gun and then slowly turned and followed Vochek to the front door.

Outside the two guards waited in the backseat of the government car. The wind and rain from the brief thunderstorm had passed; the wind gusted a cooling breath.

Ben got into the car. The guards sat on either side of him, Vochek driving, Kidwell in the passenger seat. As Vochek pulled the sedan away, Ben glanced back through the tinted windows as his lawn sprinklers surged to life and began to shroud his house in mist, like a vanishing memory.

One of the guards stuck a gun into his ribs. "Sit straight, eyes ahead, don't move."

This isn't right, Ben thought and through the shock a horrifying notion occurred to him: maybe these people weren't with Homeland Security after all.

KHALED'S REPORT— BEIRUT

NOTHING IS AS IT SEEMS. That idea is the deepest truth in this sorry world. And now I am about to live this truth, because my whole life is going to become a carefully constructed lie.

Why?

Because I write these words with my brothers' blood on my face.

Oh, I washed the stains off weeks ago. No remnant of their loss remains on my skin for anyone to see. But their blood is there. Always, an invisible mark on me.

The only cure is to avenge them.

My bosses want me to write my story as to why I have taken on this most dangerous work. I can assume that my words and my handwriting will be analyzed, to see if I'm worthy, to determine my loyalty, to do a psychological evaluation to see if I'm made of—to borrow an Americanism—the right stuff.

I am an unlikely candidate, I know, to become a fighter. I was the baby of the family, the one whom my brothers

Samir and Gebran always tried to protect, to shield from the bully, to walk home from school, to give advice so I didn't make a fool of myself. Which I am, confession time, prone to do. I do not think I am particularly smart or brave. I am angry.

My bosses should know exactly what they are getting in me. I studied chemistry for a while, then changed to business and finance. I like the cleanness of math; it is much less messy than life. I am too formal in social settings (and probably in my writing) but too easygoing with those that I love. I don't like loud people. I love old Westerns. I can be a fool but I am not foolish. I can be angry but I am not mad.

And now, I think I can kill and not weep.

Let me say this about my brothers: I do not blame them. They both always did what they felt was right in this world. Gebran was a music teacher, a talented guitar player. Samir worked at a bank, generous to a fault. They had no idea of the danger they were getting into, I suspect, but I am walking in, both eyes open, facing paradise.

Samir and Gebran were two and five years older than me, and they had a different set of friends. More political, more fiery. I was more concerned with video games and girls than defiance of Israel or Palestinian statehood or the Islamic struggle. No one in Beirut is surprised that I am supposedly moving to Europe for school, not after what happened to my family.

No one can ever know that I'm actually going to America to do my work.

So here is what happened: Samir and Gebran had, as I said, a different set of friends, far more firebrand than my lazy loafing clique.

I don't want to go when my brothers invite me to go

see a buddy of theirs named Husayn who lives near Rue Hamra—but my brothers are insistent and I have, sadly, nothing better to do.

On the car ride there from the southern suburbs in Beirut where we lived with our parents, Samir turns to me in the backseat and says, "Husayn works with a special group."

We are driving past buildings bombed out in the last fighting with Israel, mounds of rubble slowly being cleared so the buildings can rise again before they are bombed back down to their foundations. An endless cycle. Will it take twenty days or twenty years? It doesn't matter, it will happen again. The cycle never ends. "A special group," I say. I do not think my brother means the Special Olympics or volunteering with the elderly or any other helpful pastime.

"Yes, a group. Called Blood of Fire."

"Sounds like a charity," I say sarcastically.

Samir ignores the edge in my voice. "It has been dormant for several years. Husayn is bringing Blood of Fire and its ideas back to life. It is not a charity but it…does good work." Samir peers at me through his glasses, as though my reaction might be printed on my head, like a news feed.

Good work. I've heard that term used before, a justification for bombing and killings and terror. Fear worms through my guts. That sunny afternoon, I had no use for violence. None. What did it ever accomplish? The knife in the hand doesn't buy security when the other man has a bigger knife. Perhaps you get in one stab and then you're done…unless that stab pierces to the heart.

But I am a different boy in that backseat as we trundle toward fate, and I say, "So, what, Hezbollah not good enough for him?" Like I am making a joke.

Samir and Gebran don't laugh.

"Your friend is, what, a terrorist?" Try using those words together, *terrorist* and *friend* in the same sentence. Putting breath around those words feels like a pipe inching through your throat.

"Terrorist, no, it's the wrong word," Gebran says, in the patient voice he uses to teach guitar chords to ten-year-olds. He doesn't suggest an alternate term.

"You said you wanted to have peace in Lebanon," Samir says, watching me. "So do we. Peace across the Arab world."

Sweat lies cold against my ribs. I thought we were going to his friend's house for a casual dinner, nothing more. This is more. A whole new world of more, and I want no part of it.

I want to say, *Mama and Papa will kill you for buying into this,* which is true, but I don't. Maybe the trick is that I need to see this friend of my brothers. See how he's played them into joining his cause and then dismantle his approach with reason and a dose of brotherly guilt, convince them both it is a bad idea.

Strange, how a stray thought, a word unspoken, a whim followed, can change your world. If I'd told Gebran to pull over. If I'd told them, no, turn the car around, I want to go home. If I'd had a bit of courage to stand up to them immediately.

Husayn lives in a small apartment a couple of blocks away from Rue Hamra and its busy stores and crowds of tourists. The apartment reeks of onion and cinnamon and cigarette smoke but is well furnished. Books, in Arabic and French and English, crowd the shelves. Husayn looks like a man who practices his scowl in front of a mirror. He is thin like a weed, dark, with a soft, fleshy mouth. But in his eyes a flame stands, a fire that makes your bones twitch under your skin. I wonder if he is high or crazy.

Only eight or nine people are at the apartment; the only one I talk to for longer than five minutes is a young man with a scar marring the corner of his mouth; his lip looks twisted. He tells me his name is Khaled, same as mine. He seems nervous, also like me. Food and drinks, and I am introduced all around, the baby brother. Or am I the promising candidate? I nod and smile and shake hands and try to keep my hands steady.

They talk, but they do not start chatting of plots or bombs or retribution. They talk of politics—hatred for the Israelis, disdain for those who want peace with them, aggravation and fury with the West. They sound like old men, not young firebrands. The cigarette smoke thickens like a cloud because the windows are kept shut at Husayn's insistence. I notice, after twenty minutes, that I am the recipient of many sidelong glances.

This is a test.

Fine. I wish to fail the test. I smoke my last cigarette, sip at tea, and tell Samir that I'm walking down to the corner store to get some more cigarettes.

"I have cigarettes," he says, fumbling at his pocket.

"Not the kind I like." Whatever brand he offers, I will instantly hate.

"Poor students shouldn't be picky," Husayn says. Next to him, the boy with the scarred mouth nods, gives me a nervous smile, and offers to walk with me.

"No, I'll just be a moment," I say. I give a false-note awkward laugh. I want out of the room. Maybe I'll take a bus home and tell Mama and Papa that their two oldest sons have lost their minds. I excuse myself and walk into the rain.

The store sits on the corner. I buy the cigarettes and

I stand under a store awning, the warm honey of smoke calming me, in no hurry to return, watching the pedestrians a block away on fashionable Rue Hamra. My brothers. Getting involved with a wannabe terrorist-slash-bookworm who lives in an expensive apartment. Madness. I start to build the arguments in my mind, the words I will use to tell them they're making a mistake. Blood of Fire, what a name. I imagine the drive home as my brothers will try to convince me that they're serving justice. Perhaps they are. Yes, I understand their frustrations with the political system, with the West, with the rest of the Arab world, and—

The blast sounds more like a truck coughing up a ton of grit, more a rumble of machinery than death. I have heard explosions before. This one's boom grabs my bones. I freeze and then horror fills my skin. I am running down the street, the cigarette crushed between my fingers, and I don't feel the cinder scorch my hand.

The boy with the scarred mouth, the other Khaled, smacks into me, knocks me down, slams a foot into my chest as he keeps running. I get up and run toward the apartment building.

Smoke from Husayn's building roils into the rain. The third floor, where Husayn's apartment is. Was.

A body, burning, crumples from the window. Falls, arms cartwheeling, smashes into the rubble-filled sidewalk as I run toward it.

Gebran. I start to scream. His arms that carried me burning, his fingers that strummed Bach and folk songs burning, his dark curly hair burning. He lands in front of me, ten feet away. I land on top of him to smother the flames. I don't feel his flames, I don't feel pain, I feel his death pass through me.

Hands grip me and pull me up from Gebran. A mask of

surprise covers his dead face. Smoke wafts from his shoulders, his hair. Sirens wail. I bolt up the stairs, fighting against a surging tide of panicked tenants fleeing the building.

The floor is a ruin. Husayn's apartment and the one next to it are destroyed. The fire rages in the two apartments, but from the stairwell I see fragments of the dead: the remains of an arm smeared along the floor. A head and the shoulders of one of Husayn's friends, burned and torn. A fetal-shaped crisp that was once a person.

And Samir. The edge of the blast caught him; perhaps he was coming out of the apartment to fetch me on my cigarette errand, to lecture me on my rudeness for leaving and not hurrying back. He is crumpled against a far, unsteady wall, legs bent like wind-churned twigs, his face pale, gore seeping out of him as though he is melting, his whole body turning to blood.

I kneel by him, try to pick him up, and he starts to come apart. He is beyond broken.

"Kill…kill them…" His lips manage to shape the words and he looks at me as though he doesn't know me and he dies.

The ceiling begins to collapse and I run down the stairs. Out into the streets, past the sirens and the fire engines, smeared with my brothers' blood, I run home.

Mama and Papa are standing at the doorway, watching me stagger toward them. The television is full of the bombing. I have to find the words to tell them Samir and Gebran are dead. I don't even remember what I say. Probably, "Samir and Gebran are dead."

Papa shakes his head, keeps shaking his head. Mama screams. They are lost in their grief and shock; they clutch at me, suddenly their only child.

When they can speak—when I can speak—they ask questions. No, I do not know why the apartment was bombed. No, Husayn, I had never met him before, he was my brothers' friend. No, I only went to get cigarettes, I was only gone a few minutes. Papa starts to wheeze in shock.

"Who did this?" I ask, kneeling before the television to watch the news footage. "Who has claimed responsibility?" Because whatever division of the police or counterterrorism group has killed Blood of Fire will surely be trumpeting their victory.

Through his tears, Papa shakes his head. No one has claimed it yet.

Then that means the Israelis, the CIA, perhaps a rival cell. I think of how Hamas and Fatah, in the Palestinian camps, happily murder each other.

"Who is this terrible friend, this Husayn?" Mama demands. Then she is screaming a new trill of grief, because Papa's hand closes over his shirt, disappointment in his eyes but also a surprising relief. He slumps into his chair.

We call an ambulance. I am calm on the phone. Me bloodied and singed and battered, Papa dead in his chair, Mama clutching my arm. We stand, looking at Papa in his recliner, my hair smelling of burned blood, Mama sobbing.

Our world is gone. Gone, in an hour. I want to kill someone for the first time in my life, and I don't know how to, who to hunt for, who to hate.

The police talk to me in the days and the weeks that follow. I am questioned for hours. I can give them nothing. I never say the words *Blood of Fire* aloud. The papers argue that the murdered men were a peace-committed organization, cut down by the Mossad or the CIA. No arrests are made.

No one knows who the boy with the scarred mouth is. Rumors fly: the boy was an American agent, an Israeli-bribed traitor who planted the bomb and made his escape, nothing proven. But now I know the truth.

Mama sits at her window and moans and cries, and the sound of it will drive me slowly insane. The sound of her grief cuts me slow and deep, like a sword drawn over my back again and again, laying all my pain and hate and anger bare.

That night, I make a simple vow. Those who destroyed my family will pay, with blood spilled a thousand times more. My promise sounds ancient. It feels modern. Time-less. Hatred doesn't seem to expire.

It is why I am coming to America, and am eager to do my duty.

4

Teach put a motherly hand on the big man's shoulder, ran her other one across his burr of hair. "You literally dodged a bullet." The relief in her face was vivid. "Pilgrim." Teach leaned close to him. It wasn't his real name but it was the name she had used for the long, dark ten years of working together, so it was as real as anything else in his jigsaw life.

Pilgrim nodded. "I must have moved just enough as he fired and it saved me. I felt the shot pass above my head. I hit the floor and the sniper thought he'd taken me." Pilgrim stepped past Teach into the den in the rental house, which stood on a quiet bend of Lake Travis, near Austin. Teach and her assistant, Barker, had already started tearing down the scant equipment in the safe house: erasing the laptop's drive, looping cables. They always packed lightly so they could vanish quickly. She told Barker to finish loading up the cars.

Pilgrim sat at the table, rubbed the back of his head as though the bullet had left a trail in his hair. "I should have just kidnapped Adam, forced him to tell us how he found us, who he worked for." He shook his head. "I don't like losing, Teach."

"We couldn't tip our hand early that we were watching him. You made the only approach possible."

"Whoever he works for didn't want him talking."

"You should have brought him back here." This from Barker, stepping back inside the house to pick up a box containing eavesdropping equipment. Pilgrim wondered if the kid had wiped the milk off his lip. He couldn't be more than twenty-three or so, bespectacled and thin. He had more opinions than experience.

Pilgrim ignored him. "Adam thought I was a terrorist. Who knows what he told Homeland?"

"I'll derail that with a few phone calls." Teach's face was normally florid, a little plump, but now her skin was pale and her mouth a thin slash of worry. She was in her fifties, slightly built, bookish, with a polished Southern accent. "This sniper—"

Pilgrim said, "I recognized his face. Nicky Lynch. Rumor was he killed two CIA officers three years ago in Istanbul."

"I remember," Teach said. She stood next to him, inspected his head as a mother might a scrape. He shrugged her off. "Hon, give me info on his car."

Pilgrim described the car, gave her the license number. "I'm sure it was a rental, paid for under a false name. Or stolen for the job."

"Barker, track the plate when we get out of here." She nodded at Barker, still standing in the corner. "Let's get the bags in the car, hon. We're heading back to New York."

Barker nodded. He paused at the door. "I'm glad you're okay, Pilgrim."

"Thanks."

Teach waited for Barker to step outside and closed the

door behind him. "You nearly get shot and you don't call me immediately?"

"I'm having a really unpleasant idea. Only you and me and Barker knew about the operation. And foreign gunmen don't just show up in a place like Austin. Someone had advance word of our operation."

"Barker's clean." Teach went to the window, as if to regard Barker afresh as he loaded the car. "Did Reynolds give you any information before he died as to how he found us?"

"No." He went into the bedroom he'd used, started packing a few essentials into his bag.

Teach rubbed her temples. "Whoever Adam Reynolds was working for has obliterated his tracks. Barker's found nothing unusual in Reynolds's life: no unexplained money, no accounts, no suspicious e-mails or phone calls, nothing. Which scares me. We're talking very smart, very dangerous people."

"Clearly. They killed their own boy genius for talking to me."

"It narrows the suspects." She shrugged. "Terrorist organizations. Organized crime. Drug cartels. Foreign intelligence services." She offered a wan smile. "No shortage of people who hate us, hon."

Pilgrim went to the bathroom, splashed cold water on his face. A ghostly heat tingled in his hair, left over from the bullet, as though its close path had singed his scalp. Just imagination, he told himself, and he stuck his fingers under the cool jet of water. He didn't want Teach to see his hands shake. It was strange to think how close he had come to his brains painting the walls and the desk and the surprised face of Adam Reynolds. The poor dumb brainiac.

Pilgrim dried his face. "Reynolds. All he wanted to do was good."

"Exposing us is not in the national interest," she said. "It's necessary for our work that we remain unknown."

Pilgrim shook his head. "I'm tired of what's necessary. Necessary sucks. I want to do what's decent."

She put her hands on his shoulders. "Pilgrim, you do. Every day. You're tired and rattled. You'll feel better when we're back home. We'll regroup, plan our next move."

"Screw the next move. Suppose there's evidence in his office about the Cellar. Something I didn't find. What do we do? Hide? Take up new names and new lives, again?"

"You knew what our work was when you signed up. You knew it entailed sacrifice—"

"Don't lecture me about sacrifice. Sacrifice implies a choice."

"You had a choice today." Teach crossed her arms. "You should have let Nicky Lynch believe he succeeded. Track him and see who hired him. Instead you pull a brainless macho act. You probably liked him realizing he'd missed."

"Yes. I'll long treasure the surprise on his face before I blew him away."

"Lose the sarcasm. You didn't analyze the situation and I want to know why."

He sat on the edge of the bed. "I didn't think because—I don't want to do this work anymore." The realization was clear in his head, unexpected but sharp.

She came to him and touched his arm, and it made Pilgrim remember the old days, when she first found him, offered him a choice better than a lifetime in a dank hell-hole of a prison that smelled of ancient stone, tears, and blood. "You're just shaken—"

Pilgrim shrugged off her hand. "I'm done. Adam Reynolds found me when no one else ever has. He knew the aliases I used on the jobs in India and Canada and Syria. He could have plastered the news channels about us. We can't hide anymore."

"Wrong. We simply find out how he found us."

"I don't want to work for the Cellar anymore. I want a normal life."

Her frown deepened. "Stop this nonsense. You're not resigning, Pilgrim." Teach was like a mother who didn't hear what she didn't want to hear, he thought. "We're dead if our aliases can be exposed. I know you well enough that you won't walk away from us while we're under attack." She picked up her phone, started punching in a number.

He heard his own words again: *I want a normal life.* He touched his pocket; the notebook was there, where he always kept it. He wanted to go to the lake's shore, sharpen a pencil, draw the face as he remembered it, as he dreamed about it. But not now.

Pilgrim clicked on the television, surfed to a news channel. CNN showed an aerial shot of a downtown Austin building, police securing the scene. The reporter said one man was confirmed dead in a sniper shooting and another death in a nearby parking garage might be related. No mention yet that the dead guy in the garage was a known assassin. No release of Reynolds's name yet—it was too early. The talking heads droned on, the reporter on the scene parceling atoms of worthless data and trying to make her words meaty and relevant.

Teach got off the phone. "We've got seats on the evening flight to LaGuardia."

Pilgrim made a walking-away gesture with his fingers. "Have a good trip."

"You can't resign—"

Barker stepped into the bedroom doorway. He straightened his glasses. "Good Lord. Are you quitting?"

"False alarm. It's the shock of nearly getting shot," Teach said.

"Your timing sucks." A strange smile touched Barker's face.

"That's what I said, he can't leave us now—" Teach started. She turned to Barker and she stopped. Her body blocked Pilgrim's view of the young man and he stood.

Barker held a Glock 9-millimeter. Aimed at them.

Pilgrim felt disjointed, still blinking from the surprise of surviving a sniping, and the slight, bespectacled Barker reminded him of poor, foolish Adam Reynolds and he thought: *Nerds with guns.* Then his survival instinct kicked in, an engine in his chest, and he calculated—eight feet to reach Barker, with Teach between them. He couldn't get to Barker before Barker shot Teach.

"This is disappointing," Teach said.

"I apologize," Barker said. "Nothing personal."

Pilgrim was silent. Barker was stupid, tipping his hand early. Therefore he would do something else stupid. Pilgrim put the worn, tired look back on his face, one that would make Barker smug.

Teach kept her voice calm, but Pilgrim, behind her, could see a shift in her stance, a balancing to shift her weight forward.

Pilgrim said, "You work for the same boss as Adam Reynolds."

"Wow. Give me a moment to deal with the staggering awe I feel at your mental prowess." The gun gave Barker a sense of power, shining in his cocky smile. "Retirement is definitely in your future." He kept the gun locked on Pilgrim.

"Put the gun down. I'll pay you better than whoever you're working for," Teach said.

"Shut your mouth," he said with an eye roll.

Pilgrim said, "Why are you waiting?" because there was no good reason for the kid not to shoot them both. He risked a step to the left. Teach stayed still. "I'm unarmed and I still make you nervous."

"Consider it your last compliment," Barker said.

Footsteps approached, boots crunching into pebbles. Teach had chosen a rental house with a gravel driveway—the stones announced feet or tires with a growl.

"They want Teach alive," Barker said. "So cooperate and she doesn't get hurt."

Too much information, Pilgrim thought. "What about me?" he asked.

"You're dead," Barker said, and Teach rushed him, drawing the gun's aim. Barker hesitated for a fraction of a second, not wanting to shoot her, obeying his orders. Teach rammed into Barker, catching him in the door frame. Pilgrim seized the gun from Barker's hand in a swift downward wrench that broke Barker's wrist with a sickening crack.

Barker screamed and dropped to his knees.

Teach took the gun from Pilgrim and moved into the den. Their guns were gone, hidden by Barker. She locked the back door. "Three more guns, upstairs closet," Teach said.

Pilgrim ran up the stairs. In a closet, he found two semi-automatic pistols and a rifle. A crash boomed downstairs, glass breaking, a door being knocked loose from its frame. He grabbed the rifle and barreled a third of the way down the stairs. He saw chaos.

Barker still lay splayed on the floor, face contorted in pain.

Teach squeezed off a shot at the first man through the door but missed by a fraction of an inch. Before she could fire again, a dark-haired bruiser of a thug struck her in the arm with the butt of his rifle. She lost the gun, and he grabbed Teach as she staggered backward, then shoved her out the door, following her.

Two other men covered the room with semis. Pilgrim raised the rifle, tried to angle the awkward shot past the railing.

Barker screamed, "On the stairs!"

The men spun the guns toward him and opened fire.

The railing splintered around Pilgrim as he retreated upstairs. Blood wet his temple, cut by the flying debris. He reached the second floor, covered the stairs with the rifle, and backed up next to the window. He peered through the glass.

As he dragged her across the yard, Teach struggled against her captor, hitting a well-placed blow to his throat. But he had a hundred pounds and twenty fewer years on her, and with a jackhammer backhand he knocked her into the scrub. She fell like a stringless puppet to the rain-wet lawn.

Silence below. Not a cry from Barker, no feet slamming on the stairs. The men in the house were waiting him out.

Pilgrim watched the bruiser throw an unconscious Teach over his shoulder and start a hard run toward the oak thickets behind the house.

Pilgrim shattered the window with the rifle butt, took careful aim, and fired. The bruiser jerked and fell, he and Teach crashing to the grass. Pilgrim knew he should turn his eyes back to the staircase, to the immediate threat in the house, but he kept his gaze locked on Teach.

He heard an angry bellow from downstairs.

Get up. Run, he willed her.

She didn't move. Maybe he'd hit her. The idea iced his heart. He didn't see blood on her, but the way she lay slumped, blocked by the bruiser, he couldn't see her clearly.

He heard a barked, angry half curse, half command. "You can hold a gun in one hand, can't you, idiot?"—in rapid, heavily accented English; the leader must be talking to Barker—then "Position yourselves, wait for the dog to panic." Spoken in Arabic. First an ex-IRA sniper and now these charmers. It was an international gathering to kill him. He swallowed past the thick dryness in his mouth and a peculiar serenity filled him and he thought: *You guys made a really long trip to die.*

He glanced around the room. The only furnishings were a table and an office chair, not much for cover.

He calculated how long it would take him to get down the stairs if both men turned away from the stairwell, toward the window. Not long enough, not running. He moved to the lip of the floor, checked the stairs. Empty. That meant Barker and the two gunmen were taking cover, waiting for him to expose himself on the trapped boundary of the stair, where his options were limited. They, on the other hand, had an entire room in which to move and catch him in their cross fire.

He returned to the window and saw Teach's chest rise in a hitch of breathing. She was okay, just out. But two men emerged from the dense grove of oaks and ran toward her. If he fired at them—the three men waiting below would know he was aiming out the window, busy with multiple targets, not at the stairs. In moments the trio would rush upstairs and obliterate him with the semis.

Stalemate.

One of the men, with hair dyed blond and waxed into spikes, threw Teach, still unconscious, over his shoulder. He raised high a pistol, nestled the barrel against her head, where twigs tangled in her graying hair. Pilgrim understood. *Fire at us, she dies.* The man turned and ran awkwardly, Teach bouncing on his shoulder. The second man, wearing gaudy wraparound sunglasses, covered their retreat into the woods. They left the dead bruiser in the grass.

He needed a distraction. Nothing at hand but the table, the chair... He noticed the chair had wheels on its bottom. He readied his pistols, left the rifle on the floor.

The hardwood floor was a minefield, and one wrong creak would tip the gunmen to his position. He slowly opened the window over the porch roof, directly above where the gunmen had entered. He fed the chair through the window, carefully, and propped it on the windowsill, half in and half out, the wheels positioned against the lip of the frame. He picked up the Glocks and slid quiet as a cat across the hardwood to the head of the stairs.

The gunmen and Barker still weren't standing on the stairs waiting for him. Cowards, he thought.

Pilgrim held the two Glocks, lifted one, aimed, and fired.

The bullet smacked into the chair's back. The force propelled the barely balanced wheeled chair out the window. It made a rattling descent down the shingled, sloping porch roof. The noise was huge. He heard a downstairs yell, imagined the gunmen turning toward the window, believing he scrabbled across the shingles in a desperate escape attempt.

Pilgrim threw himself down the stairs, his hair brushing the ceiling, ignoring the coming agony of impact. In the flash of the fall he saw a skinny gunman at the window, whirling back toward him with surprise as the chair bounced on the lawn. Barker huddled at the window, cupping his damaged wrist. A second gunman crouched with semi at the ready, but aimed at the stairs themselves, a foot or two lower than Pilgrim's falling path. The second gunman fired and the edge of the stairs erupted into splinters.

Pilgrim fired three times with the two guns in the scant seconds before he crashed into the floor. The first bullet caught the skinny gunman in the face, the second pierced Barker's forehead, the last winged the second gunman in the leg. Pilgrim hit the floor, his left shoulder taking the brunt, debris flying around him.

The second gunman, pain twisting his face, stumbled and tried to aim again.

Pilgrim ignored the agony and fired, catching the gunman in the throat. He jerked backward, and his last spray of bullets dotted the wall above Pilgrim. The gunman collapsed.

Pilgrim's whole body hurt. *Get up, they're kidnapping her, get up.* He had just taken a full-story jump to a tile floor. His left arm raged in pain, but a good shake told him it wasn't broken. He staggered to his feet, testing the weight. The skinny gunman and Barker were dead; the other gunman still breathed, gurgled, stared up at him with confused eyes.

Pilgrim reeled out of the house. He loped along the path the kidnappers had taken into the dense growth of oaks and cedar. How much time since they took her? A minute? Two? He heard a car start, tires tickle gravel, an engine accelerate. He couldn't see the car. He lurched onto a back road and saw a silver van blast from the roadside.

He ran back to the house.

He aimed his gun at the dying gunman. "Where do they take her?" he asked in Arabic.

The dying man spat saliva and blood at him.

"I'll get you to a doctor—you can live. See your family again. Where do they take her?"

The man's eyes went sightless.

Pilgrim frantically searched the body. Just a matchbook and a crushed pack of American cigarettes. The matchbook was silver and red, with the words *Blarney's Steakhouse* in silver print, with an address in Frisco, Texas, and a phone number. Frisco, he remembered, was north of Dallas, a fast-growing suburb.

He hurried over to Barker's body. Stupid, stupid kid; but he wished he hadn't killed him in the flurry of shots. Barker could have answered all his questions. But you couldn't always shoot to wound. He found a cell phone and wallet with driver's license in Barker's pocket and he took both—maybe he could crack open a trail to whoever had induced Barker to turn traitor. He found nothing on the skinny gunman except a wallet containing a well-handled picture of an equally skinny woman and two small skinny children, shy smiles on their faces. He dropped the picture on the floor, nausea braiding his stomach.

You really shouldn't have a family in this business.

Pilgrim ran. Clean up the mess later, if he lived, but if Teach was gone the Cellar was gone as well, so what did it matter what the police found? Dead men in an empty, rented-for-cash dump of a lakeside house, a laptop wiped clean, guns, no explanations, no clues.

He dragged himself to his car and roared down the driveway.

Only one road threaded through the lakeside neighborhood. Lake Travis was a sprawling stretch of water a stone's throw from Austin, its edges lined with homes, condos, and marinas. This neighborhood was fairly quiet; several of the homes were rentals that weren't always occupied during the week. The car had four minutes on him, maybe. He nearly careened through a stop sign that fed onto Highway 620, a major, curving road that connected the northwest and the southwest edges of the city.

Which way had the kidnappers gone?

To his right, toward the bottom of a curve, a red light caught several cars. One was a silver van.

A horrible, treacherous thought occurred to him. He wanted to resign. He could just turn left, drive the opposite direction. Fewer retirement opportunities were more decisive and clear. Have a normal life, a life outside the shadow, a life in sunlight. With no one shooting at his head.

He could almost taste the beer. He had not been drunk in ten years, not out of a dedication to sobriety but because drunk meant slow and he could never afford to be slow, to be anything but constantly aware of every movement around him. No more. He would go to the airport, toss his guns in the trash, buy a ticket, pick the farthest destination from the Austin airport, get drunk on the miniature vodkas they served on the plane.

Maybe he could even try to have his old life back. No. He dismissed the thought as soon it came to him. That was an impossibility.

So just turn left. Drive away. This whole job was a trap, a trap to draw you and Teach out of the shadows. It freaking worked. They got her. So get out. Now. He had made enough sacrifices.

The light flashed green. The silver van rumbled into motion.

He remembered the first time he saw Teach. He lay on a cold stone floor in Indonesia, cursing at the stupidity of his mistake, his ineptness at getting caught. He'd been beaten with rubber batons, off and on, for a week. He'd glanced up and she stood at the bars. He first thought: *Why has a librarian come to see me?* The guard opened the cell door for her and then, greased with money, he walked away. She stepped inside the cell and inspected it with a frown. She knelt by him and said: "Listen. You say yes or no, nothing more, when I'm done. To the CIA, you're nothing; they aren't ever going to acknowledge you exist. I was in the same mess myself once that you are. I was in a prison in Moldova. The food appears to be halfway edible here. Lucky you."

He tried to speak but his mouth wouldn't work. She said, "You can either stay in prison or you can work for me. Hardest work you'll ever do. Probably will get you killed. But it's all for good. The most difficult good we can do. But everything about you must change. Nothing of the man you were will remain."

He held his breath. It was a hallucination, an offer out of here. It couldn't be. She reached and touched his face so he would know she was real.

She waited to see if he understood what her offer meant, the price he'd pay.

"Or you can stay who you are and enjoy this lovely cell for the rest of your life. Yes or no."

He watched her for ten silent seconds. Decision of a lifetime. He decided to believe her and whispered, "Yes."

"Then I'll have to get you out of here," she said. "Be patient. I'll come see you tomorrow. I'll have to negotiate a number of bribes. And we'll have to fake your death." She made this outrageous statement as though it were simply the final humdrum errand on a long list. To his surprise, she brushed the matted, dirty hair from his eyes, a caress that was kind and gentle. She got up and left the cell and vanished down the dank stone corridor and he blinked, as though she had been a dream.

But everything she promised, she did.

Shame at his doubt turned his stomach. Necessary, she'd said. You always did what was necessary.

Another decision of a lifetime to make, he thought, right now.

Ten seconds later Pilgrim turned right, easing eight cars behind the kidnappers' van as it rumbled toward Austin.

5

———•◦(((◦)))◦•———

Vochek drove the car with Kidwell, Ben, and the two guards toward downtown. Traffic thickened; a set of streets to the north had been closed by police—Ben remembered hearing the tidbit on the radio about a shooting—and the area between Austin's high-end Second Street and the restaurant-and-club-heavy Warehouse District thronged with concertgoers for a blues-focused music festival.

Off Second Street Vochek pulled up in a lot next to an abandoned, squat brick hotel called the Waterloo Arms. Every other building on the block had been redone or undone in the latest spasm of urban gentrification. An early evening crowd of well-heeled music lovers and drinkers wandered among the bars, restaurants, and music venues along the streets. A wire fence blocked the lot of the hotel, a sign announcing that the Waterloo Arms was being remodeled into premier office and restaurant space.

A thousand words crowded the back of Ben's throat, arguments in defense of his good name, but he decided to keep his mouth shut. Say nothing more until he got a lawyer. Silence was the refuge of the calm and the innocent. As they neared the Waterloo, Joanna Vochek's eyes met his in the rearview and he wasn't sure what he saw in her brown eyes: pity or confusion or disgust.

The guards tucked their guns into holsters under dark jackets.

Kidwell turned to face Ben. "We're going to get out of the car now. We're walking into the building. No one else is inside. If you run, if you scream, I will hit you so hard in the spinal juncture in your neck that I might very well paralyze you for life. Do you understand me?"

Ben saw Vochek's gaze flash again in the mirror, as though Kidwell were crossing a line, but she said nothing.

"Yes." Ben saw the shine of ambition in Kidwell's eyes. Of course. A high-profile case like this was a rocket to ride. A friend who'd made a personal plea for Kidwell's aid; a man who helps companies score highly lucrative contracts; and a notorious assassin linking the two together. The possibilities smacked of deep and headline-screeching scandal. And bringing that scandal to light was an ideal career booster for Kidwell.

They got out of the car. Vochek and Kidwell walked on each side of Ben as the guards unlocked the gates. The group walked under the haloes of concertina wire to keep out the vandals and the curious. The two men in suits peeled off from them, taking stations at the fence.

No one was inside the Waterloo; it looked nearly ready for office tenants. Kidwell, Vochek, and Ben took an elevator up five flights to a remodeled floor. They walked down a short corridor and into a windowless room. It held a table and three chairs. A palm-sized digital recorder sat on the table.

"Sit down," Kidwell said, and Ben obeyed.

Kidwell turned on the recorder, gave the date and the

time, and stated that Ben was speaking willingly. Kidwell began to pace, hands behind his back. Vochek stood in the corner. Not looking at Ben.

"Outline your dealings with Adam Reynolds," Kidwell said.

Ben leaned close to the recorder. "This is Ben Forsberg and I protest at how I've been treated. I'm innocent, I've been denied a call to legal counsel—"

Kidwell hit Ben. Once. From behind, a closed fist impacting behind his ear and Ben's face slammed down into the desk. Kidwell erased the recording, gave his intro again, stopped the recorder.

"Kidwell…" Vochek offered Ben a handkerchief for his bloodied nose.

"We're breaking him, Agent Vochek." Kidwell said it as a statement of fact. "Now."

"You don't need to assault him," she said. "Our mandate—"

"Our mandate says do the job, ask for forgiveness later."

Vochek stayed in the corner, her expression unchanged, but Ben saw a creeping of color, of anger, touch her cheeks.

Kidwell leaned close to Ben. "Ben, how much you help me is how much I help you. I'm going to turn on the recorder and you're going to talk, talk till your throat's raw, or I'm going to turn off the recorder again and I'll get one of those tough young guys downstairs and let him beat you. I bet you've never truly been beaten, Ben. I bet you don't really know how much a solid fifteen minutes of fist against flesh will hurt." He turned on the digital recorder again. "The victim, Adam Reynolds, phoned you at home to confirm a business meeting. Describe the nature of the meeting."

"You are threatening the wrong guy," Ben said. His

clients were important people; they would be his allies in clearing up this nightmare. "Sam Hector is my biggest client. He runs Hector Global in Dallas."

"I know who Sam Hector is," Kidwell said.

"He does millions of dollars' worth of contracting for Homeland Security. He'll vouch for me. He's a longtime friend."

"You're right, Homeland Security does a great deal of business with Mr. Hector. So if I call him and tell him to drop you as a consultant, he will." Kidwell glanced at Vochek. "Joanna, get Mr. Hector's number for me. We'll call him on Ben's own phone."

"I think we could learn more by asking Ben—"

"Do as I ask, please."

"Yes...sir." She started to navigate through the numbers on Ben's smartphone, a frown on her face.

"Your biggest client, you're going to lose him, Ben. I promise Hector will pick us over you. Tell me about your meeting with Adam."

"If I could help you I would." A hot tickle caught in Ben's throat.

"I'm going to call every firm that contracts with Homeland Security and tell them you're under suspicion of consorting with a known terrorist. You'll be blackballed. You'll never work in this business again."

"I can't tell you what I don't know."

"I'm also going to freeze your bank accounts. Your savings accounts. You won't be able to pay your bills. Pay your mortgage." Kidwell crossed his arms. "You'll be out on the street. You have a girlfriend?"

"No." Emily's face swam up in front of him and he blinked.

"I'm going to find someone you love. Someone you care about. Lover, aunt, uncle, neighbor, college roommate, best friend. I'm going to freeze their accounts as well."

Rage flooded Ben, surged past the fear he felt. "You can't. Absolutely you cannot."

"Whatever I do, it will be on your head." Kidwell raised his hands in mock surrender.

Ben turned to Vochek. "You seem reasonable, Agent Vochek. Please. You can't endorse what he's doing."

"I don't endorse what you're doing, Ben, which is stone-walling us. Tell him what he wants to know." She held the phone out to Kidwell. "I found Sam Hector's number. Are we calling him?"

Kidwell smiled. "Are we, Ben?"

Ben swallowed. "I'd like to know if there's any other evidence against me."

Kidwell stopped his pacing and pulled a folded piece of paper from his pocket. "You have three other cellular accounts."

"No." Ben shook his head.

Kidwell read off three numbers, all with 512 area codes in Austin.

"Those aren't my phone numbers."

"They were opened in your name a week ago."

"Tell me which branch opened the accounts. I want someone to ID me as the guy who conducted the trans-action."

"You rented office space last week, off North Lamar." Kidwell read an address off the paper.

"Wrong."

"The office was rented through an agent. Sparta Con-sulting."

"Never heard of them. I never hired an agent. Maybe this is a case of identity theft."

Vochek said, "People who steal IDs buy TVs and golf clubs and diamond rings, not rent office space."

"Does your report tell you I have new credit card accounts, too?"

Kidwell nodded. "Three. In the past week."

"Great. Examine my credit history. I don't open new accounts. I have one credit card I've had for six years, and I pay it off each month." He looked again at Vochek. "I have no motive for wanting Reynolds dead."

"Talk to me, not her," Kidwell said.

"Talking to you is like talking to brick."

A dark scowl crossed Kidwell's face.

"Do any of these new phone numbers point to Adam Reynolds or Nicky Lynch?" Ben asked. He had to keep them, he thought, on the defensive, force them to acknowledge a weakness in their case. Because they were wrong.

To Kidwell, Vochek said, "We just got the records faxed over to us. Adam Reynolds only made calls today to Ben's new cell number and home, to your office in Houston, and several calls to a number in Dallas." Vochek showed Kidwell two printouts. "Ben's new cell phone number has several calls to Reynolds's office."

"Fantastic," Ben said. "I want to know the time of all those calls I supposedly made. Because I'm betting I can prove I didn't make them." Vochek started to bring him the sheets and Kidwell stopped her.

"No. Show him nothing."

Ben spoke to Vochek, meeting her gaze with his own. "Before you start threatening me or bullying my clients, you better check your evidence more closely. You better have it be watertight. Because Sam Hector's a mover and shaker in D.C., and I doubt you want to be accusing his friends. Especially me. I helped make him a wealthy man. A powerful man."

Kidwell's lips went tight. Ben wanted the heat of the exchange to pass; he wanted to let Kidwell save face, for his own sake.

"May I please go to the bathroom?" Ben said. Kidwell switched off the recorder and nodded his assent, as if he welcomed a few minutes of quiet thought.

Vochek escorted him down the hall. Ben washed his face twice, cleaning the blood from his nose. The ache faded to a dull throb. At least it wasn't broken. He went back out into the hallway. Vochek stood with arms crossed.

"Is this when you pretend to be the good cop?"

"No."

"You can't be worse than Kidwell. You know he's breaking the law in how he's dealing with me. I can't imagine this is how Homeland Security operates. I know too many good and dedicated people who work there to believe Kidwell's typical." He shook his head. "Office of Strategic Initiatives. I don't recall ever seeing that name on a Homeland org chart. Who exactly are you people?"

She crossed her arms.

"Fine, you won't tell me. Why should I help you?"

"To help yourself."

"You've got it backward. I'm owed basic rights as a citizen, I'm presumed innocent," he said. "Until I get counsel I'm unsure why I should help Kidwell steamroll me." He shook his head. "I thought I could reason with you. I saw how you looked at him when he went nuclear on me."

"Ben..." But she went silent and Ben walked away from her. They went back into the room.

"Sit down," Kidwell said.

Ben sat. He looked again at Vochek, who lingered in the doorway.

"I'll check what you say. But you consider what's going to happen to you if you've lied to me. Think long and hard about it, Ben. Knock on the door if there's anything else you want to share to save us time."

Kidwell got up and turned out the lights and walked out. Vochek gave Ben a backward glance. The door clanged shut behind them, killing the soft envelope of light from the hallway, and Ben sat in total darkness.

"He's soft," Kidwell said, as Vochek sat down at the laptop. "He'll do exactly what we expect. Deny, plead for a lawyer, but when he gets confronted with more evidence, he'll crack."

"I'm not so sure," she said.

"Why?"

"Here's the hole in all this mess. Ben strikes me as an intelligent guy, and he barely tried to cover his tracks."

"People are idiots. Or so arrogant they think they won't get caught," Kidwell said. "I want to find every link between him and Adam Reynolds. Find this Sparta Consulting that rented the office for him, see how Forsberg's tied to it. I want to know everything Forsberg's done or bought or who he's talked to in the past few days."

She opened her laptop, saw a new e-mail from their office in Houston titled "FORSBERG REPORT." She opened it and scanned it and said, "Norman. Read this." Her throat went dry.

Norman Kidwell leaned close, read the e-mail, and smiled. "Goodness. Mr. Innocent here left out a key detail."

6

———◈———

THE KIDNAPPERS' VAN SUDDENLY powered into high speed along FM Road 2222, a winding snake of pavement cut into the side of limestone cliffs.

They spotted me, Pilgrim knew.

The van dipped and wove through traffic, rocketing along the curving road.

Pilgrim stayed with them, whipping around a minivan and a Porsche to narrow his distance from the van. The kidnappers had not waited to see how their compatriots had fared after the barrage of gunshots at the lake house. Which meant they either assumed Pilgrim was a dead man or they had orders not to look back. Getting Teach away must be their priority.

If he could grab her back, he could end this nightmare.

His eyes stung—blood running into his eyebrow and eye. His body ached like he'd been beaten with pipes.

Cars peeled out of the pathway of the van as the driver rode the horn, powering through a red light, missing by inches a honking Lexus, sideswiping a BMW, sending it into a spin. Pilgrim dodged both of the cars, stayed close to the van.

The van roared up the incline, sparks flying from a

swipe against the guardrail. The van overcompensated, veering into oncoming traffic and then easing back just in time to avoid a head-on with a pickup truck full of high school students. Pilgrim could see the teenagers' O-shaped mouths, their faces contorted in screams as the van missed them by a hair.

End this now. Pilgrim powered his BMW up close to the passenger side.

The spiky-haired blond leaned out the passenger window and opened fire with a shotgun; Pilgrim dropped back. The hail of pellets pocked the windshield.

The van skittered back into the wrong lane and wove like a drunken dancer to avoid three cars. Pilgrim saw the disbelieving faces of the drivers, all heading back to suburban comfort after an extra-long day of pushing paper or making phone calls or chained to e-mails, death suddenly inches from them, as he tried to give the van room to maneuver.

An empty stretch of road lay ahead; there must be a red light on the other side of the hill, stopping the flow of cars. Pilgrim thumbed down the passenger window, floored the BMW past the van, spun across the empty asphalt so he straddled the lanes. He aimed his gun at the van's front tires and fired through the open window. Flashes of bullets sparking against the tire cover and bumper told him he'd missed. He was hurting, his arm wasn't steady.

The van plowed past him, the spiky blond leaning past the driver and leveling fire into the front of the BMW. Pilgrim ducked as the windshield shattered. He sat up as the van passed and floored the car, trying to catch up, but he felt one of the damaged tires part from the rim, and he overcorrected as the road curved. The crippled BMW smashed through a railing onto a sharply sloping hill, sliding thirty feet downward in a dust of limestone scrabble and hammering into the cedars lining a landscaped backyard.

He blinked. Broken glass littered his hair and his lap; the passenger door was crumpled by a tree. The engine died. He opened his door, clambered to his feet.

He was unhurt, but the BMW was undrivable.

Pilgrim stumbled, then found his footing on the scrabble. He ran into the backyard's house, kicking open the back door. A family stood by a dinner table that faced onto the yard: a dad, a mom, two teenage girls. They all stared at him over their pot roast, salad, and potatoes au gratin. Dinner smelled delicious. He raised the gun, aimed it at the dad.

"Pardon the intrusion," he said. "I need your car."

The mom retreated back to the kitchen counter, tossed him the keys. Pilgrim caught them with one hand and said, "Thanks." He hated the next part. He ordered the family into a utility room without an exit. Closed the door, shoved a chair up hard against the knob. "You sit here for the next two hours. I've got a cop radio, so you call the cops, I'm back and you do not want me coming back here," he yelled through the door. He needed them scared to the bone, he needed them to give him enough time to vanish. He could hear the parents comforting the girls with whispers.

The keys were to a maroon-colored Volvo station wagon. He roared out of the driveway, turned back onto FM Road 2222. A police car stood where the BMW had peeled through the railing, and he drove by at the speed limit and didn't glance over at the officers, who would probably find and free the family in the next ten minutes. He topped the next hill and floored the station wagon. The van was long gone. He drove a couple of miles, hoping he'd winged a tire, given the van a flat. But they were gone. He headed right as FM Road 2222 came to an end and forked into two separate streets, headed down a side road, pulled into a Chinese restaurant's parking lot, tried to marshal his brain. Where would they take Teach and who could help him?

He had no one to call. That was the beauty of the Cellar—you never knew the other operatives' real names or how to reach them. Barker had a real name that wasn't Barker and probably had two or three other names he operated under. Pilgrim was just the name Pilgrim used in the Cellar, as he lived through a series of false names. No one could betray you.

Except Teach, who was the only person who knew every detail of every job.

Her brain was the prize. Her brain could break the Cellar, put every operative in the group in prison or in crosshairs.

It was an unusual opponent, he thought, who could hire an ex-IRA assassin and a group of Arab gunmen to come to Texas to do dirty work. And Barker had claimed to find nothing unusual in Adam Reynolds's bank accounts or e-mail records—but since Barker had been in the enemy's pocket, then he would have lied and destroyed any evidence linking Adam Reynolds and himself back to the enemy.

Pilgrim thumbed through the call log on Barker's cell phone. If Barker's day was to end with Teach kidnapped and Pilgrim dead, then the traitorous young man didn't have to be overly careful in erasing his tracks. The call log held what was to be expected as they'd worked their job on Reynolds over the three days: calls to Teach, calls to Pilgrim's phone. But there was a call to an Austin local number Pilgrim didn't recognize.

Pilgrim drove toward central Austin. On Koenig Lane he saw what he wanted: a small coffeehouse with a sign in its window offering free Internet access. He went inside; early evening, the shop wasn't busy. A row of three sleek computers sat on a far counter, and he sat at one and launched a browser. It opened onto a news page and he saw a scattering of headlines: Senate committee demands CIA develop more human intelligence resources in the Mideast for the War on Terror; a football star enters rehab; a sniper shooting in Austin, Texas.

He scanned the news report. No naming of the dead men, yet. No mention of a man seen leaving the scene.

"Sir? Are you all right?"

He glanced at the barista behind the counter and then realized he must look like he'd crawled out of a train wreck. She was a pretty woman of college age, and she pointed at his cut forehead. "You're bleeding."

"Oh, am I?" He went to the coffee stand and grabbed napkins, dabbed at his forehead. Blood flecked the paper. "I took a fall. I'm okay."

"Are you sure?" she asked.

"I'm fine. A medium latte, please, that's what'll fix me up." He tested a smile.

The barista nodded to him and returned to the machine. He sat, did an online search for the Austin phone number he'd found on Barker's cell.

No listing.

He waited for the barista to call that his latte was ready, but she brought it to him. "On the house," she said, as he stood to reach for his wallet.

"No, really ..."

"Sir," the barista said, "I'm guessing you've had a rotten day. It's on the house."

Kindness was a stranger, and for a moment he didn't know what to do. "Thank you," he said. "Thanks a lot."

She smiled and went back to the coffee bar. He sipped the latte—it was energy and stimulant and calories, all of which he needed. The door jingled, a man and his teenage daughter coming inside, the girl smoothing her auburn hair against a gust of damp wind. He watched them laugh and debate what to order, a heaviness filling his gut and his chest.

That should be you, he thought. *Maybe it can be. When this mess is done.* He turned back to the computer.

He used the browser to access an online database for the government, where the phone companies, both cell and landline, were required to list every issued number. He logged in, using a password Teach had stolen from a CIA officer and given to him, and searched for the number.

The database did not give him the phone's location, but it told him that the phone belonged to McKeen Property Company and the billing address was on Second Street in downtown Austin. He jumped to a maps site searched for the address.

He finished the latte and hurried to his stolen car, not looking at the father and the daughter laughing over their coffees.

Jackie Lynch sat hunched at the bar, the granite cool under his palms. He had stumbled along the downtown streets when he realized he was going to have to call the boss, explain the job was an unmitigated disaster, Nicky dead.

He'd seen a neon harp advertising Guinness in a bar window and he'd lurched inside, ordered a pint in a hoarse whisper. Drank it down fast, took a long breath, told himself not to cry. Ordered a second pint because, as his father often said, no bird flies home on one wing.

Home. He had lost his brother and his mentor. Nicky was the brains of the business; Jackie barely knew how to deal with dangerous clients, assessing contracts and their risks, devising escape routes, managing money in numbered accounts. Now they'd failed a job for a very powerful man. He stared down at the counter.

He still clutched the sealed envelope. He was supposed to have dumped it on Adam Reynolds's desk after Nicky killed the targets, but in the shock of only one corpse in the office instead of two, he had simply turned and run out the door.

He left his half-finished pint of Guinness and edged over to the bar's window. A few blocks away, the streets around the parking garage and Reynolds's office building were closed in a police cordon. If they hadn't already, he knew, the cops would discover Nicky's modified Heckler & Koch PSG1 rifle in the trunk. Someone would see the bullet-holed window in the building or find Reynolds's body, put the evidence together.

No way he could plant the envelope now. Impossible. The client would just have to understand.

A band in the corner began to tune up on a small stage, a guitarist and a piano player, playing riffs of one of his favorite Johnny Cash songs, "The Tennessee Stud." He loved music nearly as much as he loved his brother, and for a moment he was tempted to not call the client, to vanish. Go back to Belfast, listen to his records, and curl up in bed.

But no. That was selfish, running away meant Nicky's killer walked. Jackie was the family business now; he had to be a man. Nicky had always been the grown-up, but

those days were nothing but mist. Music was nothing compared to blood.

He moved to a corner table, far from potential listeners,
and punched the number he and Nicky were supposed to
call to confirm the job was done. The phone had been left
for them in their hotel room, and they were supposed to
call only once. The number had a 972 area code and Jackie
knew it was Dallas; he'd looked it up, out of curiosity, in
the Yellow Pages at the hotel the night before.

It rang three times, then a man answered. "Yes?"

At first he couldn't speak. Then he said: "It went bad.
Nicky's dead." He explained.

He could sense a simmering anger building on the other
side of the phone. "If you had called earlier, I would have
been able to warn my other team."

Jackie bit his lip. "Other team?"

"The first man you all were supposed to kill is called
Pilgrim. The job had a second component, the kidnapping
of a woman who is Pilgrim's boss. Missing Pilgrim meant
he killed four more of my men after he killed your brother."

You're going to whine and my brother's dead, Jackie
thought. *No, sir, not today.* "Not my problem," he snapped.
"You don't tell me the big picture, then don't hold me
accountable for it. That's your mistake, not mine." He tried
to put the iron in his voice he'd heard Nicky use with a
troublesome client. It was never a good idea to piss off an
assassin, no matter who you were.

A painful stretch of silence. Jackie thought, *First hand
you play alone and you screw up.*

"Did you deliver the package to Reynolds's office?" The
client's voice was ice.

"No, sir."

"Deliver the package." Now the rage was clear.

"Absolutely not," Jackie said. "Cops are crawling over that office like fleas." Best to simply assert what was undoubtedly true. "I can see them from here."

The duo began to play a plaintive Willie Nelson song, and the voice said, "Where are you?"

"Uh, a bar."

"A bar." Disbelief and fury, crammed into two words.

"I'm not drinking."

"The surviving members of the other team will pick you up. You miss the rendezvous and I'll tell them your mistake is the reason why half their team is dead. I'm not sure what they'll cut off first—your tongue or your hand."

Jackie swallowed the rock in his throat. "And then what?"

"You help them finish the job of killing Pilgrim."

Jackie wasn't eager to face a man who'd defied Nicky's bullet and killed five men today. But he had no choice, he told himself. The job wasn't about the payment, it was about payback. Nicky would have hunted this Pilgrim night and day to avenge Jackie.

Jackie tried to put steel in his voice. "Where do I meet your men?"

7

———⊰◉⊱———

SAM HECTOR SAT AT HIS DESK, five cell phones spread before him, waiting for the call that would change his life.

With one hand he clicked an antique Chinese abacus. He owned a sizable collection of abaci from around the world: ivory counters from Africa, jade calculators from China, a prized set from India that had once tallied the household accounts of a maharajah. He loved the soft feel of the beads, the click of their collisions on the rods. Ben Forsberg had given him the one he played with now, a souvenir from a trip to Beijing Ben and his poor dead wife, Emily, had taken before their marriage. It was his favorite.

With the other hand Sam Hector paged through his e-mail inbox. The list was long and from every hotspot of the world. Communiqués from Iraq, where he had close to a thousand military contractors working security details from Kirkuk to Basra. From Ethiopia, where a select team of his employees offered advice to the regime on dealing with an insurrection in the south. From Afghanistan, where his teams provided protection for both Afghan and coalition dignitaries and had helped stop a suicide bombing at a school—one of the contractors had shot the bomber dead, unfortunately also killing a local guard who'd grappled

with the bomber. Regrettable. He forwarded a note to his
Afghan operations director, encouraging him to provide a
bit of money for the hapless guard's family. Anonymously,
of course; Hector Global couldn't be held liable for doing
their job. War was full of tragic accidents, and the work
that Hector Global did was all for the common good. Not
just America's, Sam thought, but for the world's.

The next e-mail made him frown: a manager in Baghdad,
saying that many of the security workers were expressing
unhappiness with their tours and the level of violence they
faced. If they didn't like working for Hector Global, they
could get on a flight home, Sam believed. Aisle or window,
chicken or pasta, pick your seat, he thought. But it had been
a rough couple of weeks; he'd lost five men in three separate
incidents. It was a relief he did not have to pay medical benefits or life insurance; the contractors were responsible for
their own.

Worse, he'd lost the past seven contracts he'd bid on for
Iraq work, and the contracts for domestic security were
starting to dry up. He had three thousand employees on the
payroll; he needed every deal he could land.

He put aside the abacus and typed an e-mail to the Smith
woman at the State Department who'd shown the more-
than-professional interest in Ben: *Sure that Ben will call
you tomorrow, he's back from his getaway I believe today.
I'm sure we'll be able to come to agreement. Best, Sam.*
He sent it and thought: if Ben would have just bedded the
idiotic woman from State when she'd dropped her first hint,
that contract would be signed and he'd have several million
he desperately needed on the books.

But Ben wasn't going to be bedding anyone.

The last e-mail in his inbox was from New Orleans and

contained a link to a map image. He studied the map for several long, silent moments. The map was the first key to his future. He committed it to memory, felt a little thrill of excitement.

One of the five phones rang; he blinked at the number display. "Hello?"

"Homeland Security has taken Ben Forsberg into custody. Evidence linked him to a dead foreign assassin killed today in Austin."

But...Jackie hadn't delivered the envelope. The frame of Ben was incomplete. But he was not going to argue with a sweet twist of fate. "Where is Ben now?"

"At the new Homeland facility downtown, at the old Waterloo Arms. They're questioning him."

"No police?"

"No police."

"You've earned a bonus," he said, and hung up. It was useful to have people sprinkled throughout the government who were willing to give you information for a price.

Sam Hector stood and went to his window. He had not killed in years; he was done with dirtying his hands, he thought, but if the Lynches and the team from Lebanon all failed to kill Pilgrim, well, then it was time to sharpen his skills. A tremble of warmth touched his skin, made his face flush. It would be good to be back in the game.

Another phone rang and he scooped it off the desk.

"It's Jackie, sir."

"Go ahead."

"I hooked up with your other crew and we caught us a break." Jackie sounded almost joyful. "Pilgrim is two streets over from the hotel you picked as the rendezvous point."

"You're sure it's him?"

"In a Volvo station wagon, cruising, like he was checking out the property. We're ready to take him down."

Pilgrim had managed to trace a connection back to the Waterloo Arms. Smart boy.

He considered. And then Sam Hector saw a solution—an unpleasant one—but one that would serve more than a single purpose. He examined the idea quickly, from every angle, testing its strengths and weaknesses and risks. Ben Forsberg and Homeland Security were inside the Waterloo. Pilgrim wanted inside the Waterloo to find how it connected back to Teach's kidnapping.

"Jackie. You let Pilgrim get inside the building. Then you follow him in and you kill everyone. *Everyone.* Do you understand?"

"Yes, sir."

"One of you stays with Teach. When everyone inside is dead, you call me back. You'll each be paid a hundred thousand more. Except you, Jackie, as you haven't completed your original assignment. Plus, no money can motivate you more than avenging your brother."

Message clear: *Don't complain. Or I'll tell them it was you not warning them that got their friends killed.* Jackie stayed silent.

Sam Hector hung up. He started to breathe again, feeling like he'd just ordered an army to launch a devastating assault, nearly dizzy with the idea of the carnage he'd unleashed. He had just ordered a mass murder. But it was required. It was the only choice.

It was a very small sacrifice for a very big gain—an incalculably huge gain—that was going to change everything for him.

He let the smile come onto his face while he waited.

*   *   *

Jackie and the three gunmen listened to Sam Hector's instructions on how to get into the Waterloo, and then Jackie closed his phone. The three men in the van stared at Jackie, two with blank expressions, one with clear disapproval. Jackie glanced down at the old woman—Teach, Hector called her—the men had kidnapped, unconscious, hands bound in front of her, sleeping off an injection designed to keep her out for a few more hours.

"You heard the man," Jackie said. "An extra hundred thou for each of you." He announced it with casual arrogance, as if he were disbursing the funds himself.

The Arab leader was unimpressed. "You, Irish, you stay with lady." A large mole marred his chin. He prodded the unconscious woman with his foot. The other two shifted on the balls of their feet. One had a wild thatch of hair, streaked white and black; the other wore wraparound sunglasses. They all looked like freaks to him.

"No," Jackie said. "Pilgrim killed my brother. I kill him."

"No. We are used to working together as a team. Not with you."

"I'm going with you."

The leader shook his head. "Three of us, one of you."

He could let these dumb oafs do the dangerous work. As long as Pilgrim died, did it really matter who killed him? The thought shamed him. He started again to stand.

The leader produced a smile of slightly crooked teeth and a Beretta aimed at Jackie's chest. "Plenty of hate for this Pilgrim. He'll die badly. I promise. You guard the woman." Jackie could hear the sting of an implied insult in the words, as though Jackie were capable of nothing more than watching an unconscious fifty-year-old.

The gunman with the wraparound sunglasses took pity on him, squeezed Jackie's shoulder. "We'll give this Pilgrim a bullet for your brother."

Jackie swallowed his rage and he nodded. Let them go do the work. He didn't like that they'd seen his face or ordered him about like he was beneath them. He still had the knife strapped to his pants leg and he was hungry now to use it. He thought how the knife's handle might shine, buried in their throats.

He kept the smile and shook their hands to wish them luck.

8

---◦◦◦---

THE WATERLOO ARMS PRESENTED a tactical nightmare. Fences, guards, in the middle of an urban setting. Pilgrim drove past the renovated building three times and stowed the Volvo in a nearby parking garage off Second Street. Barhoppers and music lovers crowded the evening streets. Stages, with bands playing blues music, towered in two intersections. More music spilled out from nearly every bar. Pilgrim wished he could go into one of the bars, order a cold Shiner Bock, let the heat of the music flow over him, and not dwell for a moment on violence or guns, unless it was inside the lyrics of a jealous lover's song. Instead he found a vantage point, a table at an outside jazz bar, and drank a Coke. An older woman who was attired as though for church, complete with floral dress and pink hat, pounded the piano's keys with vigor and precision and sang about a no-good man that she couldn't give up, necessary as air.

He took a sip of soda. He wore a burnt-orange University of Texas Longhorns cap and a windbreaker he'd found in the stolen Volvo. The cap was pulled low on his head; the jacket was too roomy for his lanky form, but it hid his gun.

He studied the hotel lot. He didn't even know for sure

that Teach was inside. A sign on the fence said this was a McKeen property, soon to be the Waterloo Arms Court, with several thousand square feet of office and retail space and a Blarney's Steakhouse. All opening in about two more months.

Blarney's. The name of the same Dallas steakhouse he'd found on a matchbook in one of the dead gunmen's pockets. Couldn't be coincidence.

He'd watched two men in suits circling the fence, one always staying in visual range of the building's back entrance. On guard.

The suits didn't look like the other kidnappers. These two were Anglos, tall, heavy-built, military burr haircuts, wearing jackets that were no doubt hiding rigs. They looked like high-end rent-a-cops.

The two guards didn't wander as a pair. One took a clockwise orbit around the chain-link lot; the other headed the opposite direction. They roamed out of each other's sight for at least a minute, on the edge of the fence. The south side of the empty building fronted the busier Second Street; the east abutted a jewelry store and design firms; the north side was Third Street, and the west faced another construction site, also fenced. A narrow passageway cut between the construction sites.

He flipped Barker's phone to his ear—he didn't turn it on—and started a pretend conversation with an imaginary friend, pacing back and forth, just another guy in a self-made cellular bubble.

"Yeah, absolutely I'm gonna kill these losers," he said to himself. "Then I'm gonna make Teach buy me a steak dinner and accept my letter of resignation. Yeah, yeah."

He nodded, holding the silent phone, and watched the

guards continue their orbit. He could not shoot either of them on the street; too many people around. And if they were reporting back into the hotel via phone or wire, taking them out might alert the others inside. So he had to get past them.

The wooden fence on the adjoining lot wasn't concertina wired. It was the route of least resistance. He waited until the walking guard closest to him rounded a corner. Pilgrim hurried to the fence of the stripped lot. The fence loomed, and he tucked the phone in his pocket, got a running start, and took a leap. His fingers just caught the tip of the fence, and he grunted hard as he pulled himself up and over, his arms aching with the effort. He slid down on the other side of the fence and ran to the east side. He stopped to listen.

Pilgrim heard a guard amble along the fence line. At first he thought the guy was talking to himself, but then he realized the first guard was using an earpiece communicator.

"Yeah," the guard said. "It's a lot better than Baghdad. I made ninety thou but the wife complained incessantly, cried herself to sleep every night. I only want to do domestic now, or maybe Africa except for Somalia, those people are crazy. Yeah…"

Pilgrim checked his watch. Listened for either the approach of the next guard or the return of the one he'd heard. They held true to their schedule, once a minute, give or take ten seconds.

Those ten seconds might be life or death to him.

He surveyed the empty lot. A trailer sat on one side, near the middle of the lot. A forklift squatted next to it like a stout guard. He took a lockpick from his pocket and had the trailer open in five seconds. No alarm sounded.

The office was cluttered. He spotted the keys to the fork-lift hanging on a hook by a desk.

He listened for the clockwork steps of the guard, and as they passed he ran to the forklift, lurched it into life, aimed it at the sweet spot in the fence that bordered the hotel lot. Stopped it short and killed the engine. The music festival drowned out the noise he'd made. He checked his watch: ten seconds to spare.

Twenty seconds later he heard the guard pass.

Pilgrim clambered onto the forklift's roof, lying flat on his stomach. He peered over the fence, which was now about two feet higher than the minilift's roof. He saw the guard walking away from him.

Four feet separated the two fences. He powered himself over the gap.

Just enough and his feet cleared the wire of the hotel fence. He slammed into the ground and sprinted for the closest door, which stood in a shaded alcove.

He tried the door. Unlocked.

He opened the door, gun ready. He stepped into a service hallway, lit only with the faint gleam of fluorescent lights dangling in a straight row from the ceiling.

He closed the door. He listened to the silence. No sound of an alarm.

He tested doorknobs. The third door opened into a stairwell's ghostly light. Halfway up the concrete stairs, he heard the footfall behind him. He spun, and one of the suits, thick-necked, stood in the hallway, leveling a gun at him. "Freeze!"

Pilgrim thought: *I'm not going to be taken down by a rental cop.* "May I raise my hands?"

"Lock fingers together, palms up. Off the stairs, to the

ground." The rental cop didn't sound like a rental. A bite of authority lay in his tone.

Pilgrim stepped off the stairs. "Where is Teach?"

"On the ground. On your knees. Last warning. Then I shoot."

Definitely not a rental cop. Pilgrim started to kneel. He bent his knee until he had the right amount of leverage, and then barreled hard into the man, gunning his head straight into the guy's stomach as they slammed into the concrete wall.

The guy was solid muscle. He hammered Pilgrim's chin using a short, sharp blow derived from Muay Thai, a martial art. Pilgrim was surprised, and he ducked the second punch, slammed a fist into the man's temple, once, twice, and then caught him in the back of the head with a pistol butt. The guy staggered, for one moment, all that Pilgrim needed. The man collapsed, and Pilgrim whipped him again with the pistol butt to keep him down. But when he saw the guy's ear, cupping an earpiece, he knew that the other guard would hear and respond. He frisked the guy for a second gun. He found only flat plastic in the guard's pocket. An ID card: Hector Global Security.

He dropped the card on the unconscious man's chest.

Wait for the second guard to respond or go? He pressed his back against the wall, flicked off the light.

Ten seconds later the door flew open and the second guard bolted into the hallway. Pilgrim launched a kick at the back of the man's head.

9

---•◦•---

THE LIGHTS FLICKERED TO LIFE, and after the coffin-like darkness Ben blinked hard against the harsh dazzle. He'd sat in the darkness, perfectly still, trying to steel himself against what might come next.

"Nice to have quiet and time to think." Kidwell shut the door behind him.

"Sitting in the dark didn't make me smarter."

"Didn't it? I thought you might be ready to talk about Emily."

Ben felt a slow rage fill him. He said nothing. Ten seconds. Thirty seconds.

Kidwell didn't blink. "You got a real ugly streak inside you. I see it now."

"You're mistaken."

"It's just fascinating"—he pointed his fingers into little guns—"to me that, you know, your wife was shot to death two years ago, case never solved, and today your business card's in a sniper's pocket. Because I don't believe in coincidence."

Ben stared at the floor.

"Is that why you kept mewling for a lawyer, Forsberg? You didn't want to talk about the way your wife died?

Surely you weren't stupid enough to think we wouldn't make the connection."

Ben stood up from the chair.

"Sit down." Kidwell snapped fingers, pointed at the chair.

The finger snap pushed him in a way that the threats had not. "Shut your mouth," Ben said. "You don't talk about Emily."

"I see the nerve remains raw."

"I'm done here. My wife was killed in a random shooting, the police exonerated me. You haven't arrested me and I'm not saying another word to you. I'm leaving and I'm going to hire a lawyer and I'm going to sue you personally so that your bank account's emptier than your brain."

Kidwell lifted his gun, in a slow, lazy motion. He aimed it at Ben's chest. "I told you to sit down. I'm going to call the police in Maui and the FBI office and inform them that I've got a new development in your wife's murder."

"Call away."

"Or I'll leave it alone. Just tell me how you and Reynolds and Nicky Lynch all connect."

"We don't connect." Ben tested the doorknob; it was locked. He turned back to Kidwell and the gun went against his forehead.

"You're not going anywhere."

Ben was too angry to be scared. "I'm tired of your threats and your insinuations. Fine. You call the cops. Because they'll make sure I get a lawyer."

Kidwell slammed the pistol into the side of Ben's head, and Ben collapsed into the chair.

"You had her killed, didn't you, and it's caught up with you."

"No—"

"You had Lynch kill your wife two years ago, then you had him kill Adam Reynolds today."

"No." Ben stood. "Shut your mouth!"

A wife killer, Vochek thought. Ben didn't seem the type, although a sociopath could camouflage himself beautifully in normal society, show guilt and remorse enough to convince the gullible. She'd made herself look stupid, defending the loser, before she'd seen the report that his wife had died very much like the way Adam Reynolds died.

She glanced through the police report again. A number of windows had been shot out in properties near Lahaina in a forty-minute period, a prank gone horribly wrong when Emily Forsberg took a bullet in the head. No arrests ever made, no gun ever found.

Nicky Lynch having Ben's business card pretty much made her sure Emily's shooting wasn't an accident.

Vochek hunched over her laptop, quilting together information, determined to see if she could poke holes in Ben Forsberg's story and find more links between him and Adam Reynolds. She had access, via Homeland Security, to a major credit-tracking database. A phone call resulted in a list of charges on all accounts for Ben Forsberg being e-mailed to her computer. Ben's credit cards did show two flashes of activity in Marble Falls, where he had claimed to be; both in the evenings, purchases at a liquor store and a grocery. But they also showed activity in Austin in the past three days. She compared the times; one of the Marble Falls charges was at 7:15 P.M., one of the Austin charges was at 7:46 P.M., which also coincided with a dinner appointment with Ben on Adam Reynolds's calendar.

You couldn't get from Marble Falls to Austin and eat a dinner that quickly.

So one charge could well be fraudulent.

Kidwell was not going to be happy.

She opened her cell phone, scanned the phone company printouts, looking at Adam Reynolds's call log. He'd dialed one number four times. She dialed the number. The answering machine said, "Hello, it's the moon base, not here, you know the drill."

Moon base? She summoned a government database of phone numbers. The phone number belonged to Delia Moon. She did an online search for the name—nothing. Did a criminal check. Nothing. Found Delia Moon's driver license photo on the Texas Department of Public Safety database. Twenty-eight, five-ten, attractive, with an address in Frisco, a Dallas suburb. So who was this woman to Adam Reynolds?

Vochek left a message, introducing herself and asking Delia Moon to call her back, that it was important. She could hear the mutterings of the guards below on a radio monitor and she turned it low and dialed her phone. Her mother should be home now.

"Hello?"

"Mom?" she said. "Hi. Listen, I had to come to Austin quick, on a job, I can't do dinner tonight, I'm really sorry."

"Oh, honey. Okay. Well, maybe this weekend, will you be back?" Mom sniffed, a reminder that her allergies had been a constant burden this spring. Piling the firewood of guilt on the flames.

"I don't know yet."

Her mother couldn't, or wouldn't, hide the disappointment in her voice. "Well, then. All right..."

"I know it's hard, Mom." Her mother had moved to Houston from Long Island, where Vochek had grown up, to be close to her only child. Houston had been a difficult adjustment. It was a friendly city, but her mother had not quite found her footing. Couldn't or wouldn't, Vochek thought again. "I'm really sorry to miss the dinner you made."

"Well, I won't go hungry." Mom tried a laugh, brittle and forced. "Will you call me when you know if you'll be back? I won't make plans until I know."

"Well, maybe you should," Vochek said, and she realized, with a drop in her stomach, that she sounded thoughtless. "I just mean, Mom, if there's something you want to do, go. Go to the movies, or the museum, or shopping. Don't wait on me." *Please,* she thought. *Find a friend. Make an effort. Don't let your life just slide by, Mom.*

"I don't mind waiting." And then Mom launched into a summary of her gripes about Houston: the humidity, the traffic, the lack of a good New York–style pizza, missing her friends back in Oyster Bay. Vochek gave her two minutes of free daughter-guilting and said, "Love you, Mom. I'm sorry. I got to go. Okay, bye."

She turned back toward the door and a pistol was in her face. A big-built man stood behind the gun.

"That's nice that you love your mama."

Vochek didn't speak. She clutched her phone tighter.

"I don't want Mama picking out a casket for you," the man said. "Where is Teach?"

The gun in her face made it hard to talk, but she managed. "I'm a federal officer. Lower your weapon."

"Nice bluff, but I saw the soldiers downstairs are hired. Where is she?" the man repeated.

"I'm the only she here. I'm a Homeland Security agent. Lower your weapon. Please." She knew she shouldn't say *please*; she needed the edge of authority in her tone, but the word slipped out before she thought. The gun was an inch from her face and she thought: *If he shoots me this close, Mom won't even recognize my face.*

A telescoping baton lay next to her purse; she'd kept it in case Ben Forsberg had to be subdued without deadly force. Her purse blocked the weapon from the man's view. No way she could go for her gun, in the rig under her jacket.

"My badge is in my purse," she said. "May I get it? It should convince you."

"No. Lock your hands on your head." The man reached under her jacket, liberated Vochek's service piece, stepped back. Both hands holding guns.

She threw her phone at his face.

The phone nailed him in the forehead but he ignored it. He clubbed her with the pistol, hitting her shoulder. She lurched hard against the table. And grabbed the baton.

It snapped into its two-foot length with a click, and she spun, whipping it at his face. He dodged. She swung the baton back, nearly catching the top of his head as he ducked. He hit her wrist hard and the pain bolted along her bone like flame. The baton fell nervelessly from her fingers.

No, she thought. He took her down without even having to fire either gun. An unexpected bolt of humiliation cut through the fear and the hurt.

The man tucked her gun into the back of his pants. He stepped back several paces from Vochek, still keeping his gun leveled at her head. "Don't blame you for trying."

"I'm Homeland Security," she repeated. "Kill me and the penalty doubles."

"Turn around."

"Shoot me in the back. Nice." Vochek's chin lifted in defiance. "I won't turn around."

"Don't make this worse." The man gestured with the gun.

Vochek turned. She didn't want to show fear, but as she turned to face the wall her lips twisted, her throat tightened. She thought of her mother and never having another dinner with her.

"Sorry," he said, and she thought: *He's really going to shoot me. This is how it ends.*

The blow, direct into the nerve juncture at her neck, crumpled her to her knees.

"I'm sorry," he said again. Then blackness folded over her eyes as the tile of the floor rushed toward her.

Pilgrim fished the ID out of the unconscious woman's purse.

Department of Homeland Security. Office of Strategic Initiatives. Joanna Vochek.

It was either a very good fake or she was telling the truth. Pilgrim dropped the ID onto her stomach. He picked up her phone, turned it off, and tucked it into his pocket; phones could be useful sources of information. If Homeland was attacking the Cellar, then the situation was far worse, because he would then be fighting the resources of the American government.

Which meant his battle was against a far more dangerous and powerful enemy than a bunch of gun-toting kidnappers with a grudge against the Cellar. The thought dried his mouth.

He dragged the unconscious Vochek into a storage closet and locked her inside. One less person to worry about.

He returned to the hallway and closed the door behind him. He hurried down the hall, gun straight out, listening.

Pilgrim heard voices, arguing, from behind a door.

10

———◆◉◆———

KIDWELL SHOVED BEN BACK into the chair. Pain sparkled like a spinning firecracker in Ben's skull.

Kidwell leveled the gun at Ben. "Amazing how a bullet in the knee loosens a tongue."

"I've quit believing that you're with Homeland Security," Ben said, "and—"

Boom. For a second Ben thought Kidwell's gun had fired. The door flew open from a kick.

A man stood there with a gun. He aimed at Kidwell, who lifted his pistol to fire.

The man shot first. He nailed Kidwell in the leg. Kidwell collapsed with a scream. The man rushed Kidwell, freed the gun from Kidwell's grip with a vicious kick.

Kidwell wore a look of utter surprise.

The man regarded Ben, who stayed in the chair as though locked to it. Kidwell kept screaming. Ben thought: *He's right, a bullet in the leg does make you talk.* He felt like slapping himself to set his mind back to order.

"Where is Teach?" the man asked.

"I don't know what you mean." Ben frowned at him as if he were speaking gibberish.

"Identify yourself," the man said. He looked first at

Kidwell, who writhed in pain on the floor, blood seeping between his fingers as he gripped his leg.

Ben managed to speak. "He's Agent Kidwell, Homeland Security. Supposedly."

"Where is the woman you took from the lake house? Tell me or I shoot." The man stood over Kidwell. "Did Barker work for you? The Arabs?"

"Don't know...what you mean..." Kidwell gritted his teeth, closed his hand over the flesh wound in his leg.

"You. Up. Against the wall." The man's gun tracked him as Ben obeyed.

"I haven't seen any woman," Ben said. "I'm not with Homeland Security; he brought me here."

The man glanced between Ben and Kidwell again. "Who are you?"

"Ben Forsberg."

The gun wavered and naked shock crossed the big man's gaunt face. "Say again." As if Ben had spoken in Latin.

"My name is Ben Forsberg," Ben repeated. Then in panic the words seemed to spill from his mouth: "They think I knew some hit man and I don't, I shouldn't be here—"

The man shushed Ben, bringing his gun to his own lips like a hushing finger. He blinked as though thinking. Then Ben could see a decision made, in the man's sudden resolve. "My name is Pilgrim. Come with me. Help me find her."

"No...other prisoner here." Kidwell had pulled himself up to a sitting position and leaned against the wall, clutching at his torn leg. "Just this man, and you've shot a federal officer, and you're in deep trouble."

Pilgrim said, "You. Come with me."

Ben wasn't inclined to trade in Kidwell for this new jerk, but he had no choice. He followed the man into the hallway.

Pilgrim ran to the other doors, yelling "Teach!" and listening for a response.

"Who are you?" Ben asked.

Pilgrim didn't spare him a glance. "I'm the guy who's getting you out of here."

At the middle of the hallway, between them and the room they'd left Kidwell in, the elevator door pinged and opened.

"Get behind me," Pilgrim said.

KHALED'S REPORT—
BEIRUT

MY RECRUITMENT WAS A SEDUCTION. Not in the physical sense; there was of course none of that. But in the long crush of weeks after my brothers and my father died, I began to realize I was being followed. By a man I now know as J.

At first I was very afraid. No one had been brought to justice for the bombing, and I wondered if my brothers' enemies—whether they be domestic or foreign—might target me. Paranoia is not a healthy life, but often I noticed J—in the market, as I made my way home from the university, returning home from my aunt's house with my mother. J watched us, followed us. I said nothing to Mama; her worries were already crushing her.

He approaches me at the school library. Sits down across from me at a table. We are alone.

"Hello, Khaled."

I say nothing.

"I know who killed your brothers and their friends," he says.

I look back down at my financial analysis textbook. The charts and tables swim before my eyes.

"Don't you wish to know?" he says after my silence becomes uncomfortable.

"Yes," I say.

Then he surprises me. "Why do you wish to know?"

"Because I want to fight back against whoever killed them. I want them dead. I want them suffering."

Now it was his turn to be silent.

"You seem a stuffy sort and you are thin. I'm not sure you will be useful." J puts his hands flat on the table.

I let all the strength gather in my body. "I'd like to be useful."

"Come with me," he says.

I do. Over the next day he shows me the proof— financial trails, photos, a picture of the Khaled boy with the deformed lip, now lying on a morgue slab.

"I killed him," J says. "He cried before I shot him. I didn't much like him. He wouldn't betray his friends, he wouldn't work with us."

I don't take any relief in seeing the dead man, even though he planted the bomb. He is just a cog; I want to break the machine. "You could give all this evidence to the police."

"They would do nothing," J says. "You could do something."

"What?"

J leans back in his chair, lit his cigarette. "Join us."

"No."

He offers the cigarettes to me and I shake my head. "I expected you to say yes."

"I'm not a fool."

"No, you're not, Khaled. That's why I'm issuing the offer to you. You are ideal. You're young, smart, and motivated."

"I'm just one man."

"We have several young men lined up for this sort of dangerous work."

"Where would I go?"

"America." J almost says it with a growl.

I hesitate on how to answer. I want to strike back at the murderers. I want to make something happen so another family does not go through this horror. I put my face in my hands. If Papa hadn't died...maybe I could say no to J. But my brothers' deaths have shown me the ripple effect. My brothers' murderers killed more than themselves. Blood of Fire's enemies remain unpunished. And if I decline J's offer...am I suddenly, well, dangerous to J and his people? I know about them. The thought chills.

It is the single biggest moment of my life. Decide whether to avenge my family or whether to walk away and be safe. But there is no safety in this world.

"What do I have to do?" I ask.

"First? You have to sneak into America, Khaled," J says.

"Will I have help?"

"Yes. But if you're caught, we do nothing for you. You never heard of us. You speak of us, and I don't think American prison will go very well for you."

I swallow. The decision makes itself. I nod. "When do I leave?"

11

BEN SAW TWO MEN—HARD-FACED, pale, wearing jeans and dark T-shirts. One sported wraparound sunglasses, the other a punkish thatch of black-and-white hair. He didn't see the guns until the one in sunglasses raised a pistol and the other gunman hoisted a rifle.

"Run," Pilgrim said, putting himself between Ben and the gunmen, firing at them as he ran. Ben turned and sprinted down the hallway. In the narrow corridor the sudden blasts of two shots boomed like thunder yanked close to earth.

Ben headed for a stairwell at the end of the hallway. An exit sign hung above the door, and as he bolted toward it the sign shattered, a stray bullet slamming through the X.

As he reached for the door, heat hissed past his ear. He tried the door. Locked. Then Pilgrim jerked Ben back from the door, fired a bullet into the lock, a punch of fire and metal. Pilgrim kicked the door open and shoved Ben into the stairway. A faint, dying-bulb glow lit the stairs.

"Stop," Pilgrim said. "There could be more downstairs. I'm sure there are at least three of them. I'll kill these two here."

Okay, fine then, you'll kill them here. Ben couldn't

believe Pilgrim's calm. Ben took a step backward onto the stairs. "They'll shoot us—"

"We need to get to the ground level."

They heard a man down the hallway, pleading "No," then the bang of a shot.

Kidwell, Ben thought. Where was Vochek? The two guards? He wasn't going to stand here and get shot. The solution was distance between him and the guys with guns. Including this one.

He doesn't want to give away his position—he won't shoot you. Logic was a beauty.

Ben turned and ran for the rooftop door.

"No," Pilgrim hissed. "Get back here"—but Ben hit the door to the roof and it opened.

He ran out onto the roof's concrete expanse. The day was dying, the sun halfway through its low slide into the hills. He saw another roof entrance on the opposite side, with a jumble of industrial AC units and ventilation equipment in between. And he ran straight for the door, an escape hatch, a way out of this nightmare.

The door opened.

Pilgrim couldn't protect the idiot if said idiot wouldn't listen to orders. He hated extraction jobs and hadn't done one in over ten years; it was a bother to worry about keeping a frantic civilian alive in the heat of dirty work. But he had to keep Ben Forsberg alive. Because Ben Forsberg was clearly the key to understanding what was going on, with Teach, with the Cellar, with this attack.

First things first. The two gunmen in the hallway. Keep one alive to talk, to tell him where they'd taken Teach.

He considered. The staircase was concrete, with metal

railings. He peered down into the gloom. The pit of the stairwell dropped down six stories and offered no nooks or crannies in which to hide. No cover.

But there was the bend of the stairs. Where the stairs forked at the landing, the plain metal railing met the dusty concrete. The railing's post stood close to the gap in the stairs.

He could hide in the gap, just below the landing.

Pilgrim eased himself over the railing, tested to see if his feet would reach to the railing below. No. If he braced himself in the gap, his head and shoulders would show, and they'd blow his brains out in the first few seconds. But if he held on to the railing one-handed...

He tested the idea. Only his fingers, wrapped around the metal of the railing post, were exposed. He held the Glock in his right hand; he couldn't see the landing, but the gunmen, if they came through, would be standing just so—he pictured the positions in his mind—and he screamed, in hysterically tinged Arabic, "I give up, I surrender, truce, let's talk."

They would know he was on the landing, and they'd fire suppressing rounds to clear him off the landing before they set a foot inside.

He heard the broken door kicked open, a spray of bullets hitting the steps where a man would stand. If they saw his fingers gripping the bottom inches of the post they would simply blast the bones of his fingers away and he'd fall. The stairwell went dark, the lights blown out.

The shooting stopped.

Pilgrim raised the gun above the lip of the landing, emptied the clip at an angle he hoped would catch the knees. Bullets pocked against skin and bone, and screams echoed against the concrete. He released his hold as a bullet smashed against the post he'd been gripping, the screams fading, and he landed, feet hitting the railing below, bouncing from the rail to land like an awkward cat on the steps.

Pilgrim scrambled to his feet, drew the gun he'd taken from Kidwell, and ran to the landing. The punk-blond gunman lay dead, guts ripped, heart hollowed. The one in the cheap wraparounds had caught shots in the chest and the groin. He cupped one hand around the blood welling from his jeans while reaching toward the blond's gun.

Pilgrim shot him in the hand and the man shrieked.

"Where is the woman you took?" he said.

The man cussed him and Pilgrim answered in Arabic, "I will get you a doctor and promise protection for you if you tell me."

"She is dead," he screamed. He drew his knee up to his bloodied crotch.

"You wouldn't kidnap her just to kill her. Where is she?"

He mumbled an answer, gasped in exquisite pain.

"Who do you work for?"

One of the lenses on the man's sunglasses was shattered, either from the crease of a graze or from falling on the floor, and it resembled an empty eye staring back at Pilgrim. The man grimaced and frowned, and shuddered a final breath.

Then a shot thundered on the roof. Pilgrim remembered the person he needed to keep alive.

The roof door opened and Ben bolted for the cover of the closest AC unit. He was down and hidden before whoever came through the door had closed it.

Ben crouched against the metal of the unit and tried to

breathe silently. He listened, trying to hear which way the man moved. Instead he heard the hubbub of the ordinary world: brakes on the street, music rising from the festival nearby, a car honking, the hiss of the air-conditioning system.

Then he heard a footstep. Close. As though the hunter were taking the measure of the wind, breathing the scent of Ben's fear.

Ben had no weapon. Nothing. He had the clothes on his back, shoes, a belt...He stopped and carefully slid the belt free from his pants. He grabbed the end of it, opposite the buckle. The silver buckle wasn't heavy but it would hurt if it hit a face, a nose, a mouth.

Fighting a killer with a belt? He was an idiot. He tried not to shiver.

"You're not the one I want," a voice, accented, called.

Ben didn't move. No point—the man knew where he was. He just didn't know if Ben had a weapon, was trying to urge him out rather than fight.

"You tell me where Pilgrim is, and I'll let you live. I have no gripe with you. Him I want. He killed my cousins."

The man stepped around the corner of the unit, a heavy gun in his hand. Ben swung the belt overhead, as hard as he would swing an ax. The buckle cracked against the wrist bone, the shot blasting into the ground, close to Ben's foot.

The man—Ben saw heavy shoulders, a mole on his chin, a snarl of teeth—instinctively grabbed at his wrist, more surprised than hurt, and Ben barreled into him before he could lift the gun into Ben's chest.

Pilgrim ran up the stairs. The shot probably meant Ben Forsberg was dead. He needed someone still alive to tell him what was happening. He went through the door low, gun out, and halfway across the expanse of roof he saw Ben struggling with another man. The gunman was trying to shoot Ben in the head, but Ben fought hard, if not well, keeping the man's gun aimed upward. But Ben was quickly losing the battle.

Pilgrim lifted his gun, aiming to shoot the gunman in the shoulder as the two men fought.

Then the gunman saw Pilgrim and head-butted Ben. But Ben didn't release his grip on the gunman as he fell backward, and the bigger man toppled. The two of them vanished behind an electrical unit.

Pilgrim ran to the mechanism. The gunman cradled Ben Forsberg in a headlock, the gun aimed at his temple, a thick arm around Ben's throat. He held Ben up as a shield. Pilgrim aimed at the man's head. "Let's talk," he said in Arabic.

"Stop or I'll kill him," the gunman said in English.

Pilgrim shrugged. "Kill him. I don't care."

The gunman retreated toward the other door, hauling Ben with him.

"I'll shoot right through Ben if I have to," Pilgrim said.

"No!" Ben yelled.

"Then do it, big mouth," the gunman said.

"But you," Pilgrim said, "get to live if you tell me who took the woman from the lake house. Where is she?"

The gunman said, "You came to the roof to save this man, so you want him alive."

"Don't let him—" Ben started but the gunman yanked on his throat and Ben went a shade of blue for a few moments. He fell silent.

Pilgrim shrugged. "Shoot him; he keeps interrupting

me." If only Ben Forsberg would have the guts or the stupidity to fight, to break away and run, then Pilgrim could shoot the gunman in the knees, get the answers he needed. "I've killed everyone you people have sent at me today. But you, I'll let you walk, just tell me where she is."

Ben remained silent, but Pilgrim saw rage win out over fear in his eyes and thought: *If Ben decides to fight, it'll be interesting. Be ready.*

"Your only way out is to talk to me," Pilgrim said.

Ten seconds passed that felt like ten days, and the gunman said, "The woman. She's in a silver van a couple of blocks away. With an Irishman."

"No. I killed the Irishman."

"You left another Irishman behind. A brother."

"What's his name?"

"Jackie."

"Who do you and Jackie work for?"

The gunman shook his head. "I told you enough. You, idiot, open the door." He pivoted Ben slightly—he didn't have a free hand, without releasing either Ben or his gun, which was aimed at Pilgrim—and he turned Ben toward the door so Ben could grab the handle.

Two heads together, struggling, with one square inch of suddenly clear temple, and Pilgrim nailed the open space. A thunking round powered through scalp, bone, and brain. The gunman sagged, Ben sinking to his knees with the body.

Pilgrim started toward the gunman, pistol out and down toward the body, making sure the man was dead.

Ben reached over and grabbed the gunman's pistol. And raised it at Pilgrim.

"Uh, hello," Pilgrim said. "Your life. Just saved. By me."

"Okay, thank you. Thanks. Appreciate it." Ben didn't let go of the gun. His muscles felt thin and taut as wire.

"Ben. Put the gun down."

"No. I'm getting out of here. You stay put. I'm just going to head downstairs and call the police..." The gun started to waver.

"And they'll give you back to Homeland Security," Pilgrim said. "They suspect you were involved in killing Adam Reynolds. They found your business card in Nicky Lynch's pocket. Right?"

The gun wavered in Ben's grip. Every nerve ending warned him to run, to put distance between himself and this nightmare. But he couldn't make a stupid move. Not now. He needed the truth about the past day if he had a prayer of clearing his name. "Who are you?"

A distant rise of sirens. The police, approaching.

Pilgrim lowered his gun, raised a palm. "I can answer your questions and you can answer mine. We can help each other. But not if we're both in custody. Which is where we will be in five minutes if we don't move."

"This is all a mistake."

"What it is, Ben, is a double. A special kind of frame, done to you and me both. We've both been set up to take the fall here. We've both been screwed."

"I don't understand."

"I work for the government, but I can't go to the police. Neither can you. Not yet. Not until we know who framed you, who tried to kill me. This Teach I'm searching for, she's my boss. And whoever took her," Pilgrim said, "is the same person who framed you and set me up to die."

"We have to go to the police."

The sirens drew closer. Someone had heard the rattle

of gunfire over the hum of nightlife. "Police will defer to Homeland, to Kidwell's special group. You want a buddy of Kidwell's to start beating you again?"

"No..."

"Then come with me. Now. We need to find out who's targeted us and why. Later, you want to walk away, you want to go to the police, I'll let you. But right now, we have to run."

"It looks worse if we run."

"Forget looks. Worry about reality."

The sirens grew louder. Ben handed him the gun.

They ran down the stairwell to the top floor. "Vochek," Ben said. "There's a woman with Kidwell..."

"I knocked her out and locked her in a closet. She should be safe. I don't think they found her." They paused at the room where Kidwell lay. Nothing to be done—the gunmen had shot him once in the head. The granite face was still.

"Let Vochek out."

"The cops will. She'll be okay." He grabbed Ben's arm and hurried him down the hallway.

They ran down the stairwell to the first floor.

The hallway was empty, except for the guard Pilgrim had knocked out. The man lay dead, two bullets marring the skin behind his ear. Another guard lay dead by the closed back door, open-eyed, two bullets in his face.

Ben made a choked noise.

"The gunmen came in to kill everybody," Pilgrim said. He turned Ben to face him. "Listen. This Jackie may be waiting outside, to kill anyone trying to get out. You stay low, you follow me, and if I get shot you keep running."

Ben nodded. "What if I get shot?"

"Then I keep running," Pilgrim said.

On the other side of the building, sirens blasted their arrival. Pilgrim and Ben ran for the chain-link fence and went through the gate.

And no sign of a van where Teach would be. But there was practically no street parking, and the closest parking was the garage where Pilgrim had stashed the Volvo.

"Come on." He grabbed Ben's arm and they ran down Second Street, toward the parking garage. A couple of blocks away, the gunman said. Maybe he lied. Maybe he didn't. Pilgrim's eyes scanned the garage's levels—if Jackie Lynch was parked there, he'd be waiting for the trio of gunmen. He'd know what Pilgrim looked like. Jackie Lynch could be watching him and Ben right now, seeing them approach, knowing that their survival meant the gunmen's failure.

"We may not be able to get to my car. We'll have to steal one if we can't."

"Steal a car. Are you kidding me? I am not stealing a car."

"Borrow, then. We'll bumper-surf." He spoke to Ben in a voice of utter calm, thinking, *Give him a problem to worry about other than getting shot.* "It's easy; you hunt for those little magnetic boxes under the bumper that hold a spare key so people don't lock themselves out . . ." As they navigated into the meandering crowd spilling from the bars and the streets, Pilgrim slowed down, keeping Ben close to him.

"What are we going to do?" Ben said. He was calmer now.

"I'm going to get you to a car, and then I'm going to find my boss while you wait."

They muscled through the crowd, headed east for two

blocks, and ran to the garage's stairwell. They climbed the stairs up to the floor where Pilgrim had parked.

"Wait here," Pilgrim ordered Ben. Pilgrim eased into the row of cars, gun out, up, watching. The garage was quiet. He scanned the parked cars. No sign of a silver van. Many slots remained full, either people working late or downtown for the music festival. But he didn't see anyone leaving or heading toward a car.

The stolen Volvo sat where he'd left it. Pilgrim turned back toward the stairwell door and gestured an all-clear.

He saw the door closing. Ben Forsberg was gone.

12

BEN RAN DOWN THE CONCRETE STEPS. Get away from the lunatic, find a policeman now and tell him everything. Yes, maybe he would end up back in the hands of this freaking weird division of Homeland Security, but he was a witness to murder and he wasn't going to steal a car and he wasn't going to run. The idle suggestion—*We'll steal a car*—had been the proverbial bucket of ice water, clearing the shock from Ben's mind. That was not the responsible course of action. He had a business to consider, a reputation, and this horrific night could not redefine him as a person. Once he had a lawyer, the world would shift back to its normal orbit. Sam Hector and his vast connections in the government would get Ben's good name cleared.

He could get to the ground floor faster taking the stairs than Pilgrim could in a car.

He heard the stairwell door bang open, a flight above him. "Ben!"

Run.

Ben didn't continue down the stairs—they were empty. Pilgrim could fire down at him or catch up with him, the guy was obviously a soldier of a serious stripe. But people might be on one of the levels. Attendants. Barhoppers. Someone who could help him.

He hit the door. The second level was empty. No people, just cars in most of the slots.

He ran across the level, arrowing for the opposite stairwell. *Get as far away as you can,* he told himself, *just run run run—*

A van peeled fast down the incline between him and the far stairwell door, and he raised his hands, beckoning for help as the van cornered and roared toward him. Ben saw a young, soft-faced man with stringy dark hair behind the windshield.

The van didn't stop. The kid's arm jutted suddenly from the driver's open window and a blinding red light caught Ben's eyes. But not before he saw that the kid held a gun.

A silver van, the gunman on the roof had said.

Ben flung himself between a Saab and a BMW. A shot cracked, shattering the BMW's window above him. The van's brakes squealed as though the driver stood on the pedal. Ben didn't huddle under the sedan; he rolled under two SUVs parked next to it, grease staining his shirt and pants, trying his hardest to be silent.

Nowhere else to run. Nowhere to escape. The kid could just get out of the van and shoot him dead, ease down, smile at Ben in his temporary fortress of undercarriage and concrete.

Ben waited to hear the van door open. But instead he heard an eruption of gunfire.

Pilgrim barreled out of the stairwell—he'd caught a glimpse of Ben running down the stairs, hitting the second-level door—and saw Ben dodging a van, a laser sight dancing, a glow seeking flesh, then a shot fracturing the rear wind-shield of a car behind where Ben had stood.

The van. Jackie Lynch. Teach was inside that van if the gunman had told the truth.

Then the laser sight swung toward Pilgrim, caught between the stairwell door and a parked car, as the van braked to an awkward, neck-snapping stop.

The shots sang a warble of *th-weets* and Pilgrim retreated backward, the sting and burn of steel ripping through flesh in his shoulder and his arm. He staggered, missing the door as Jackie leaned out the window to tighten his aim and fin-ish the job.

He retreated, blindly, no place to run, and threw himself over the concrete lip of the garage wall. He dropped into emptiness. How far up was he? he wondered. He couldn't remember past the pain.

Now in a burst of speed the van powered past where Ben hid.

The guy could kill him easy—why was he running?

Because he just shot who he was really after. Pilgrim.

Ben crawled from under the utility vehicle. Bullet holes scored the wall along the stairwell door, a spill of blood decorated the lip of the edge. Where, presumably, Pilgrim had stood in chasing him.

He started to run toward the other stairwell. He heard a screech of brakes. He stopped. Pilgrim could be lying back there, dead, dying.

He leaned against a parked truck. His and Pilgrim's lives were somehow connected, tied to each other, because of the murder of Adam Reynolds and how Ben had been framed for it. *I can answer your questions,* Pilgrim had said, *and you can answer mine. We can help each other. But not if we're both in custody.* If Pilgrim died, Ben might never be able to prove his innocence. Homeland Security could threaten him all over again, his reputation would be destroyed, he would never know the truth. Pilgrim must know the reasons why Ben's life had been targeted and ruined.

Pilgrim had saved him from Kidwell, from the gunman on the roof.

Ben ran back to the edge of the garage and peered down the side. Pilgrim lay, a story and a half below him, in a row of crushed yaupon bushes, moving his arms, groggy, hurt, barely lifting his head.

Halfway down the incline to the ground floor, a crowd of college kids were laughing and piling into their cars, debating through the open windows which club to visit. Jackie guessed they hadn't heard the sounds of the silenced shots or had attributed the bangs to festival noise. But the kids were taking their own sweet, slow time, calling from car to car while they inched out of the parking slots, blocking the passage. Jackie slammed on his brakes to keep from veering into them.

Jackie rolled down the window. "Move it, now!"

"Hey! Politeness, dude." A boy his own age, sitting in one of the cars, slurred his syllables and gave Jackie a beer-soaked smile. Jackie wanted to shoot and knife them all, but the cars were full, six kids in each, and it was too many, it would take too long.

"Please," Jackie said. "Please. Sorry I yelled. I'm in an awful hurry. Please move."

"See, politeness works," the loudmouth said. The car inched up enough to let Jackie roar past.

Jackie yanked up his pants leg, pulled the eight-inch

steel knife from its sheath. If Pilgrim lay hurt on the ground, he'd dispatch him with the knife. Quiet and it wouldn't draw the attention a gun would. If there were witnesses helping Pilgrim, the knife was fast—he'd killed a quartet of late-paying drug dealers in a small Dublin room once with the knife, in under thirty seconds.

Nicky, I'm going to make it right, he thought.

Ben sprinted down the stairwell again, hands skimming the railing. He hit the exit, and the cool night air washed over his filthy and bloodied face. He turned the corner and Pilgrim was trying to stand, favoring his leg. Bleeding, shot in the shoulder.

"C'mon." Ben looped Pilgrim's arm over his shoulder. Pilgrim was only a couple of inches taller than him but he felt much heavier. Pilgrim—hurt—leaned hard against him. They couldn't run down the street; the van would be here within seconds, and the shooter in the van was bound and determined to be sure Pilgrim was dead.

"I'm *shot*..."

"I know, come on, come on." Ben pivoted Pilgrim, half-dragged, half-carried him back into the garage. They needed to hide. Now. Or the maniac in the van would cut them both down.

The crash of a wooden barrier breaking boomed on the opposite side of the garage. They ran, Pilgrim gasping, for the elevator. Ben thumbed the Up button. The doors slid open at once and the two of them fell into the open elevator.

Ben rose on his knees and jabbed the controls. The roar of a car approached, and he'd gambled wrong; they were trapped. He dragged Pilgrim into the far corner of the elevator, where they couldn't be seen.

The elevator doors slid closed as a van powered past and onto the street, its headlights sweeping the broken bushes and the empty sidewalk.

Pilgrim was gone. Jackie Lynch circled the parking garage twice, peering at the entrances, letting his headlights spill along the streets, lighting the couples and singles walking along toward the restaurants and nightclubs. He could guess Pilgrim's point of impact from the mashed bushes— but Pilgrim wasn't there. Which meant he wasn't hurt, and he was running.

He turned around to drive back into the garage, but a large crowd of pedestrians—festivalgoers, he guessed— were pouring into the garage as a light rain began to fall again. Too many people there now, too many witnesses.

Maybe they hadn't gone back into the garage.

He drove up and down the neighboring streets, rage building in the cage of his heart. He scanned the crowds for a limping, bloodied man.

Nicky wouldn't have missed him, not that close. Then he thought, *Kick Nicky off the pedestal. Nicky sure missed when it counted.*

The phone rang. He put the knife on the seat and clicked on the cell phone.

"Report." It was Sam Hector.

"They're dead, they're all dead . . ." Jackie started.

"You better mean Forsberg and Pilgrim."

The name Forsberg meant nothing to him, but he said, "No, I mean your bloody Arab hired guns. All dead. Pilgrim killed them all."

"It's just you left?" Hector didn't show any emotion; the iron control made Jackie dislike him more.

"Yes and I'm going to find Pilgrim and kill him...He's gone; I hit him but he's gone, he's gone."

"Get out of there. Now. Get Teach to my place. I'll text directions to your phone."

"But Pilgrim's still—"

"Do what I tell you or I'll forfeit your payment."

Maybe I'll just keep the woman, see how you like that, he thought in a blistering rage. But no. Sam Hector would be an extremely dangerous enemy to have. Better to deliver the woman. Get his money. Then see if there was any way to use Hector to find this Pilgrim again.

Jackie drove until he saw the sign for I-35 and found an entrance ramp, heading toward Dallas, four hours north. Leaving the town now where his brother had died, and for the first time he wondered what would happen to Nicky's body, where it would be buried, how he could ever get it home to Northern Ireland. He suspected he couldn't. He started to tremble, not with grief. With rage.

Today wasn't supposed to be this way.

Several blocks to the west a Volvo station wagon worked past the crowds.

13

———◦◦◦———

"Pain is nothing," Pilgrim muttered in agony. "Pain is a friend. If you don't feel pain you're dead." He repeated it like a mantra.

"Pain says you need a doctor." Ben drove west on Sixth Street, heading out of downtown, watching his rearview, trying to make sure he wasn't being followed. He made a sharp turn, headed north for a few blocks, then turned east again. Brackenridge Hospital was on East Fifteenth Street—he could be there in a few minutes.

"No doctor. No hospital." Pilgrim gritted his teeth.

"Don't be stupid. You're hurt."

"No. I'm lucky. Haven't ever been shot before. Haven't ever fallen from a building. What a day."

"I'm taking you to a hospital."

"No. Can't go. We'll be right back where we started. You'll be in custody and I'll be…"

"Where?"

"Hurts too bad to talk. Keep driving." Pilgrim pressed his fist hard against his shoulder. "A federal agent pulled a gun on you and a killer had your name in his pocket and another killer just tried to shoot your head off. You might want to stay under the radar."

"I'm still taking you to a hospital."

"If you want to stay alive, get us to Dallas. If I pass out, get me into a motel, cheap, get a first-aid kit."

"First aid. For a bullet wound."

"And a tool to dig the bullet out. Don't forget that."

"I'm not digging a bullet out of you. Get real." He turned into the Brackenridge Hospital parking lot, the emergency sign a beacon.

Pilgrim grabbed the wheel. "No. I am begging you. Please. If you bring me here, we're both dead men."

Ben hesitated as he started to pull into the overhang by the entrance.

"We're guaranteed dead. We have to get to Dallas."

"Why do we go to Dallas?"

"Because the matchbook I found on the gunman is from a Dallas restaurant; Barker betrayed me and his driver's license address is in Dallas. Those are my only leads." And then he added: "The guard I knocked out had a Hector Global ID in his pocket. The back of the ID badge gave an address near Dallas."

Ben tightened his grip on the wheel. "The guards weren't Homeland agents?"

"Nope. So I'm thinking this Hector company's connected to this whole mess."

Ben swallowed. "Sam Hector, he owns Hector Global, he's a client of mine. He's one of my closest friends. He wouldn't be involved in anything illicit or illegal. I spoke with him not three hours ago..."

Pilgrim stared at him. "Awful big coincidence. Our friend Kidwell should have Homeland agents working as his guards—not hired guns."

Two paramedics came out, began to walk toward the Volvo.

"We can't stay here, Ben, please. Drive!"

"Hector Global must have a contract with Kidwell's group...Sam can help us, can tell us what's going on..."

"Maybe." Pilgrim leaned against the door, putting pressure on his shoulder wound. "If he's really your friend, okay, let's ask him for help. But not here. Get us to Dallas, Ben, please."

A car behind them honked and Ben pulled back out into the lot, past the paramedics. He turned east onto Fifteenth Street, then headed north onto I-35, toward Dallas.

"That's the first smart move I've seen you make."

"I'm only doing this because...Kidwell implied..." Ben swallowed. "Two years ago my wife was killed. Murdered. On our honeymoon. Shot to death. It was a random thing."

"Damn. That sucks. Sorry."

In its odd, awkward way it was one of the most sincere expressions of sympathy he'd gotten. Most people said nothing more than *I'm sorry*. A few shared horrors like *At least she didn't suffer* or *You're young, you'll marry again*. And some said nothing, which was somehow worse, as though Emily had never existed. "Kidwell suggested I'd had her killed. Like I had a history with hired killers like Nicky Lynch."

Pilgrim watched the road spill past, breathing in rhythm to control the pain. Several minutes passed.

Ben broke the silence. "Let me call Sam. Hector Global's a huge company. Sam might not even know he's got people working for Kidwell. He could tell us who Kidwell is."

Pilgrim twisted slightly in the seat. "I'll make you a deal, Ben."

"I'm listening."

"I can help you clear your name, Ben. But only if you help me."

Ben considered. "What's to keep me from driving straight to a police officer, then? They'll force you to talk."

"If the police get ahold of me, I'll get turned over to the government and you'll never see me again...and then you're trapped under suspicion of the worst sort. I don't officially exist anymore, I can't help you if we're caught. You're going to have a rotten time clearing your name. Might never do it." He stared out the window as they went past the suburban spread of Round Rock, letting the weight of his words settle down on Ben.

The idea made Ben's skin prickle. He'd already endured the rot of suspicion before, after Emily's death, because the husband was always a prime suspect. "So what are you, a government agent or an undercover cop?"

"I'm a strange breed."

"What does that mean?"

"It means I'm not telling you what I do. Not until you help me. I need your help, Ben, I'm asking for it."

Ben swallowed. "Why me? Why is this happening?"

"I can hazard a guess. Your wife."

"I don't—"

"Ben. You were a suspect in her murder, weren't you? It would only be natural."

His throat closed and he coughed. "Briefly. But the police cleared me. I had no involvement."

He'd had to fly home to Dallas from his honeymoon alone, the worst flight of his life. Her body lay in the plane's cargo hold. He arrived alone at the house they had shared; her parents, shattered in their own grief and blaming him because the world had been cruel and capricious, did not meet him at the airport. Sam was on a trip and couldn't get back in time. Within a few more days he realized that Dallas had gone dead for him, and he'd moved back to his hometown of Austin, where there were fewer whispers about him behind cupped hands.

"If you wanted to frame a person, a man who's already been suspect once is a much easier sell. To the police. To the media."

"But why me—"

"I'll explain why you were framed. Just get me patched up and get me to Dallas." His words slurred, his eyes fogged with pain. "It's a fair trade. I'm trusting you, Ben. Do we have a deal?"

"Yes. I give you my word," Ben said. "We have a deal."

"I need some water."

Ben took the next exit, stayed on the frontage road until he reached a gas station. He went inside. The cashier said hi and he said hi back. He bought two bottles of water. He hurried back to the Volvo. Ben opened the bottle for Pilgrim, watched him gulp the water down.

"I should have thought of getting you water sooner. Sorry. I'm not used to dealing with gunshot wounds."

"I can't make it to Dallas without getting patched up."

Ben pulled back onto the highway. "I'm going to find a Walmart, and then a motel, and get you cleaned up, stop the bleeding."

"Thank you."

"Can I use a credit card? Will the police or Homeland Security be looking for me? Kidwell said he'd freeze my accounts."

Pilgrim said, "I got a credit card we can use." He laughed. "Can you forge a signature?"

"Um, I've never tried."

"Trust me. It's not hard to learn. You look like a quick study." Pilgrim sagged against the door, eyes at half-mast. "I'm not in good shape here, man..."

Ben floored the car down the highway.

14

———◆———

Jackie Lynch's throat ached from singing. The van's broken radio hissed static and he couldn't bear the silence, so he sang, slow and low, the entirety of Johnny Cash's *At Folsom Prison* album. The rereleased version had been his and Nicky's favorite. He'd started with "Folsom Prison Blues," then sang his way through the poetry of the other eighteen songs. He knew every lyric, but on Nicky's favorites it was a struggle to finish, to link the words together. He sang the album in an hour, listened to the quiet again for five minutes, then started singing it again, like he was a busted music box doomed to spill the same notes for eternity. His stomach began to growl as he reached the small city of Hillsboro, ninety minutes south of Dallas. Hillsboro boasted a huge outlet mall and a large collection of fast-food chains and gas stations. He figured no one would remember him in the constantly changing crowd. Jackie hated the necessity of his hunger; it reminded him he was alive, and Nicky wasn't.

He bought his dinner at a McDonald's drive-through, keeping an eye on the prone form of Teach lying bound in the back of the van. He regarded her with a cordial hatred. He bought her no food in case she awoke—the woman could starve, for all he cared.

He pulled over at the far edge of the parking lot to eat his hamburger and fries. He sipped hard on a soda to cool his throat and bit into the burger. He couldn't shake off memories of Nicky. They should be eating lobsters and steaks, drinking a fancy wine, savoring a kill that would have made their reputations even more sterling; now he'd be eating alone all the time, with Nicky dead, and the realization made his face ache.

Jackie set the burger and fries into the passenger seat. The tears came hot and hard and he bent his head over the steering wheel, happy images swimming before his eyes. Nicky teaching him how to ride a bike because Da was always busy with his interrogations and his meetings; Nicky showing him how to kick a football, how to shoot a semiautomatic, how to cut with a blade so you opened the carotid on the first try. His brother shouldn't be, couldn't be, dead. He used his napkins to mop up the tears and the snot and then he used his sleeve and, looking up, he saw the boys laughing at him.

Three of them, a shade younger than him, nineteen or so. They stood four parking slots away, getting into an old, weathered sedan, but they'd seen him crying like a baby and one acted embarrassed and the other two smiled, amused at his pain.

Behind him, the woman stirred and groaned. He glanced back at her; she lay still again.

Now two of the three boys had gotten into their car but one stood there and mock-rubbed his cupped hand on his cheek, wiping away pretend tears.

Jackie opened the van's door and stepped out into the cool. The hum of the highway made a throaty murmur and the night sky spilled stars across the darkness. His fist felt primed to hit, his feet ready to kick. He didn't need a gun. Or the knife.

"What's your problem?" Jackie asked.

The boy kept his smile locked in place and said, with a twang, "Buy some pride, dude."

"My brother died today." He walked faster toward the smiling boy, whose grin faded. "Maybe I should laugh? Do a freaking jig?"

The boy ducked back into the car, started shutting the door.

Jackie caught the door handle. Fury made him strong and he reached in and dragged the boy onto the pavement. The boy twisted and hollered. Jackie punched his mouth hard; the teeth in the vanished smile cracked under his fist.

The two other boys spilled from the other side of the car. One was bigger than Jackie, with the bearing of an athlete, but Jackie didn't see muscle and speed, he saw only weaknesses born from overconfidence: a throat left unprotected, a crotch to be kicked, an eye to be gouged. He slid across the trunk to engage the athlete. Take the biggest first, Nicky told him. Jackie nailed him with a hard kick in the guts. The athlete doubled over and Jackie slammed him into the side of the car. The car door stood open and Jackie shoved the athlete's head into the opening, knocked the door hard against him. The athlete folded, bleeding from both ears.

"See," Jackie said to the last kid, rounding the car to come at him. "That's pride."

He bounced while the last kid threw a reckless punch; he stepped under it and delivered three close-in blows, to groin, stomach, and jaw. Nicky had taught him the moves. The last kid folded, mouth wide in a gasp. The athlete lay unconscious on the asphalt. Jackie ran around the car and found the once-smiling boy, dazed, trying to crawl into the driver's seat, blood dripping from his mouth and chin.

Jackie yanked the boy out of the car. He grabbed the keys from the ignition, knocked the boy to the ground.

"Cry," Jackie said.

"Don't, please!" The boy's tears welled, real ones of stark terror.

He pressed the boy's head to the pavement, jabbed the ignition key into the soft corner of the eye. The boy screamed his own throat raw. Jackie's grief vanished in the flame of his rage.

Blind him, he thought. *Do the other eye.* But he glanced up, noticed a couple of people gaping at him in shock from their cars in the drive-through line.

Time to go. He turned and the van was gone.

He dropped the keys and forgot to breathe. Then he saw the van, creaking along toward the exit, the woman driving but weaving. Like the drugs still hobbled her mind, like she hadn't figured out the relationship between accelerator and escape.

Jackie ran, leaving the boy screaming and writhing on the pavement. The van was thirty feet from careening onto a thoroughfare that bisected the highway. Thirty feet for him to catch her and please don't let her gun the gas. He cut across to the van's right side, trying to remember if he'd locked the passenger door. Hoping that she, dazed with drugs, hadn't.

The van jolted up onto the curb, flattened the spring grass, lurched out of the McDonald's lot and onto the road.

Ten feet. He ran out into the street and reached the passenger-side door, caught the handle. The van surged out into traffic. He fumbled at the handle, clicked open the door as the woman veered the van back toward him, trying to knock him down and nearly planting him on the pavement. He jumped through the door, landing on his abandoned dinner, a slick of meat and lettuce and pickle.

Now Teach hit the accelerator, ignoring the cavalcade of honks as she dodged through traffic. She veered into the wrong lane, screeched past another car. Jackie grabbed her arms with one hand, seized the steering wheel with the other. Her head bobbed as if she were only half awake.

He slammed his door shut. "Lady, no." Jackie grabbed the wheel from her, steered a clear path to the road's shoulder. He hit her, hard and precise. She went limp. He yanked her from the seat, shoved her into the back of the van. He eased into the driver's seat, roared back into traffic.

Idiot, he told himself. No control. Why did he care if small-town jerks saw him crying? His bad judgment had gotten him noticed, cut, and bruised, and nearly lost him Teach. He zoomed back onto I-35. He'd have to find another car, dump the van, steal another car, fast. He imagined Nicky's ghost crouched on his shoulder, thumping Jackie's head in disappointment. No more stupidity. It would get him in jail or dead.

The first mistake, he decided, was in feeling grief. Not again. From now on he would simply cause it for others. Gouging the boy's eye had eased his pain. That was the way to deal with grief: lose yourself in your work.

Two hours later, Jackie parked a different van at a shopping center on the edge of the growing Dallas suburb of Frisco. He'd abandoned the gunmen's van and stolen a new one from an apartment complex in Waxahachie, between Hillsboro and Dallas. The stolen van reeked of weed, and this gave Jackie his first, borderline hysterical laugh of the day.

A joint didn't sound bad at all, but then he reminded himself he was running the family business and CEOs should remain sober.

Especially when facing a very irritated customer.

So maybe it would be responsible and smart—both aspects of being the mature and executive-minded Jackie, he told himself—to have a bit of leverage over Mr. Sam Hector.

He pulled into a corner of the lot, far from the few other shoppers, far from the lights. Teach lay on the floor of the dirty van, half-watching him. He stared at her and she closed her eyes. But he could tell from the focus he'd seen in her eyes that the drugs were wearing off.

"Most old ladies been kidnapped, they would have run screaming from the van. Shrieking their throat raw for help. But you wanted to slip away, unseen, unheard."

Now Teach opened her eyes. Under the gag, under the wicked bruise on her face, the merest trace of a smile appeared. Then wavered and was gone. He went back to the rear of the van and lowered the gag.

"What are you, lady? What's your line of work?"

"I'll make you a deal," she whispered. "A million dollars if you let me go."

He laughed. "A million. Handsome offer. But my brother's dead. So money's not my reason for the game now, sorry."

"The offer expires in one minute."

She was used to hardball, he thought. "I don't need ten seconds to tell you no."

"All right," she said. Almost respectfully. It impressed him that she didn't beg.

"This Pilgrim fellow's a friend of yours."

Teach opened her eyes. "He's going to kill you. It's guaranteed."

"I shot him and he fell from a parking garage, and so odds are he's dead." Better if she had no hope.

"A man thought he'd killed him this afternoon. He hadn't."

Jackie put his mouth close to her ear. "If he's not dead, I'm going to kill him, and when I'm done, if you're still alive, I'll bring you his head and you can kiss him good-bye."

"Where are the guys who grabbed me?" she asked.

Jackie's mouth went thin; he didn't answer, and the woman shook her head.

"Let me guess. Pilgrim's killed everyone you work with today. Do you really want to take him on, little boy?"

He ignored the bolt of anger and decided not to kick her teeth down her throat. Hector wanted her unhurt. He went back to the driver's seat and she asked, "Where are you taking me?"

"I hope to a highly painful death."

In the rearview, he saw her eyes widen, very slightly. Yeah, he thought. Telling her that was better than giving her a kick in the face.

A grand place the man's house was, Jackie thought. The complex covered rolling farmland west of Prosper, a small town on the verge of great growth, but still rural enough that you had space to breathe. Jackie had driven through the iron gates—a long stone fence ran along the whole perimeter of the acreage. There were stables, a private airstrip with a hangar and Learjet, a three-story manor of Tuscan lines and arches, a seven-car garage at the end of a winding driveway, not visible from the road.

Sam Hector and Jackie stood in the garage. The back of the van was open, and Hector stood staring at Teach.

Sam Hector wasn't what Jackie had expected. Hector was taller than Jackie, a solid six-five, fiftyish, graying hair trimmed close to his scalp, a hard body shaped by weight lifting, a craggy face. His eyes reminded Jackie of gray clouds right after lightning flashes against them. It was the sort of face that made Jackie want to defend himself.

"I nearly got Pilgrim and the other—"

"Ben Forsberg." Sam Hector's voice was low and quiet.

"Forsberg. But they got away. Pilgrim's hurt bad." Pride inched back into his tone.

"The envelope, please."

Jackie handed it to him. Hector glanced at the seal, to be sure it was undisturbed.

"I wouldn't boast about your competence. How hard is it to leave an envelope behind?" Hector said. "The only thing you've done right is get her here to me."

An odd itch in the back of Jackie's brain made him say, "Yes, sir, but she's here and we could use her as bait for this Pilgrim."

Teach didn't look at him.

"That's true, Jackie." Hector gave him a cold smile. "Pilgrim will come after her."

"I hope he does." Jackie lit a cigarette and focused so his hand didn't tremble. "I want to kill him."

"I already killed Pilgrim once," Hector said. "I'm sure we can do it again. If you'd carry her into the house, I'd appreciate it. Just follow me."

Jackie carried Teach, dangling over his shoulder, and dropped her into a chair in a conference room. The table was smooth granite, with a state-of-the-art presentation system hooked into the table, a giant plasma screen on the wall.

Jackie turned to leave.

"No, Jackie, stay," Hector said. "You'll find my sales pitch interesting."

Jackie wanted to go be by himself, clean up his torn and soiled clothing—although he realized he had nothing to wear; his suitcase was in Nicky's trunk—but he stopped and stood behind Teach's chair.

Hector sat on the edge of the granite table.

"I want to make a deal with you," Hector said.

She waited.

"You've cost me a great deal today," Hector said. "In money, in blood, in risk."

"Perhaps you should reconsider your investments," she said evenly.

"I'm not going to contact your people and demand ransom. I'm going to contact your people and demand loyalty. You're going to help me."

"I won't."

"Adam Reynolds, he's found ten of your people. I'd like to know how many of them you have total. I'm guessing twenty to thirty. Former and discredited CIAs, maybe a few former KGBs who want to live and work in Europe and Asia, a hacker and a thief thrown in for good measure that you've recruited."

She watched the tabletop.

"I could torture you," he said, "but it's just so distasteful and ineffective. And I'd probably end up killing you—you'd lead me down several false paths, I'm sure, and I know my own temper well enough to know I'd kill you in a rage." He offered her a smile that reminded Jackie of a fracture in a window.

"What do you want?" she said finally.

"I want the names and details of everyone who works for you in your private little CIA, Teach. Every account you have. Every resource you have."

"This is the part where I tell you to go to hell, I think," she said.

"Hell is crowded," he answered. He clicked on the laptop, opened a video chat file.

The screen kicked to life. It showed a young man in his late twenties, bound to a chair, mouth gagged. His eyes were blackened, as though he had been beaten already, a dried trickle of blood inching down his chin, past the gag. He blinked into the camera, flinching at the harsh light on his face.

"He used to be Antonio De La Pena," Hector said. "Ex-CIA field operative, missing and presumed dead after a botched job against narco-terrorists in Colombia. His cover was blown and he had nowhere to go except witness protection, but you made him a better offer. He's worked under about three different aliases for you, most recently in Mexico City." Hector leaned closer to Teach. "You're going to cooperate, or he pays."

"Cooperate." She said the word as though she were testing its taste in her mouth.

"You're going to come to work for me, Teach. You and everyone in the Cellar. You'll follow my orders without question. You will not let any of your agents know that there has been a change in leadership. If you do not cooperate, I will expose your entire illegal operation. The government will disavow you like you're lepers, and probably most of your people will end up in those lovely foreign prisons in those delightful countries where you've made so much mischief over the years."

Teach did not tense her shoulders; she did not tremble.

"Tell me the ten you know," she said.

Hector rattled off a list of names. Teach closed her eyes, bit her lip. She nodded toward the screen. "Why grab him?"

"He's the youngest and most inexperienced. If I have to kill one to prove a point, he's the most expendable." Hector shrugged. "Purely a business decision."

"I take my orders from very few people," she said. "I can't fool them by taking orders from another source."

"Let me guess. The president."

She shook her head. "No. The president never knows about us to preserve deniability. A senior cadre of career officers within the Agency—they give me direction."

"You'll continue to take their direction and will report to me all the orders you receive from Washington. But you will work for me. Not them."

"And if I decline?"

"De La Pena dies. After I've killed his whole family." Hector crossed his arms. "He has a mother, two sisters with husbands, who have five children between them." He glanced at Jackie. "Jackie, could you kill a kid?"

"I don't much like kids," Jackie said. "I'd be game. Probably pays less, though, since they're easier."

"I'd give you a family rate." Hector turned back to Teach. "None of your people want to be exposed, want to go to prison, want to be disavowed and prosecuted by the government they serve. But they certainly don't want the people they cared about in their previous lives to be dead because of them. You either work for me, or I'll gut the Cellar."

She said nothing, watching De La Pena on the screen. The man closed his eyes above the gag.

"We'll tell De La Pena that this was a training exercise. I'll let you live, and a lot of innocent people keep breathing."

Teach was silent and Hector seemed willing to wait her out. Finally she said: "What do you get out of this arrangement?"

"I'm a firm believer that private firms are more effective than government agencies," Hector said.

"Not in our line of work," she said.

"Spoken like a true bureaucrat." He opened a folder. "Two months ago you had a chance to kill a leading terrorist in Istanbul. But you missed. Three weeks ago you flub an opportunity to destroy a narco-terrorism cell in Ecuador. Not inspiring."

Anger reddened her face. "Those failures had nothing to do with the skills of my people."

"Under my guidance, you won't make so many mistakes."

"Who hired you?" she asked, and Jackie thought, *Ah, now that's a million-dollar question.*

"No one."

Her laugh was brittle. "Contractors don't work for free."

"I'm making an investment in my company's future. And I'm going to pay you and your people, Teach, better than the government ever did." He knelt close to her, lifted her chin with his fingertips. "The fact you recruited and maintained an off-the-books organization for so long is brilliant. You have the Cellar's collective history in that librarian's head of yours. You know every detail of every agent, of every job. I need you. We can do great, great work for our country together. I don't want to destroy your group. I want to give it new life."

"You tried to kill Pilgrim."

Sam Hector smiled at Jackie. "He got too close to Adam Reynolds. It was nothing personal." And Jackie saw that yes, it certainly was personal, a flash in the man's eyes as he turned away from Teach. Interesting.

"Let's not leave your poor guy in suspense, Teach," Hector said. "Does his family live or die?"

"Live," she said. She cupped her hand on her forehead, as though a migraine bloomed behind the bone. "I'll cooperate."

"Good. Jackie, Mr. De La Pena is in the next room. Would you please untie him from the chair and bring him in here. You can tell him this kidnapping was a field exercise, one that he failed." He watched Teach for a reaction.

"I have a job for him and for Teach, and several other agents." He leaned close to Teach. "You have an agent in Denver. Get him to Dallas by early tomorrow morning. You tell him or your people anything, they and their families are dead. Then we need to select at least six others for another project."

"Project," she said.

"The Cellar's going to kill a group of very bad guys for me," he said. "In New Orleans."

KHALED'S REPORT— NEW ORLEANS

THERE ARE SIX OF US NOW in New Orleans—preparing for our moments of glory.

Six of us passed the first test: to enter America without being caught. I suppose our bosses could have easily snuck us in across the Mexican border in the dead of night, but they clearly want to weed out those who lack daring or are ineffective.

The unspoken deal is if I'm caught, I'm on my own. No one will help me.

Two months ago, I followed the instructions in a phone call, and in a locker I found a ticket, a thousand euros, and a French passport in a new name for me. I boarded a flight in Beirut to Frankfurt. In Frankfurt a man walked past me and slipped a new ticket and passport into my coat pocket.

First real problem. One does not want to walk around in a Western airport with an Arabic face and multiple passports. I destroyed the first passport by ripping it to bits and flushing the torn strips down the toilet. I used the new Belgian passport and the ticket, flew to Geneva, then to

Rome. I picked up a paged message left for me at the airline counter—to meet J at a hotel not far from St. Peter's Square.

I took a roundabout route to the hotel, thinking I could lose any tracker in the crowds and expanse of the massive square. I was wrong. At the hotel I was told by the fellow they called J—he has the bearing of a math teacher, if you ask me, and I am sure he is reading this—that four men shadowed me, following in a cascade so I would not notice, one moving ahead of me and then picking me up again, an invisible dance as I moved through the streets of Rome. J advised me of ways to circumvent such techniques; I will practice more in America, J tells me.

One must move without leaving a shadow, J says, and I quite like that phrase, that idea. Because the alternative is to be caught and to die.

J let me keep my Belgian passport with its French first name and Lebanese last name and provided me a rental car to drive to Paris. In Paris I flew to Miami. My seatmate was one of those tiresome boors who take a simple nod of hello as an invitation to interrogate you about every aspect of your life: where you went to school, where you live, what you do, what you like—and then must bury your every answer under his opinions. I am sure such people simply cannot abide the sound of silence or the shallowness of their own thoughts, but then I realized I need people like that—they give information. Information is power. This is my job now.

I was frightened for a moment that either this inquisitor was not an innocent nosy passenger, but rather either friend or enemy determined to catch me in a lie seven miles up, either to teach me a lesson or to unmask me. He told me that he sells enterprise software to large financial institutions, and I decided he was telling the truth. I learned some important basics about banks and their operations; this might be useful to me one day, in selecting a target, in interpreting data.

At immigration they looked hard—without trying to seem so—at my Arabic face and they asked for my reasons to come to the United States. I explained I was here on business, as the sales representative of a start-up software company based in Brussels. J had given me brochures and I had memorized the product features. They asked their useless questions and I sailed through.

What would have happened, though, if I had been caught in a lie? Would I have been abandoned? I suppose I very well might have been; secret warriors can never be acknowledged. It would have been a harsh lesson.

From Miami, a seductive jewel of a city, I flew to New Orleans, a seductive ruin.

I expected that I would be followed at the airport—them trailing me to see if I had been trailed, to avoid a repeat of my Roman debacle, when I thought myself so clever. A necessary precaution. I spotted one man following me, but I am sure more lurked in my wake, and I'm not going to claim a victory I did not earn. Following J's instructions, I took a cab first to the Audubon Zoo, trying to lose any shadows in the milling crowds, then I walked to Tulane, eyeing anyone who might be following, then another cab to the Superdome. I walked through a hotel, checked into a room using my false name, but never set foot in it, walking through the back of the hotel, grabbing a final cab to a chain hotel in the suburb of Metairie.

New Orleans is a strange half city now. It reminds me of a once-treasured plaything abandoned by a child. Entire stretches of the city remain utterly devastated—here in a country that prides itself, incessantly, on its wealth, its ambition, and its (shall I be frank?) superiority. Yet here is this blister on America's soul. The neighborhoods that have returned to a semblance of normalcy still give the sense of lives lived on an edge, of a hope tempered by the possibility that the city will never regain its former life.

I know how New Orleans feels. It is the way I feel.

And so, I arrived two months ago, and we started our work. Because it is a city where people are constantly coming and going, staying, leaving—no one will notice us here in the ruins.

I had no instructions at the final hotel. How was I to find my new colleagues? Adrift, I thought perhaps I would show initiative. I went for a walk, heading toward a local mall, and they grabbed me shortly after I arrived at the mall, escorting me into a dark Lincoln Navigator. I wasn't afraid. We exchanged assigned code phrases, ones J gave me in Rome. They drove me to a large home outside the city proper—near a swath of a nice neighborhood ruined by the recent hurricane, close to Lake Pontchartrain—and to a large house, which had fresh paint, a new roof, a sense of restored solidity. The neighborhood remains mostly abandoned; those who can afford nice houses can afford to leave.

The leader here is Mr. Night. Is he reading my words? If you are, Mr. Night, you must admit, your name is the definition of pretentious. But it suits him: dark, unknowable, yet somehow comforting. If we listen to him, we'll stay alive as we go to battle.

I am honing my skills. I am learning how to travel and lose someone if followed, how to follow someone without him knowing, how to encode information so I can pass it undetected, how to communicate back to my network without being discovered or found, how to identify people who need to die, how to get close to them.

And they will teach me how to kill. Not simply the techniques of murder. But they will teach me not to hesitate. J said this is the secret to killing. You cannot hesitate.

In three days, on Sunday, the holy day here, we will head out into the world, us six, to do our duty without a moment's hesitation.

15

———◄●►———

THE MOTEL WAS OLD AND CLEAN, owned by a smiling Pakistani couple. Ben signed Pilgrim's counterfeit charge card (in the name of James Woodward) with lip-biting care, trying to make it identical to the tight scrawling signature on the card. Ben asked for a room on the side of the motel away from the highway. He drove the car around to the back and half-carried, half-walked Pilgrim into the room and onto one of the twin beds.

He'd found a store near Georgetown, a small city north of Austin, and purchased clean clothes, towels, a duffel bag, snack food, a large bottle of antiseptic, bottled water, boxes of bandages and Coban medical wrap, saline solution, peroxide, and the most elaborate first-aid kit offered. He also bought a pair of forceps in the pharmacy section, thinking, *As if I'm really going to dig metal out of him.* Down the street was a grocery store and he bought two bottles of cheap Chianti.

He peeled the blue shirt and khaki pants off the groggy Pilgrim and dumped the bloodied clothes on the floor. Hard strength wired Pilgrim's body; not gym or tennis muscles like Ben's. A scar wandered like a river on a map across Pilgrim's stomach; another seam of healed tissue bisected his shoulder. It was as if the story of a life lived in shadows was burned into his skin. Now a neat puckering wound marred the other shoulder. An awful purpling continent of a bruise extended from hip to knee on the leg. A tear across the forearm revealed where a bullet had pierced and exited. Ben gently inspected Pilgrim's legs and arms, testing for broken bones. All seemed whole.

"Bullet's still in my shoulder," Pilgrim said. "Gonna tell you what to do. Trusting you, Ben."

"If I screw up, I'm sorry."

"You'll do great."

Ben followed Pilgrim's directions: He eased Pilgrim to the tub, irrigated the wound with water, disinfected both wound and forceps. Then, back on the bed, towels beneath the shoulder, Ben probed gently with the forceps into the wound.

"I don't know what I'm doing, so it's going to hurt like hell," he said.

Pilgrim never screamed. In the meat of his flesh the forceps touched, then closed on a slug of metal. Ben inched the bullet free, holding his own breath along with Pilgrim. Ben dropped the bullet on the side table with a plunk, swallowing a trickle of bile that rose into his throat.

"Okay," Pilgrim mumbled. "Irrigate it. With force. Hard."

Ben helped him back to the tub and chugged water over the wound, emptying several bottles, then pouring saline, then rinsing with peroxide. Pilgrim gritted his teeth. Ben smeared a generous spread of antibiotic ointment on gauze for the bandage. He applied pressure with the bandage, and then secured the pad with stretchy self-adhesive medical wrap colored bright blue.

He opened one of the screw-cap bottles of cheap-jug

Chianti he'd bought for Pilgrim to kill the pain, and Pilgrim took a giant swig of the red wine. Then Ben cleaned, disinfected, and wrapped the forearm wound.

Pilgrim let out a long sigh. "Okay, Doctor, you're done. Thank you."

Ben went to the sink. Blood speckled his hands, the new beach towels he had bought, his pants he'd slipped on when he got home, back when his life was normal. His hands stayed steady, though, and he stuck them under the jetting water.

"I'm gonna down more of this premium vintage." He inspected the label. "Did you get you some wine, Ben?"

"I never drink before surgery." Ben noticed Pilgrim had gulped down a third of the bottle. Pilgrim closed his eyes, breathing through the pain.

Ben collected Pilgrim's torn and bloody clothes. He felt a weight in the pockets, both front and back. The front pocket held a small black notebook, which tumbled to the floor as Ben laid the pants on the chair.

He picked it up and opened it. The notebook's pages were unlined, and half of them were filled with delicate ink and pencil drawings.

A range of images were carefully inscribed on the ivory pages: a baby swaddled in a father's strong arms; a toddler, dancing in a garden of roses, her pudgy hands reaching toward a fleeing butterfly; a teenage girl, bent reading a book on a park bench, shaded by a wall of pine trees, pushing a hank of dark hair from her face. A gentleness pervaded the drawings—the way that light captured the expressions of serenity and joy and concentration on the girl's face.

"That's mine," Pilgrim said, opening his eyes.

Ben handed the notebook to Pilgrim, embarrassed, as

though he'd stepped into another person's dream. He could feel another weight in the back pocket—where Pilgrim had drawn the credit card from—but Pilgrim's stare scored his back and he dropped the pants back on the floor. "You didn't strike me as the artistic type. Those are really well done."

"I'm not artistic." Pilgrim closed the notebook, kept it in his grip, close to his chest. "It's just good to have an eye for detail. See things as they really are."

"So. Really. How are things right now?" Ben went to the medical kit, poured six ibuprofen into Pilgrim's hand, watched him swallow them with sips of the Chianti.

"You got questions. I hate questions."

"I got questions."

"Get a glass. I don't want to drink alone," Pilgrim said.

Ben didn't want a drink but he got a glass. If Pilgrim drank to kill the pain, it might loosen his tongue. Better to be sociable, to get him talking. Ben found a clean plastic cup in the bathroom, dumped an inch of wine in it.

"Life changes fast, doesn't it?" Pilgrim said.

"Yes." He thought of the moment when his life divided, married one second, widowed the next, the echo of the shattering window.

"I killed seven people in the past four hours. I'm like a freaking serial killer, all in one day." Pilgrim downed more of the Chianti. He wiped his mouth with the back of his hand and Ben saw his hand tremble.

"You need some food." Ben heated water with the room's tiny coffeemaker, poured the hot liquid into a ramen noodle cup, watched while Pilgrim ate the spongy mass of noodles, studded with chunky dried vegetables.

"So your questions."

"Your boss, you, this secret group. Who are you?"

A long pause. "Teach is the general," Pilgrim said, "and she's the only one who knows the troop strength, the battle plans."

Ben decided to let Pilgrim tell this his own way, to let the answers unfurl, because he could guess from Pilgrim's grimace that he was unused to discussing his life. "And the bad guys want to know what you and Teach and this group do. Or keep you from doing your work."

Pilgrim emptied the cup in an unsteady slop and reached again for the wine jug. Ben didn't stop him. Pilgrim gulped more Chianti, didn't look at Ben. For the first time the intense gaze in his eyes dimmed, as though he were tired of glaring at the world.

Ben decided to prod him. "The credit card was for James Woodward. Is that your real name?"

"Promise me you won't freak out."

"I don't have a lot of freak-out left in me."

"I could tell you were thinking of going through my wallet. I know you'll do it as soon as I'm asleep. Go ahead."

Ben went to the pocket, dug out the wallet. Opened it.

A Texas driver's license lay under a plastic window. Pilgrim's face on it. The name read "FORSBERG, BENJAMIN LARS."

Ben thumbed through the rest of the wallet. Visa, American Express, health club membership: each one in Ben's name. A business card that was a near-twin of his own. Tucked into the wallet was an American passport: Pilgrim's face, Ben's name.

His breathing grew ragged and a slow rage rose in his chest. He threw the wallet at Pilgrim, who caught it one-handed.

"I'm you, Ben," Pilgrim said. "I've been you for the past three days."

"You're the reason...Homeland thinks I'm guilty," Ben said. "It doesn't have anything to do with *me,* or my life..."

"It has everything to do with your life," Pilgrim said. "You were framed as much as I was."

"You stole my identity."

"No. Your identity was given to me by a traitor. He set me up to be you because someone wants us both destroyed."

"You could have told me this immediately...back in the car..."

"I couldn't have. I needed your help. And earlier I was too busy saving your life. Sit down. Drink your wine."

"Don't expect me to thank you." Ben went and picked up Pilgrim's gun off the table.

"I don't think you're a fool. You and I both got played, both got nailed with a single shot. We've got a common enemy." He paused. "I'm not your enemy. If I were, you'd be dead. I would have grabbed you when you were checking the last of the bandages and broken your neck. I didn't."

"Wow. Thank you." Ben put the gun back on the table. "Tell me why you're pretending to be me."

The silence stretched between them like a wire drawn tight. The only noise was the distant ripple of highway traffic and the drone of cicadas in the trees. "You told me you trusted me before I dug that bullet out. Prove it."

Pilgrim cleared his throat. "The group I'm with does the dirty work that is necessary at times to identify and neutralize threats and protect the country."

"Dirty work."

"The activities the other agencies are legally blocked from doing."

"You do the jobs no one can take credit for or be blamed for."

Pilgrim blinked. "Excellent description."

"Where's your budget hidden—FBI? CIA?"

Pilgrim looked at him with a bit more respect. "Only Teach knows for sure, but I think the budget's hidden inside the CIA, cobbled together from miscellaneous funding. We're a back corner. A forgotten room." He paused. "It's called the Cellar."

"And you routinely hijack other people's identities."

"No. At least never before. A little jerk named Barker created my legends—my identities—when I was on a job. Normally he spun them out of thin air, invented a name, a history, a financial background. He gave me your identity; I had no idea you really existed. He also betrayed me and Teach; he worked with her kidnappers. Which means his boss—whoever that is—gave him your name to use." He paused. "I didn't know you were real."

"But why me?"

"I'd say whoever Barker worked for hates your guts."

"No one hates me."

"Or you're a huge threat to someone. You just don't know it."

Ben rubbed his forehead. "What was your job where you needed my name?"

"To investigate Adam Reynolds." He took another long sip of the Chianti. "Over the past few weeks, every alias or false identity used by myself or one of my Cellar colleagues was being tracked. Credit checks were run against the fake names, inquiries were being made, our aliases brought to the attention of police in New York, London, Atlanta, other cities. When we're done with a job we walk away from the aliases—but we keep an eye on them for a while after the job is done, in case someone tries to track us through the false identities."

"Adam Reynolds tracked you."

"He was a software designer, so he had to be using technology to find and discover our activities. But we have no idea how he did it."

"And you dragged my name in."

"We needed to find out why he was after us and who funded him. Teach got an old CIA contact to tell Adam Reynolds a contractor consultant named Ben Forsberg might be able to help him land funding for a start-up software company, to build products based on his ideas. But I thought Ben Forsberg was just an identity Barker made up along with a history."

"Barker bought the cell phones in my name. Opened the credit accounts. Rented the office space." Ben shook his head. "Sparta Consulting, that's what he used as a cover."

"Sparta's a front company for the Cellar, a way to camouflage our financial dealings." Pilgrim coughed, winced at the pain. "I got three meetings with Adam and I told him I represented a bunch of government contractors interested in backing his software ideas. I could help him set up his own company, fund the work, share the profits. Of course all I wanted to do was find out how he'd found us and who'd paid him to hunt us down."

"You wrote the business proposal, with my name on it, that Kidwell and Vochek found in his office," Ben said. Nausea clawed into his guts.

"I wanted to learn how he found our aliases, see who his business contacts were, find who funded his search for the Cellar."

"So why did he get killed?"

"He knew this afternoon that I wasn't Ben Forsberg. I tried to make him understand I could protect him, but he told me he'd called Homeland. But I don't think he worked for Homeland in trying to find the Cellar."

"Why?"

"Homeland Security doesn't hire Arab gunmen to kidnap people. They're not into assassination. And they have no reason to frame you."

"So his boss is who?"

"No idea. And if his boss knew Adam was bolting... clearly he didn't want Adam talking about his search for us."

"And the Cellar is the threat to national security he described to Kidwell?"

"Clearly he viewed us as a threat."

Ben got up from the bed, walked to the window. "So Nicky Lynch killed him and you killed Lynch. You put my business card in Lynch's pocket." The rage swelled in his chest, held its breath, and then was gone; replaced by an exhausting realization of how bad his situation was. He couldn't afford the distraction of anger. He shivered as he stood by the window, even though the room was warm.

"Ben, listen, I didn't know you were a real person...my cover had been blown. I thought I was leaving a nonexistent man as the fall guy, an empty trail for the police to follow." He shook his head. "I didn't know I would be pointing a finger at you."

Ben sat down on his bed. "If Nicky Lynch killed you and Adam, it would come out quick enough that you weren't me. So I'm not convinced that whoever your enemy is, he's also mine. Your guy Barker could have just decided to use my name since I'm in the line of work you needed for your cover story."

Pilgrim refilled his cup with wine. "I don't think it's a coincidence that when I'm in Austin, pretending to be you, you're out of town. Who knew you were gone?"

Ben hesitated. "My clients. I told them so they would know I wouldn't be answering phone calls or e-mails."

"And Sam Hector—whose people were guarding you for Homeland—is one of your clients."

"Yes. My most valued client. My friend."

Pilgrim studied the empty plastic cup, frowned.

"The government contracting world is a small one," Ben said. "Hector probably has dozens of people working on Homeland projects. Just because he has a security detail working with Homeland—"

"Then imagine this. Nicky Lynch shoots straight, I'm lying dead, with a wallet with your name inside. The authorities would want to know if you were connected to me."

"They'd just assume you stole my identity. It seems… incomplete as a frame-up."

"But let's say the government thought we were working together. You, a contractor, and me, a guy who's not supposed to exist who works for an off-the-books group. Your reputation in the government might die the death of a thousand small cuts. You very well could lose your business."

Ben shifted on the bed. "Kidwell's Office of Strategic Initiatives. Did you ever hear of it inside Homeland?"

Pilgrim eased himself into a new position on the bed, trying to get comfortable. "No. But I don't much pay attention to bureaucracies. They're poison."

He put the wine cup down; exhaustion filled his face.

"Kidwell's team could be as dirty as yours," Ben said. "He sure wasn't about to give me due process."

"The only way we get free and clear of this mess," he

said, "is to expose whoever took Teach. They framed us. We get caught, we have no means of nailing whoever hired Adam."

Ben got up, began to pace, to think.

"I need to sleep now." Pilgrim closed his eyes, exhaustion gripping him. "We'll get to Dallas in the morning."

"One minute. Who would attack the Cellar?"

"Any number of enemies. Terrorists, for sure. I'm sure that certain foreign governments would be glad for the Cellar to shut up shop. They might suspect we exist but they can't prove it. Fewer than five people outside of the Cellar even know we exist."

"And now me."

Pilgrim nodded, his eyes closed. "And now you. Lucky you."

Ben watched him fall asleep over the next several minutes. If he ran now—abandoned Pilgrim—he might very well be walking straight into a bullet's path. Whoever had attacked the Cellar had used his name. Pilgrim was right; it couldn't be coincidence. It was safer, for now, to stay close to Pilgrim. See what he could find out, because he could find out nothing from a jail cell or a Homeland Security interrogation room.

He wondered if Vochek was still locked in the closet.

Ben lay down, pressed his face into his pillow. He felt like he'd fallen into an alternate world, a Wonderland gone dark, where a crazy guy used his name and police hunted for him and vicious men held guns to his head. This morning he had woken up on a low-key vacation; now his life was in tatters.

Don't kid yourself. Your life has been in tatters since Emily died.

He couldn't sleep and he sat up and turned on CNN. And saw his name, his face on the television. His driver's license picture. The anchor described Ben as a person of interest—public-relations-speak for "suspect." Homeland Security wanted to know his connection to a purported contract killer with ties to terrorist cells who had been found dead in Austin after shooting a victim who also had connections to Forsberg. The anchor announced Ben had escaped from Homeland custody in a shoot-out in which a respected, decorated Homeland agent died. Anyone with information on Forsberg or his whereabouts was asked to call a special number at Homeland Security.

He had barely managed to rebuild after Emily died; he had survived the stares, the whispers, but never the guilt: the pointless guilt of taking her to Maui for the honeymoon, the endless guilt of being alive when she was dead. Now something far more poisonous than guilt—suspicion. His wife had been murdered and his name was tied to a contract killer. He wasn't going to get a second chance, in the judicial system or the court of public opinion, unless his name was absolutely cleared.

Escaped from custody. He heard the anchor's words echo in his head. Ben touched his own face on the television screen. He was now a hunted man.

16

Vochek didn't much like kids; but she could never forget the two dead boys.

She had first seen the small, crumpled bodies when she stepped into a bullet-blasted living room six months ago, in Kabul, Afghanistan.

As she entered the ransacked house that awful gray morning, she had pulled tighter around her face the hijab she wore out of deference to tradition. The scarf masked the burned smell of gunfire, and hid the trembling of her own mouth as she stood over the pitiful bodies. She reached to touch the children, but her fingers stopped just short of their dark mops of hair. One was nine, the other ten, both boys. If they had been American children their pajamas would have featured Scooby-Doo or Power Rangers or Spider-Man. But these two boys wore PJs with a repeating pattern of soccer balls, with rainbow arcs of speed drawn behind each ball to suggest a powerful and accurate kick.

They lay on their stomachs and she realized that they'd been shot in the back.

There was no sign of the children's parents, people she knew, freelance translators who worked with the State Department. She knew them because she was here to help the Kabul government shape and refine its own version of Homeland Security. The boys' father had called her an hour earlier, waking her from a deep sleep. *I wonder, Ms. Vochek, if you could come by and talk to me and my wife. We have information of value. Time is critical.*

"It's two of your people," the Afghan officer in charge of the scene said.

"My people." She tore her gaze away from the children. "I don't understand."

"Yes. The killers. Two men from the State Department."

"The people who killed these kids work for State?" Horror filled her voice.

"Yes. In the security division. They grabbed the parents, stuck them in a trunk after they shot the family. Wife is dead, husband is wounded. May not make it through the night." The Afghan officer shrugged. "What is wrong with you people?"

She was placed in charge of the interrogation of the two State Department employees. The Afghan government fed the media a careful fiction, announcing that two unknown gunmen had attacked the family.

Vochek's questioning of the two State Department employees showed yes, they worked for State—but they were taking orders from a secret group within State, operating in Kabul, as a private information network. This group was driven by its own agenda to spy on the insurgent Taliban. The group believed the parents knew of the locations of key Taliban figures. One of the two gunmen, trigger-happy, cut down the children as they fled from their parents' attackers.

"Didn't mean to," one of the men told her. "We were just going to take the parents to force them to talk. The kids

freaked. Ran. We couldn't have them waking the neighbors"—as if gunfire wouldn't shatter the quiet—"and I just
shot them." The man wept. "Because no one could know
what we were doing. No one."

The idea that a small rogue group could be operating
independently, secretly, and illegally inside the vast maze
of the government made her sick. Washington smoth-
ered the story; the two State Department employees, who
worked in the Bureau of Diplomatic Security, were sent
back to the United States, charged with far less serious
crimes. Vochek protested. She was told to forget the inci-
dent. And she had no idea what had happened to any other
members of the rogue cadre inside State—if they had been
charged, or dismissed, or told to proceed a bit more cau-
tiously with their under-the-table work.

It was grossly unfair, and she complained about it in
memo after memo to her supervisor.

The only response was a maddening silence, until Margaret Pritchard appeared in her office one afternoon.

Pritchard was in her late fifties, a carefully groomed
woman with ash-blond hair and slightly oversized eyeglasses. She introduced herself as being from a Homeland
task force in Washington that Vochek had never heard of.
She shut the door of Vochek's office. "You don't like the
idea of these unapproved covert groups."

"No, I don't."

"They offend you." It was a dry observation. "I've read
your memos and your e-mails. You certainly love your out-
raged adverbs."

"I don't love outrage, but it serves a purpose."

Pritchard leaned forward. "Would you like to help me
shut these groups down?"

"No, thank you."

"Why not?"

"Because the government doesn't want these dirty dogs shut down. They had their chance. I saw two men who killed a family get slapped on the wrist. I don't want to participate in another charade."

"Dirty dogs. I like that term. But this isn't a charade. The administration wants these groups closed and ended but with no publicity, no acknowledgment that they ever existed. This is a problem that's been building over time—too many agendas, not enough accountability, too much leeway given to produce intelligence and hard results. I've been put in charge of a team to find the illicit groups, gather evidence against them, build a strong case, and then gut them." She leaned back, crossed her arms. "You and the rest of the team will have enormous latitude."

"I haven't said yes yet. How many groups are there?"

Margaret Pritchard shrugged. "I don't know. Sometimes groups have formed then dissolved. I suspect there's a very private CIA hidden inside the CIA. Establishing whether or not they exist will be our first job. We have our suspicions." She reached into her briefcase, unfurled a long piece of paper. A web of colored lines connected circles; the circles overlapped the names of the agencies and the departments: CIA, FBI, NSA, Defense, State, Homeland.

"We suspect certain activities—assassinations, thefts, sabotage—were ordered by a cadre of people inside the government, contrary to our current foreign policies. They might produce good results, but this isn't how our government operates. We're unsure where the groups are hiding inside the bureaucratic maze—where they get their money, their people, their resources."

"You're forming a secret group to find a secret group." Vochek gave her a bitter laugh.

"It takes a thief." Margaret Pritchard leaned back from the chart. "You'll work out of the Houston office. I don't want people in D.C. knowing what we're doing. We'll keep our numbers few, very low-profile, make heavy use of outside contractors so word doesn't spread among the people we're investigating."

No good deed could bring back the Afghan boys in pajamas. But if there were no secret groups, then there were no rogue operations, there was accountability. She would have to keep her silence, for the sake of the government, but the rogues using government cover and resources to advance their own agendas would be gone.

She wanted to make the first mark for right in the ledger. She thought she had with Ben Forsberg.

She opened her eyes at the sound of the hospital door opening, and Margaret Pritchard stood at the foot of her bed. Vochek blinked against the early morning light hazing in from the window. "Not a word other than pleasantries. We'll talk shortly."

Vochek nodded.

"Your notoriously hard head seems to be undamaged."

"I'm fine." The attacker had left her with a bad knot.

"I took the liberty of bringing you some of your clothes from Houston." Pritchard held up a bag. "Clearly I'm paying you too much."

"Does my mom know I was hurt?"

"Not from me. That's for you to tell her, Joanna."

"Thank you." Vochek went into the bathroom. She had showered earlier that morning—awake at four, restless. She opened the bag: two of her Chanel suits, summer-weight gray; two Armani suits; and silk blouses, shoes that matched, hosiery, underwear bought from a store. Clothes were her one vanity, but she had found it paid to look like she meant business. Pritchard was a thorough soul, and she'd included in the bag basic makeup, deodorant, toothpaste, toothbrush, and floss.

Vochek wished for a moment that her mother had half the initiative and poise of Margaret Pritchard. She would have to call Mom today, but better to wait until she was out of the hospital so she wouldn't have to lie by default.

Vochek used the toiletries and dressed in her favorite suit. It felt like putting on armor; she was ready to go face the world again. She felt entirely herself again for the first time since Pilgrim's gun smacked into her head.

"The hospital's set you free," Pritchard said. "Come on."

They walked down in silence to a back exit of the hospital—away from any curious press—and a waiting Lincoln Town Car. Pritchard had a driver-cum-bodyguard, a powerfully built man who raised the bulletproof privacy partition as soon as the car pulled away from the curb.

The car left the hospital complex, drove past the interstate into east Austin. The morning traffic on the highways was spiraling toward dismal—she had read Austin had the worst congestion of any midsized city in the nation—and the driver stuck to side roads. "I'm sorry about Kidwell," Pritchard said.

Vochek thought that Pritchard was probably closer to Kidwell than she was, but she said, "Thanks."

"What exactly did you tell the police when they found you?"

"I stuck to the story Kidwell ordered me to tell if we ever ran into trouble." Vochek looked out the window. They drove past brightly painted taquerias and Mexican bakeries, the lots full of commuters and workers grabbing breakfast and coffee. "That I work for Homeland Security on a classified project and cannot discuss my assignment. Repeat as needed."

"The local police have taken a breath," Pritchard said. "It has been explained to them that the shootings bear on a highly secretive operation relating to national security. They're keeping their mouths shut and responding to our requests for assistance. FBI has charge of the official investigation. They only know that yours and Kidwell's work was classified and is not to be publicized. You will have to give them a statement later today, but I've already written it for you." Pritchard handed her the morning edition of the Austin paper and she scanned the story.

A photo of Ben Forsberg stared back at her. The story described a brazen attack on an office rented by Homeland Security in downtown Austin. One agent slain, one survived, two contractor security guards assigned to the building killed. Three suspected attackers were dead. All three men were unidentified but, the paper suggested with a nod toward terror, were described as Arabic. This followed hours after two shootings downtown, one of a software programmer, the other of a man at a parking garage who remained unidentified but had a Canadian passport and fit the description of a known assassin from Northern Ireland. Forsberg, a local businessman, was missing; the paper darkly hinted that he might have information on the attackers—he was described as a person of interest to the police. A state official warned about terrorists bringing their fight to American soil. A spokesman at the Washington headquarters of Homeland Security had no immediate comment. Neither did the FBI.

"There's no mention of the man who attacked me. Does everyone think the gunmen committed suicide?" Vochek couldn't keep the acid out of her voice.

"Of course not," Pritchard said. "This job is aging me faster than my teenagers. Tell me everything."

Vochek did. Pritchard had the disconcerting habit of listening to detailed accounts with her eyes closed. When Vochek finished, Pritchard opened her eyes.

"This man was looking for a woman named Teach. Do you have any idea who she is?"

Vochek shook her head. "But I'm real interested in her."

"Why?"

"Because he is."

Pritchard leaned back against the leather. "A statement from Homeland's going to be issued shortly. We have identified the three Arabs as being part of a new terrorist cell. They attacked the new Austin facility because of scant security."

"Is that true?"

"Well, I'm told that there's been increased cell phone chatter to make Homeland and FBI believe that terror organizations are trying to create more cells here. Al-Qaeda, Hezbollah, a couple of small but ambitious groups like Sons of the Sword and Blood of Fire. The gunmen might be Lebanese but we don't have confirmation yet."

"So why say they're terrorists until we're sure?"

"Because we need the cover. Four more people died at a lake house near Austin. Three of them were Arabs as well. If we say it's a terror cell, then we don't have to explain in much more detail; the idea of hired guns from Lebanon attacking our office creates more questions, actually, than saying terrorists did it. Because here's the next problem. This was the fourth corpse." Pritchard slid a picture toward her. The young guy was bespectacled, skinny, with a bitter expression on his face, unhappy at having his picture taken.

"Who is he?"

"His name was David Shaw. He was a black hat hacker, suspected of breaking into a Department of Defense network. His hacker name was Big Barker. He was awaiting trial when he vanished a year ago."

"How does he connect with the Arabs?"

"Other than lying dead with them on a floor, I've no idea." Pritchard tented her fingers, put them against her lip.

Vochek tapped Ben's picture on the paper. "I did not mention him to the police."

"Ben Forsberg became a falling row of dominoes. The Austin police listened to Kidwell's recording of Forsberg—the one left in the interrogation room. They know Kidwell suspected him of involvement in the Reynolds murder. Then when Forsberg's name went out on the wire, the media searched on his name, hit accounts of his wife's death. The press got ahold of him, and he's the only answer they've got."

"So Ben's their focal point."

"Yes, and that's fine with me." Pritchard opened a laptop, tapped a few keys. A video began to play—two men running, one clearly injured. "Someone tried to kill your attacker and Ben Forsberg last night in a parking garage off Second Street. Bullet holes all along one wall, blood. We got a solid image of Mr. Nice Guy's face from the security camera." Pritchard tapped more keys; the photos blew up, focusing on the men's faces. One was Ben Forsberg. The other was the big-shouldered man who'd hit her and locked her in the closet and inadvertently saved her life.

"Yes. That's him."

"We've had facial recognition programs running to see if we can find a match on him." Pritchard tapped her fingertips together. "Kidwell, poor idiot, he was much closer to striking gold than he knew." She clicked on another file, conjured another photo on the screen.

In the picture, the man was a decade younger, had brown hair. His old jaw was more pointed and his nose was thicker, more hawkish then. He was plain, neither handsome nor ugly. A face that you wouldn't remember. But the eyes—the blue eyes that watched her over the barrel of the gun—were the same. Intense. "I think it's him. He's had minor surgery, there on the nose and cheeks and chin. Who is he?"

"Randall Choate," Pritchard said. "He was a top CIA assassin. He massively screwed up a CIA mission in Indonesia ten years ago, got caught. He was jailed near Samarinda, and then died in an escape attempt while crossing the Mahakam River. An Indonesian police captain testified he shot Choate four times in the back."

"I thought corpses didn't keep so well in humid climates."

"The body was never recovered. Police assumed that it was swept down to the Makassar Strait and out to sea."

"The police captain lied."

"Clearly bribed," Pritchard said. "Choate's the key, Joanna, he's the smoking gun." An odd joy tinged Pritchard's voice—driven by the scent of the prey close at hand, Vochek thought. "He's been working for someone for ten years, and it's not the CIA, it's not any agency. We find him, maybe we find our first real unapproved group inside the government. Our first major success in bringing down the unauthorized, illegal dirty dogs."

The big prize; this guy could be *it*. The key to the

suspected private CIA, the biggest of the illicit groups. Shivers of anticipation, of fear, of resolve, traveled down Vochek's spine.

She studied the man's face. It held no weakness, but last night he had been weak; he should have killed her when he had the chance.

She would bring him down.

Margaret Pritchard closed her laptop. "Your work has never mattered more, Joanna. This is our best chance. I want to feel this group wriggling right under my thumb. Especially if Choate killed Kidwell." She gave her a half smile. "I'm counting on you to give them to me."

"Yes, ma'am." She paused. "He could have killed me, he didn't; why would he kill Kidwell?"

"Unknown. And we don't know the relationship between Forsberg, Choate, and these Arabs. Make no assumptions. These people could have all been in league together. These alliances often fracture into bloodshed."

"And what, Choate and these Arabs kill Kidwell and the contractors, and then Choate kills the Arabs?" She shook her head.

"Well, we'll only find out how they all connect by finding Choate and Forsberg."

"My cell phone's gone. I'm assuming that Choate took it and still has it."

"So here's a new one. Call them." She handed Vochek a phone.

Vochek dialed her old number, said after her voice mail greeting, "I'd like my phone back. And to talk. Maybe we can help each other." She gave her new number and hung up. "They may not turn the phone on so it can't be traced. What now?"

"You say good-bye to me. I've got a private jet ready to take you to Dallas. Adam Reynolds tried to call this Delia Moon woman there four times yesterday, before he died. I'd like to know why. She was in no shape to answer questions when I called her; she didn't know about Adam's death. She went into hysterics. I warned her, rather sternly, she was not to speak with the press." Pritchard glanced out the window; they were turning into the Austin airport, heading toward a section for private planes. "And I want to know if there's any connection between Ben Forsberg and Nicky Lynch, other than that business card. If Forsberg is working with Choate, there has to be an earlier time in their lives where they intersect. And see what else you can learn about Ben's life with his wife. She died in Hawaii, but they lived in Dallas. Anything else?"

"Yes. The security guards that died...they worked for Hector Global."

Pritchard paused for the barest moment. "Yes."

"Hector Global's based in Dallas. I should stop by and extend my condolences."

Pritchard shook her head. "Best to keep a distance. I'm getting massive grief for hiring contractors for security, but when you're hunting dirty dogs in your own yard, they're easier to trust."

"Forsberg said Sam Hector was a major client of his. Hector might be able to give me some insight into Forsberg."

Pritchard shook her head again. "Sam Hector's going to be under a press microscope because his people were killed. I don't want you showing up on his doorstep and creating more questions for the media. Stay out of sight. Focus on what I've asked you to do. Hector will provide us information if needed."

"All right. I feel the need, though, to clear up a problem

before you set me loose." She crossed her arms. "I'm not Kidwell."

"How so?"

"He was crossing lines with Forsberg. I don't want to criticize the dead . . . but he was threatening Forsberg's family, friends, with arrest. Threatened to destroy his career, get all his contracts canceled."

"Threats can work wonders. We have a mandate, Joanna. Shut down all illicit covert operations. If I have to bend a few laws to catch the lawbreakers that we normally have little to no chance of catching otherwise, I'm not going to worry about it, and neither should you." Pritchard put steel in her stare. "You wanted to come to work for me, Joanna, because you were tired of these people doing dirty work and not being held accountable. Don't complain now."

It wasn't an argument she was going to win. "This Choate guy . . . what will he do to Ben?"

"Depends on how useful Forsberg is." Pritchard shrugged. "Choate's been rogue for ten years. I doubt that has inculcated loyalty in him. Forsberg could be dead real soon." She put on her sunglasses. "Kidwell's service will be in a few days. I'll let you know the arrangements. Hopefully our dirty dogs will be brought to heel by then. And call your mom. Give her the new number. I doubt you want her chatting with a man like Choate."

Pritchard's small and secretive group of "dirty dog hunters" lay tucked in a back corner of the Homeland Security department. Given their low profile, they were not about to tip a hand by asking the CIA for Randall Choate's file, if the man in the parking garage photo was the Agency's not-so-dead former agent. But Pritchard's worker bees had put together a rushed dossier for Vochek since the face had been tentatively identified, and she studied it in detail as the Homeland jet made the fast flight to Dallas.

Born Randall Thomas Barnes thirty-six years ago in Little Rock, Arkansas. Randall was his mother's maiden name, Thomas a grandfather's name. Father died, drunk behind the wheel, when young Randall was age two. Mother moved around taking a variety of secretarial jobs, from Arkansas to West Virginia and finally to Lafayette, Indiana, where her fortunes took a considerable leap upward when she got a job working as a secretary in the foreign languages department at Purdue University. One of the junior professors, Michael Choate, who specialized in Russian literature of the nineteenth century, took an interest in the young widow and her son. Randall soon acquired a stepfather, who eventually adopted the boy and encouraged him to apply his considerable intellect to school. His stepfather also taught him Russian from an early age. Randall double-majored in Russian and history at Purdue, graduating with honors. The file included a scattering of old photos of Randall from the Purdue student paper and yearbook.

Randall was a nondescript boy, pale, but with a strong body and those eyes of certainty, of intensity. In most of the photos, he was alone or standing off from the group. In one photo taken at an intramural football game, his teammates had arms around him; Randall Choate smiled like he'd rather go play the game all on his own. She recognized the smile—same as the one he'd given her after he'd knocked the baton from her hand, one of amused respect.

At the suggestion of a faculty colleague of his stepfather's who had contacts at the Agency, Randall applied to the CIA and was accepted. And there the file ended, except for the note that he was reported killed while escaping prison in Indonesia four years later. The mission he'd supposedly botched remained classified, and the busy bees at Homeland were working to glean more details without directly asking the Agency.

Personal details: His mother and stepfather still lived in Lafayette. His wife Kimberly, daughter Tamara, were all unaware of his status as an assassin. Wife had remarried five years ago; the new stepfather adopted Tamara. History repeating itself. Family told that he had been involved in drug smuggling in Indonesia, died during a prison escape. A nasty story for the disavowed. No evidence of contact of the family by Choate in the intervening years.

Vochek closed the file.

The CIA either knew that Choate was still alive, and his death a decade ago had been a cover story to pull a screwed-up agent out of jail, or they didn't—in which case it would be easy to ascribe sinister motives as to why Choate faked his own demise.

The plane dipped into the northern stretches of urbanized prairie, and to Vochek's surprise the runway appeared, stretching along a row of high-end houses, in a square formed by four busy thoroughfares, lined with shopping centers and restaurants.

"What airport is this?" she asked the pilot.

"Plano Air Park Ranch," he said. "Private air park, with a runway right alongside the homes. Buy a house, get access to the runway, park your plane in your backyard. Got built before Dallas boomed this far. Homeland bought a house here a couple of years back. More private for our comings and goings than flying into Addison or DFW. Ms. Pritchard said you could stay at the house. I got a key for you, and we've got an extra car we keep there you can use." He paused. "I've flown a few bad guys out from there, flown 'em to Mexico or the Caymans and I don't know where they get shipped to after that." He paused. "Sometimes them bad boys cry during the flight, knowing they don't know where they're going."

"Uncertainty's not a good feeling," she said. The plane landed, and the pilot drove the plane to the Homeland house, parked it under a covered hangar, and handed her a set of car and house keys.

"Holler at me whenever you're ready to fly out your bad guy," the pilot said. "I'm on call."

"I won't be bringing back a really bad guy," she said. "I just have people to question."

"The day is young." The pilot smiled. "You never know what you're gonna find."

17

---◆❮◉❯◆---

Indonesia, Ten Years Ago

THE MAN THEY CALLED the Dragon hadn't shown up for the rendezvous. Fine, Choate thought. He hated working with a partner and particularly disliked one being forced on him.

One more hour, he decided. Night began to fall on the park. The pond turned a hazy purple as the sun began to dip below the smoggy rooftops of Jakarta. Choate sat near the gazebo; a trio of young musicians, slightly drunk and out of key, sat on the steps and picked out Beatles covers on their guitars.

Choate's orders from the CIA chief in Jakarta had been clear: *We have a freelancer working for us. His code name is the Dragon. He has information on a financial trail to a terrorist group here. You're going to help him. Meet him at this park at seven this evening.*

Choate waited as the park's sunny-day crowd began to thin, just him and the musicians left and a couple of old sisters tossing scraps of bread into the water for the ducks.

He got up as the trio started on an off-key rendition of

"Hey Jude." Done. He walked past the gazebo, scattering a few coins into the open guitar case.

"He's not coming," a voice behind him said, and Choate turned. The trio of musicians stood, smiling, one of them pulling a gun from behind his guitar, the other pulling one from a weathered knapsack.

Choate froze. "I don't know what you mean," he said.

"Your friend the Dragon," the guitarist said. He laughed. "Stupid name; is it supposed to make him sound fearsome? Dragons are false, they're nothing. He's gone into hiding. For good reason."

"I don't understand," Choate said. "What do you want?"

"You'll come with us," the guitarist said. "Only to talk."

Choate took a step back. One grabbed his arm. The shot rang out and the guitarist's chest gashed a red fog and he collapsed onto the stairs. The crack of the shot was as loud as a whip.

The two old sisters at the pond screamed. They fell behind a bench, still screeching.

Choate slammed a fist into the second man's face, spun him around. Choate closed hands over the man's wrists; they grappled for control of his gun. Choate could smell the man's breath, reeking of fish and garlic. Another shot echoed across the parkland. It caught the man's head, a bare two inches from Choate's, jerked him off his feet and spattered Choate with gore.

Choate yelled and dropped the corpse.

One left, the tallest musician. He turned and ran. No avenging shot from the distance rang out, so Choate grabbed the gun from his attacker, steadied his aim, and fired. Missed. His second shot caught the man square in the calf. He collapsed with a choking howl, clutching his leg.

Choate heard running feet behind him. He spun, leveled his gun at a man hurrying toward him, a sniper rifle in his hands. The man had a shaved head, was about ten years older than Choate, big-framed. He spoke with a British accent.

"Grab him. Let's find his car. We need to know who he works for."

"You're the Dragon—"

"Wow, you're green," the man said. "Stupid of you to let yourself be followed here and listen to their bad music for two hours."

"I wasn't followed—"

"Clearly," the Dragon said, "you were. Let's go. The police are actually responsive in this part of Jakarta." He grabbed the wounded man, hurried him to his feet, and spat words in Indonesian while pressing the barrel of the rifle against the man's throat. The man gestured toward a parking lot on the east side of the park and gasped what Choate thought was a plea for mercy.

Choate fished car keys out of the man's pocket and they rushed toward the lot, Choate pressing the Auto Unlock button in wide sweeps. One of the car's taillights blinked. They shoved the man into the backseat with the Dragon; Choate drove.

"Thank you," Choate said.

"What?"

"Thank you. You saved my life." He felt dizzy with adrenaline.

"Ah. Well. Of course." The Dragon spoke as a man unused to niceties. In the rearview, Choate saw the Dragon watch the road ahead and behind, making sure they were not being trailed, and that Choate knew how to navigate the tangled maze of Jakarta streets. He asked the prisoner a question in Indonesian and got a reply in English: "Yes. A little English."

"Who do you work for?"

The prisoner hesitated.

"I have one more bullet in my gun. Just for you. You talk, you live."

The prisoner licked his lips, shuddered. Choate thought maybe he was nineteen.

"Blood of Fire. But I am new. Please. I don't know names, I can't help you."

"Blood of Fire?" Choate said.

"Small terror cell. Big ambitions," the Dragon answered. "And the target for the job we were supposed to discuss tonight is tied to Blood of Fire. Which means they know. We have a leak. They know we were rendezvousing and they tried to take you out."

Choate's throat went dry. Life was easier when the targets were unsuspecting.

"How did you know CIA's after you?" the Dragon asked.

"I don't know . . . My friend told us. He was the first one you shot. I just follow their orders. They feed me," he added in a small voice. "I am a nobody."

"You're not convincing," the Dragon said to the prisoner. To Choate he said, "Do you know where the Deepra garbage dump is?"

Choate nodded.

"Drive there."

"Shouldn't we take him to CIA—"

"No. I'm freelance, remember? I'm not official CIA, and on this job, neither are you. We're both deniable."

Choate kept his mouth shut and put his gaze back to the road.

It is unholy the amount of garbage eighteen million people can produce. The junk dumps of Jakarta covered thousands of acres, populated by scavenger families wise in the ways of salvage. The Deepra dump loomed like a miniature mountain range, the discarded steel of cars purple in the starlight, flocks of gulls hovering over the waste, the smell of refuse like a slap from the hand of death.

They drove inside, Choate following the Dragon's directions to a secluded area. Scavenger tents huddled on one side, but as the car approached, the waste finders ducked back into their hovels.

"You know why they hide?" the Dragon said to the prisoner. "They hide because they don't want to be witnesses. A nice sedan does not come here after nightfall to dump a ton of garbage. Nice sedans only come here to dump bodies."

The prisoner made a soft, wet noise in his throat.

"We should take him back to CIA," Choate said again. "They can interrogate him."

"I don't do interrogations on CIA property. I'm all about deniability." He jerked the prisoner by the shirt. "How did you know about our meeting?"

The prisoner stared at the waste.

"Worst case isn't killing you and dumping your body out there. Worst case is hurting you really badly and leaving you out there. To have all the flesh on your bones picked off by the birds. The scavengers won't help you. No one will help you. Now. In an hour you can be free, with a doctor to tend your wound and a nice hot bowl of soup to eat. Your choice."

The prisoner said nothing for thirty long seconds and Choate thought: *Just tell him, answer his question.*

"Gumalar knows that you are targeting him," the prisoner said.

"Who is Gumalar?" Choate said.

"Financier. Got Allah in a big way and he's the one funneling the money to terrorists," the Dragon said. "His brother's a big deal in the Indonesian government, so that's why taking him down is such a quiet job. The CIA wants him taken down but not in a way that can be traced back to them. Hence, me."

The prisoner said, "I require a doctor."

"How does Gumalar know this?" the Dragon said. "Where's the leak?"

"We found people working for you," the prisoner said. "Over the past few days. Five of them. They gave us enough information to know about your meeting, to know where to watch for you."

"Where are my people?" The Dragon's voice went low and cold.

The prisoner shrugged. "I don't know."

"You have a staff?" Choate asked.

The Dragon didn't look at him, stare locked on the prisoner. "I have informants. Who feed me info I sell to CIA."

"You *had* informants," the prisoner said.

The Dragon gave the prisoner a jaw-snapping slap. "Where do I find Gumalar?"

"You can't touch him." The prisoner finally spoke with defiance in his voice.

On the radio, a news report began to play. Two men identified as agents of Badan Intelijen Negara, the Indonesian government's intelligence service, had been found shot to death in a park.

"Oh, man," Choate said. "You killed good guys."

"Good is relative," the Dragon said. "Our target has the good guys on his payroll."

"You can't touch Gumalar and I don't know where he is," the prisoner said.

"Then what use are you?" the Dragon said. He fired once, the bullet making a hard, percussive noise in the tight confines of the car.

"He could have told us more!" Choate yelled.

"Hardly," the Dragon said. "Pop the trunk."

Choate, hands shaking slightly, obeyed. The Dragon got out of the sedan, went to the back. Froze.

Choate hurried out of the car. In the truck was a large plastic bag. Inside of it, smeared with gore, were a bunch of severed hands. Big, calloused ones; smooth feminine ones; ones wearing rings; others bare of jewelry.

Choate leaned away from the car and fought down the urge to vomit.

"Ten," the Dragon said after a moment. "There are ten. My five informants."

"So...what do we do now?" They sat in the dark throat of a Jakarta bar, miles from the park, miles from the dump.

"Gumalar's leak is because he has someone big inside BIN in his pocket. So this stays an off-the-books job for the Agency."

"I was told to follow your orders," Choate said. He wasn't comfortable with this, but orders were orders.

"Then we stick with our original plan. We need to find the money trail this Gumalar is using to finance terrorism. We find the money, we tie him to it, and we kill him along with his terror cell contact. We make it look like the terrorist turned on him. Keep CIA's nose out of it."

"And you need me to find the money trail."

"Gumalar owns a large bank here. It's going to undergo a cyber attack in twelve hours. You'll be called in as a representative of the IT support company to repair and inspect the databases. You'll need to run a query against the five aliases that Gumalar's terror cell contact has been using. We'll use that information to find him, so we can get him and Gumalar together for a meeting and take them both out."

"Running a query will leave an electronic trace. Gumalar may have those accounts tagged to take note of a query."

"You're supposed to be smart. Deal with it."

Choate said nothing.

"I'm not big on coddling, kid," the Dragon said.

"Not expected or wanted."

"You won't have long to do the trace. Get the account information and then get out. I don't want you stuck inside his bank all day; you'd be a target if they know your face."

"How did you get these aliases?"

"My contacts."

"Did your contacts know about our targeting his bank?"

"No," the Dragon said after a moment.

"I really dislike the hesitation you just showed."

"They didn't know."

Choate tapped fingers on the table. The adrenaline rush faded. "We need to report back to the Agency."

"Of course. But the mission goes on."

"That's for the Agency to decide."

"The Agency can decide what they want. These scumbags don't get away with killing my people. I run my network like a nice little family business. I took care of these folks, their families. I had their loyalty. They have mine."

"All very noble," Choate said. "But I'm not going on a suicide mission."

"Fine. Get Agency approval. Be sure and mention I saved your life." The Dragon got up, finished his beer. They got up, left money on the table, went to a small house of the Dragon's on a quiet street.

Choate called, got connected to the CIA chief in Jakarta. Explained. Listened. He hung up.

"We're a go."

"You forgot to mention I saved your life."

"I'm not big on coddling," Choate said. "When do we go to the bank?"

The Dragon cracked a smile. "Tomorrow morning. Review the files. Get some sleep. You can bunk down at the room at the end of the hall." The Dragon went into another room. Choate put an ear to the heavy door. Soundproofed.

He went to the room and collapsed on the bed.

He didn't like this at all, but he had his orders. He curled into a ball and let sleep close over him, trying not to think of the bag of severed hands or the shocked face of the dead prisoner, staring up past the mounds of garbage toward the star-kissed sky.

18

HIS FIRST MORNING AS A FUGITIVE. Ben was afraid the maid would come early to the room, or that the motel owners would see his face on CNN. This was a new kind of fear; it didn't pass when you turned on the lights in the darkened room, or reassured yourself the midnight tap at the window was a tree branch, moved only by the wind. This fear stayed with you, it worked on your mind, it made every moment urgent.

At 7 A.M. Friday they left the hotel. Ben drove, heading north toward Dallas. Pilgrim wrote directions down on paper, told Ben, "This is where we go first in Dallas." The *X* on the map was near the Dallas/Fort Worth International Airport. Pilgrim dozed fitfully in the back, still in pain, but his color was much better than the night before.

They got a bag of breakfast tacos at a stand in Lorena, south of Waco. Pilgrim woke and ate with a lion's appetite, drank a giant bottle of juice. Ben swapped the license plates off the stolen Volvo with those of a Subaru parked close to the Baylor University campus in Waco. Ben did the work quickly, using a wrench he'd found in a miniature tool set in the back of the station wagon.

Now I'm a fugitive and a thief, he thought, *and the day is still young.*

"College students are slow to notice things like changed plates," Pilgrim said. "I find it useful to steal plates from fraternity parking lots on weekends. Not to stereotype, but they're too drunk."

"It's a Baptist school. Baylor kids are not supposed to drink," Ben said.

"Then I hope they're distracted by spiritual matters." Pilgrim closed his eyes and slept again.

The traffic wasn't heavy until they hit the southern suburbs of Dallas, a long trail of cars heading into downtown, and Pilgrim woke up.

"Questions for you," Pilgrim said. "About Sam Hector." He sounded stronger now, more alert. Ready to rumble. "How big's his operation?"

"One of the biggest. Three thousand employees. Huge training complexes, one an hour east of Dallas, the other in Nevada. Most of his execs are former military, decorated officers. Security, training, software...if the government uses it, he sells it." Ben gave a soft laugh. "Sam joked once about using that as a company motto."

"And you worked with him for how long?"

"My wife, Emily, worked for Sam. That was how we met. She was an accountant in one of his divisions, he hired me to help him win new contracts. After she died, I left Dallas, I became a consultant and he kept me busy. His revenue's grown 500 percent since I've been working with him."

"So you're just a really good pimp," Pilgrim said.

"Excuse me?"

"I read about some of those contracts these guys land.

The government gets in a hurry—like when we invade Iraq—and they don't take lots of competing bids."

"Yeah, sometimes. There are huge time pressures to get the work done."

"And these contracts, they have profit built in. No matter how bad the contractor screws up or goes over budget."

"Well, these are often high-risk operations," Ben said.

"News flash, Ben. Every business is a risk."

"Not every business can get you killed. For about every four soldiers who die in Iraq, a contractor dies. They don't get medals or military funerals or army benefits. They don't get military hospitals. They don't get a parade when they come home."

Pilgrim was silent.

Ben couldn't resist: "And I don't think it's bad if a business makes a profit."

"But *guaranteed* profit. How many regular companies are guaranteed a profit? Sort of takes quite a bit of the risk and the responsibility out of the equation."

Ben returned his gaze to the road.

"I hit a nerve," Pilgrim said.

"Sure, there are crooked contractors, people taking money for work they can't or won't do. But abuses happen anytime millions of dollars are dangled."

"But you're not part of the problem, right, you're part of the solution."

"If you want to insult me, I can stick that bullet back in your shoulder. At high speed."

"It might be interesting to see you try, Ben."

"The reason contractors exist now is because of choices made by the governments we've elected," Ben said. "People don't want a draft. They don't want a huge military.

And they don't seem to mind that gaps in military infra-structure are being filled by private companies. I don't see protestors at my clients' offices very often. These guys are making a good return on investment."

"I doubt it's a good investment for America," Pilgrim said. "What if the fighting gets too tough? The contractors can quit; soldiers can't."

"That hasn't happened."

"Bull. Certain engineering firms pulled out of Iraq because they're spending way too much on security. If that's the Army Corps of Engineers doing the work, and the army providing the security, they have to stay. It's called account-ability."

"Odd the interest in accountability, since you stole my name."

"Given, not stolen. Back to Hector. Background?"

"Longtime military, worked as a liaison to officers of foreign armies, then went into security consulting."

"Ah. So Mr. Hector lets the military spend a fortune training him, and instead of being a career officer, he takes that investment America made in him and goes private."

"Being in the army isn't an automatic lifetime enlistment."

"But most people don't profit in the millions when they chuck their dog tags."

Ben frowned. "When Emily died...Sam Hector was a good friend to me. He paid me even when I wasn't up to working. Steered contracts my way. Gave me my first work when I was ready to get back in the game...He's a man of exceptional loyalty."

"Loyalty. Then Sam Hector and I have something in common." Pilgrim pulled a cell phone from his pocket, examined it, turned it on briefly, shut it off. "Barker called a cell phone owned by the hotel you were held at before all hell broke loose. The hotel owner is a company called McKeen. You know them?"

"No."

"You ever heard of Blarney's Steakhouse?"

Ben nodded. "There are a few in Dallas."

"I'm interested in the one in Frisco. You eat there?"

"Once. It's the original one in the chain."

"I found a Blarney's matchbook in the pocket of one of the gunmen. The construction signage indicated that a Blarney's was going in at the Waterloo Arms."

Ben tapped fingers on the steering wheel.

"There's a connection there we need to understand." Pilgrim tossed Barker's phone to the floorboard, pulled another one out of his pocket. "This belongs to the lovely Agent Vochek." He rolled the phone along his fingers. "If I turn the phone on they can trace it."

Ben had a thought. "When I was arguing with them about the cell phone numbers you bought in my name, Vochek told Kidwell that Adam Reynolds made several phone calls to Dallas yesterday afternoon. She might have tried to call the same number."

Pilgrim powered on the phone. He switched to the call log. "She called her mommy last. Nice girl." He thumbed further down. Read a number aloud, shut off the phone. "That's the most recent Dallas phone number. Ah. There are two new voice mails. I bet they're for me." He hit the key that played the voice mail, held the phone so they could both hear it.

The first voice mail was a woman, sounding cautious. "Hi, Ms. Vochek…this is Delia Moon. You called and left a message for me. So I'm returning your call. You have my number."

The second voice mail was Vochek asking for her phone back. Pilgrim switched off the phone. "I don't think I want to call Ms. Vochek today." He tucked the phone back into his pocket. "We need to know who this Delia Moon woman is. She might know who Adam was working for."

"A lot of choices. What do we do first?"

Pilgrim considered. "Stick to the plan. We get resources. Then a base of operations." He leaned down, pulled a wallet from his bag. "Then we go visit my friend Barker's house and see if we can find out who turned him traitor."

Pilgrim kept his "resources" in a nondescript, three-story, air-conditioned storage facility. They walked under the regular, pulsing roar of departing flights from DFW as they went inside the building. They walked past a couple carrying a case of fine wine out of storage, past a mother and son retrieving a few boxes. Ben faked a sneeze to cover his face as they passed both groups. Pilgrim gave Ben's attempt at camouflage an amused eye roll.

"Oh, man, that's brilliant. The Sneeze and Hide. Let me borrow that technique."

Ben felt his face redden.

Pilgrim, leaning down with a wince, opened the lock, not with a key—he didn't keep one on him—but with the silvery needle of a lockpick. Ben stood fidgeting, behind him, hoping no one would come into the hallway. Pilgrim stepped inside the unit and flicked on the light and Ben followed him, shutting the door behind them.

The unit held metal boxes. Pilgrim opened each one: an assortment of pistols and matching ammunition, a cache of identity papers: drivers' licenses, passports. A laptop computer of recent manufacture. Thick bricks of American dollars.

Ben gaped at the armaments and the money. "Where did you get all this?"

"Leftovers from Cellar jobs. Teach doesn't know I have it. I thought it wise to have a stash in case I needed to run and hide someday." Pilgrim opened and closed each container. "I don't have a water gun for you, Ben. Do you prefer a Glock or a Beretta?"

"I don't want a gun."

Pilgrim laughed and then winced at the pain in his shoulder. "You understand we're in pretty dire straits, Ben. We are going to war with these people."

"I've been thinking..."

"I thought I heard a clicking sound." Pilgrim opened a pistol, eyed its innards.

"We get proof of whoever hired the gunmen, whoever hired Nicky Lynch, we give it to the police and we're done."

"You'll be done. I won't be." Pilgrim inspected, cleaned, and oiled the guns, then showed Ben how to load, check, and unload each weapon. "Most important advice. Count your bullets. Always know how many you have in the clip."

"I don't plan on using large numbers of bullets. I patched you up, I'm not phoning the cops, I'm telling you what I know. But I'm not shooting anybody. I really don't like guns very much."

"I'll make sure that's mentioned in your eulogy next week."

"No, I mean...I don't want to."

"You pointed a gun at me just last night."

"I was in shock. I know I can't shoot another human being."

"I suspect you have stretches of your soul you've never

really explored, Ben. Could you kill the person who killed your wife?"

Ben put the gun he was awkwardly holding—a Beretta 92 pistol—back in its case. "I kill him, I'm no better than he is."

"I would think you'd consider the person who killed your wife to be pure evil," Pilgrim said. "True?"

"Yes."

"I'd say he was absolute pond scum. But you, Saint Ben, you won't lean down from your golden saddle on your moral high horse and kill him. News flash: we're going to be dealing with people who are probably even less scummy but just as dangerous as your wife's murderer is. I guess you're planning to spare all the interesting people we're gonna go meet. Golly jeepers, Beaver, I feel better with you watching my back."

Ben started to speak, stopped. "That isn't what I meant."

Pilgrim shrugged. "It's what you said. Be honest with yourself, Ben: do you have a spine? I deserve to know before we get in any deeper."

Ben picked up the Beretta, set it down. "There are a lot of ways I can help you without being something I'm not."

Pilgrim took the Beretta from Ben, loaded it, tucked it into his own waistband under his jacket. "We take money and the guns." He turned away from Ben, and Ben knew he'd failed on a test, that Pilgrim thought him more an anchor than an asset. And that, Ben realized, was a very dangerous position.

19

I'M VERY SORRY FOR YOUR LOSS." Vochek folded her ID into its wallet. "Please accept my sympathies."

"Thanks. Kind of you," Delia Moon said, and the clear anger on her face seemed to retreat behind an expression of neutrality. She opened her front door wide, and Vochek stepped inside the cool of the foyer. The home was big, newly built, in a development in the booming suburb of Frisco. The surrounding lots were either empty, under construction, or had For Sale signs in their yard.

"I understand my supervisor at Homeland asked you to not speak with the media or discuss Adam's case..."

Delia was taller than Vochek; she wore her thick dark hair pulled back in a hefty ponytail. She wore a batik print blouse of browns and blues and greens, faded jeans, sandals with turquoise stones on the straps. A night of tears had left her eyes puffed and red-lined. She had a gentle face; it wore anger awkwardly. "She so kindly broke news of Adam's death to me. I barely slept last night. Would you like coffee while I yell at you?"

Vochek silently cursed Margaret Pritchard's lack of finesse. "You can yell away and coffee sounds wonderful, thank you. Listen, my supervisor—"

"She told me I would be putting national security at risk if I talked to anyone. Not just police or press, but even our friends," Delia said. The words fairly exploded out of her. "Sympathy and threats. I thought I was in a Mafia movie." Delia went into a large, bright kitchen, Vochek following her. A warm smell of cinnamon coffee greeted her; a plate with rye toast, uneaten, lay on the black granite countertop.

"Ms. Pritchard didn't handle this well, and I apologize," Vochek said. "You have a lovely home."

"Thanks."

"I understand you're a massage therapist."

Delia poured Vochek her coffee, didn't look at her. "Adam bought the house for me."

"I wasn't asking how you could afford—" Vochek began but then she saw the battle lines drawn in Delia's eyes. Grief and Pritchard's clumsy approach during this woman's horrifying loss had hardened Delia against Vochek. She said: "If we're going to catch the people responsible for Adam's death, I need your help."

"I understand."

"We're trying to determine what happened in the hours before his death. He tried to call you four times—"

"I turned my phone off," Delia said, and emotion cracked the anger in her face. "I'd gone to the library, forgot to turn it back on." Regret tinged her voice and Vochek wanted to say, *It didn't matter, it wouldn't have saved him if he'd managed to reach you.* But she couldn't share details yet, even ones that might comfort, with this woman.

"We accessed his voice mail—he left you a message saying he might have to vanish for a few days. Do you know why?"

"No." Delia refilled her own cup.

"But I take it if he bought you this house," Vochek began, "you would be close."

Delia set her coffee down, crossed her arms. "We met through friends here in Dallas. Adam does—did—most of his work in Austin, but he came to Dallas a lot. He grew up here, his mom's in a nursing home here." She cleared her throat. "Adam and me...it's complicated. My life was a train wreck. I was in really heavy debt from school, I lost my job...he always made fantastic money, contracting for the government. He wanted to take care of me."

"So you were a couple."

"No, he wanted that...but I wasn't ready."

You were ready enough to let him buy you this very nice house, Vochek thought.

Delia crossed her arms. "I loved Adam. He was my best friend. He said he was going to buy a house in Dallas as an investment, I could live here till I was ready to move to Austin. I just needed more time...to know that I loved him, more than a friend." The words came in a spill.

Or to string him along, Vochek thought. She felt sorry for Adam Reynolds, a guy who loved a girl who apparently didn't love him back, at least enough, and kept his scant hopes alive. "Tell me what you know about his work."

"You think a dumb charity case like me understands his work?" Delia raised an eyebrow.

Vochek thought: *I've got to refine my poker face.* "I'm sure you do. I'm equally sure your well-placed anger toward my boss won't get in the way of your desire to see justice done for Adam."

"Trust me, my only concern is justice for Adam," she said, but a bitter undercurrent made Vochek believe she had a different view of justice. "He wrote lots of software for government agencies. Mostly about financial analysis. Detecting spending patterns, trends, tracing payments back to specific budgets, boring stuff." Delia started wiping the spotless counter with a dishrag.

"Could he have found financial evidence of a crime? Is that why he said he'd have to vanish?"

"He never told me anything specific. I know he was working on a new project—something to do with querying financial information across multiple databases."

Maybe he found a financial trail that led back to the secret group, Vochek thought. "Was he doing this work for a government agency?"

Delia narrowed her gaze. "No, on his own. He wanted to make it into a product, sell it to the government. He thought the government would pay him millions for it. I don't know what will happen to it now." Her voice rose slightly on the last word.

"I suppose the ownership of it will pass to his heirs."

"Heirs," Delia said. "Adam doesn't have any kids. His dad died when he was thirteen. His mom's in a rest home, early-onset Alzheimer's. It's bad. I take care of her for him, make sure the home's being good to her." She pressed her palm to her forehead. "He never mentioned he had a will."

"Did Adam ever mention a man named Ben Forsberg?"

"That's the guy the cops are looking for. I saw his picture on TV."

"Yes."

"Adam mentioned a couple of days ago he was talking with a consultant named Forsberg who might help him get investors to start his new company. Was this guy working with the people that killed Adam?"

"I'm trying to find out."

"Listen, I don't care about the money Adam's software might make . . . I just don't want Adam's work to be stopped. I mean, he was killed by a *sniper*! He and the project must have been a threat to somebody powerful. Maybe someone in the government."

"Tell me more about this new project. Because I haven't heard of any notes, or software found on his system, that would be dangerous." But then, she thought, she hadn't gone through Adam's stuff. Pritchard had had everything in Adam's office seized and put under her control.

"Homeland Security has his project data, his prototype of the software," Delia said slowly. "You've got the goods. You don't need to ask me."

"I can assure you his property won't be stolen or misused."

"I'm wondering if that's why your boss put a choke hold on me. Because you've got his software and it's valuable to Homeland?" Delia's voice rose.

"Of course not. Our technical people will go through all the programs and files on his system, to see if we can find who might have targeted him, but nothing will be misappropriated. Really, Delia, do you think we're robbers?"

"I don't know what to think. Who to trust."

"Then *I'll* trust *you*. Adam contacted us about a serious threat. Maybe terrorism. That might be why he wanted to disappear for a while. Is there a place where he would go if he was in trouble? Maybe he kept details about this threat in a safe place."

"He would come here." She gestured at the lovely, mostly empty house.

"But if he wanted to keep you out of danger . . ."

"He never went anywhere. He lived for his work. He . . ."

She stopped. "We drove to New Orleans a few times when we first met, with friends, and we love it. The people, the food, the music. Then this week he made an odd comment about it. We haven't been since Katrina hit and he said he didn't want to go anywhere near New Orleans, not anytime soon."

Vochek frowned. "But he didn't say why?"

"No."

Vochek hesitated. Pritchard had warned her to stay clear of Hector Global, but there was no harm in a question, especially since Hector's name had come up more than once. And Adam was a government contractor, too. "Did Adam ever mention a man named Sam Hector?"

Delia took a long sip of her coffee. "Sam Hector. Not a familiar name."

"He owns a huge private security firm. Multi-million-dollar government contracts."

Delia shrugged. "I'm sorry I'm not being of help. Adam didn't tell me much about his work. It was technical, and I'm not...I'm afraid Adam knew computer theory was about a thousand feet above my head." Her voice went raw.

"Did Adam say anything else unusual?"

"No. He was excited about how his work was progressing. I..." Delia stopped abruptly, like a weight had dropped on her. "I'll call you if there's anything else I can remember. I have your number from when you called yesterday."

"I lost my cell phone." Vochek wrote down her new number on a notepad sitting on the kitchen counter.

"Can I tell his mother that he's dead? She may not understand. But I can't not tell her."

"Of course. If there's anything else you can tell me..."

"I don't think so." Delia folded Vochek's note in half.

"And I'd appreciate knowing when Adam's body's going to be released. I have a funeral to plan."

She knows something, Vochek thought. *But if you press her, she'll just clam up more.*

Find out the body's disposition, that would earn a point. Vochek headed back to her car. Delia Moon, far from being the grieving girlfriend eager to help the investigation, was going to be a problem; Vochek was going to need warrants to find out more about Delia. She called Margaret Pritchard, left a message asking to be updated on what the computer team found on Adam's computers and also when the body would be released for burial. She tried to call her stolen cell phone again. No response.

She paged through her file and found the name she wanted next. Bob Taggart, the police detective who had assisted the Maui police in investigating Emily Forsberg's murder. He'd checked into Emily and Ben's life in Dallas to see if a motive could be uncovered for Ben to kill his new wife. He lived south of Dallas, in the town of Cedar Hill. She called, explained why she wanted to talk to him, and Taggart told her she was welcome to visit him.

She pulled her car away from the curb and in the rear-view mirror she saw Delia Moon watching her from a window. Then the curtain fell and Delia was gone.

Delia Moon stepped away from the front window. The day was cool and clear and the wind, gusting, sighed against the glass. The house felt like it was closing in on her, a crushing fist. Every corner seemed full of Adam, and she shuddered with grief. Delia could imagine what Agent Vochek thought of her, the flicker of dislike that the woman had tried to hide and failed, for the briefest moment.

Well, high-and-mighty Agent Vochek was wrong. She didn't care that she might not be Adam's heir. She wished she had loved him more, or at least loved him better. She did not have a copy of his software designs, but she knew he was nearly finished with a project that might be worth millions, and now Homeland Security had seized his intellectual property. Computer files could be copied and stolen. His project could be hijacked. Even if she never saw a cent, that money was rightfully Adam's, and money that could help his mother with her exorbitant health-care costs.

He'd bought Delia this house, helped her straighten out her chaotic life; she'd protect his interests now. Resolve filled her, like water flowing into a bottle.

Please tell me about his project, Miss Judgmental had said. Not very likely, Delia thought; she wasn't going to give away his trade secrets. If someone had killed Adam, he'd found someone he wasn't supposed to find. Which meant his ideas worked.

She might need a lawyer to pry free his laptop, his papers, and his electronic files from Homeland Security.

She knew who to call. Because, yes, Adam had mentioned Sam Hector to her, as a man who was going to give him money to help develop his product. She found his name in Adam's address book on the computer they shared when he was here in town, and found a number for Hector marked "direct private line."

Delia Moon reached for the phone.

20

⊰●⊱

BEN AND PILGRIM FOUND A CHAIN MOTEL, one so new the landscaping wasn't finished. It sat near the LBJ Freeway that cut across the northern stretches of the city. Pilgrim paid cash for the room. He left the money and the rest of the gear, except for one cloth bag, in the back of the Volvo.

Pilgrim looked pale as they headed up the stairs.

"Are you all right?"

"My bandages. I might need you to rewrap them."

"Okay," Ben said. They went inside the room; it was clean and neat. Ben turned on the television and started hunting for a news channel; Pilgrim tossed the bag onto one of the twin beds. Pilgrim went into the bathroom and closed the door.

Ben found CNN. The deaths in Austin remained the lead story, his face still on the news, still being sought as a "person of interest." But then a photo of Emily appeared on the screen, and his throat plummeted into his chest.

The reporter, with perfectly arched eyebrow, said: "Forsberg's past includes an unsolved murder—that of his wife, Emily Forsberg, two years ago." Ben grabbed the remote and switched off the TV. No.

He missed Emily with a grief that made his body ache. Fragments of the past spun into his mind: glancing up the green spill of hill that backed to their rental house, seeing no one, in the moments after Emily died; the Hawaiian police telling him someone had shot out windows at four nearby properties that morning, so this was probably a *random shooting,* his life destroyed for no reason; Sam Hector speaking at Emily's memorial, of her grace and her remarkable work ethic and her dignity; Ben finally leaving their home in Dallas, knowing he could not stay, crowded by memories of her, and yet believing that abandoning the house they'd shared would be a final betrayal.

Pilgrim came out of the bathroom, stopped in the doorway. "I need you to check the bandages."

"Sure," Ben said. He stepped inside the bathroom and a bracelet of plastic closed around his wrist.

"What the—" He struggled and fought, but Pilgrim shoved him hard to the tiles and had already closed the other side of the plastic restraint around the pipe on the bottom of the toilet.

"Sorry, Ben, it's better this way." Pilgrim stepped back, breathing hard.

"You can't do this!" Ben yanked hard; the pipe didn't give. Panic surged in his chest. "You would be dead if I hadn't helped you."

"I'm protecting you. I don't know what I'm going to find at Barker's house. And it's best that you stay out of the way."

"Fine, I'll stay here, just take the cuff off."

"Ben...I can't have you slowing me down. Or me not being able to count on you. I'm sorry. I'm sure your name will be cleared."

Ben lashed a kick out at him and Pilgrim dodged. "Please, I need you to tell people you stole my name."

"You're safer in jail than you are with me."

Ben yanked hard on the plastic handcuff. "Let me go."

"Ben. Listen, you don't want to go into the world I live in. It's not an adventure, it's a giant pain. It's not for you. I'll find out who set us up and I'll make sure they pay. You'll get bail. You're an upright citizen."

"You think I'm a coward? Well, you are."

"Doubtful," Pilgrim said.

"You're getting rid of me because you don't even know how to accept help that doesn't involve killing people. And after I patched you together, you ingrate, I thought we were on the same side. You're not brave enough to keep a deal you make."

"I just . . . I don't believe you have what it takes to do what we need done. So let me handle the dirty work." Pilgrim stood. "Get a very good lawyer who will ask Homeland Security the hard questions about this Office of Strategic Whatever that Kidwell and Vochek work for. Good luck, man, and thanks."

He turned and walked from the bathroom.

"Pilgrim!"

"It's for the best, Ben, for the best." As though assuring himself of the truth.

And the next sound Ben heard was the click of the hotel door closing.

Pilgrim was sure he'd done the right thing. The police would find Ben, and turn him over to Homeland. He'd tell them about Pilgrim and eventually he'd be believed; no one was going to think Ben Forsberg had escaped from the shoot-out in Austin on his own. Finally he would be shuttled to the CIA and the FBI for debriefing. Then released.

Unless...unless what was going on was a group inside the government declaring war on the Cellar, and they didn't want Ben talking in public about Pilgrim or the Cellar. An unexpected cold prickle raced along his skin. But Ben had government connections; Ben would be fine. This Sam Hector guy could get him a squadron of lawyers.

I thought we were on the same side. A sentiment of sheer stupidity. Ben lived in a normal world where, yes, you could become acquainted and think a person was your ally. Even your friend. Pilgrim remembered that world; for a brief second, he wanted to pull out his sketchbook, sharpen a pencil, draw the girl as he remembered her, bearing daisies in her cupped hands, her laughter dancing with the sunlight.

Ben's accusation rattled in his head. *You're not brave enough to keep a deal you make.* No, maybe he wasn't, but it didn't matter. He worked alone. It was the only way to survive.

The address on Barker's driver's license was on a street in east Dallas, and two of the houses had For Lease signs in the front yard. The neighborhood was quiet, dominated by mature oaks and single-story ranch houses. Most people were at work, but he saw a pregnant young woman kneeling in the shade, weeding a flower bed. She glanced up and waved at Pilgrim as he drove past. He waved back.

Barker's lawn needed a mow, and nuts from the pecan trees lay scattered and forgotten on the driveway. No police cars stood outside, which meant Barker's body, presumably lying in the Austin morgue, had not been connected to this address. Taking his driver's license had been a smart move.

Pilgrim drove past the house three times, saw no sign of life, no sign of surveillance. He parked his car two houses down, at one of the For Lease homes, and headed for Barker's front door. He knocked, rang the doorbell, knocked again. He fixed a picklock, shaped like a small gun, against the lock, squeezed the trigger, and the mechanism eased the lock open. He was inside.

The chirp of an alarm began; this was, after all, a Cellar property, and he'd expected security. He pulled a PDA from his pocket, popped off the plastic cover on the alarm keypad, wired the PDA to the keypad, tapped a program. It scanned the alarm deactivation setting on the pad and fed the system the right combination eighteen seconds into its search. Pilgrim unclipped the PDA from the alarm, memorized the displayed combination, and replaced the keypad cover. Then he relocked the door and reactivated the alarm in the Stay setting so he could move through the rooms. If anyone came inside, he wanted to create the illusion of an empty house.

The house was dark and still. It was furnished simply, with goods from Ikea, just enough to give the impression of a minimalist bachelor pad. Pilgrim moved through the rooms, not turning on any lights. He searched for the obvious places to hide a gun: the freezer, the narrow kitchen drawer closest to the back door, a spot inside the pantry. Nothing. The kitchen was nicely stocked, as though Barker expected to come home. Well, why wouldn't he? Teach was supposed to be captured and Pilgrim to be dead. An unopened bottle of French champagne chilled on the refrigerator shelf, awaiting a celebration.

He searched the house. In the den were a portable TV, a scattering of travel magazines, pages turned down on articles about the Bahamas and Aruba, notes about availability the following week jotted in the margins. Barker was planning a vacation with his traitor's coins. The built-in bookshelves were bare. It felt like home to Pilgrim; his own lodgings, usually changing every few months, were similarly plain.

At the back of the house, he found the master bedroom. Clothes, awaiting laundry, piled at the foot of the unmade bed. A worktable, wide and deep, occupied one corner. No computer, no papers. No trail. A cordless phone with an answering machine. He played the tape; it had been erased.

He began his search. In the back of a drawer he found three pairs of handcuffs, lengths of silk, sexual gels. A few magazines that showed couples lashed and bound to each other in more than love and mutual respect. Whatever, Pilgrim thought. Those in the Cellar led highly stressful lives.

Hidden at the back of the desk drawer he found two fake passports for Barker, under different names, which looked to be Cellar issue. Teach used superb forgers. But Barker didn't need to be going overseas with his work. Teach used domestic support in operations; she had Europeans to handle European ops, Americans to handle American ops. Barker and a couple of others were based near American airport hubs, to go quickly where they were needed.

So why had he been overseas?

He found one passport stamped for the United Kingdom, then Switzerland, all of two weeks ago. The other passport journeyed to Greece and then Lebanon.

The United Kingdom. Maybe to Belfast to hire the Lynch boys. Lebanon. Three weeks ago, for three days. Perhaps to hire the group who took Teach.

But then who'd hired Barker?

Pilgrim tucked Barker's passports into his pocket.

He heard the front door open, the distinctive sound of the lock being eased, probably by the same kind of pick-lock he had used. The alarm began its chime. He went to the corner of the room. He heard the door shut. Fingertips tapping in a code. Then silence.

Whoever was here knew the entry code. Pilgrim liked this visitor immediately. This visitor could tell him things.

The soft creepy-crawl of footsteps, two hushed voices, both male. The conversation—he couldn't hear what they said—murmured on for thirty seconds.

Which meant they didn't know he was here.

He waited. It didn't take long. But only one came into the bedroom, and Pilgrim put the gun on the back of his head as soon as he stepped into the room. The man was wiry and compact, in his forties, head shaved bald, and he went still with professional surrender. Pilgrim moved back from him and around him, raised a finger to his lips, and kept the gun firmly locked on the man's head.

"Call your partner back here," he whispered. "Politely and quietly."

"I found something," the bald guy said in a normal tone. Pilgrim pulled him back out of the line of sight of the hall-way, put the bald guy between him and the door as a shield. He heard footsteps approaching, then another man, a young, heavy-built Latino, came into the room. He sported evidence of a rough day: two black eyes, a bruised mouth. He wore a suit slightly too small for him: black jacket and pants, a white dress shirt, its creases indicating that it had been recently removed from its store packaging, no tie. He stopped when he saw Pilgrim, tensed for his gun.

Pilgrim said, "Don't."

"You're Pilgrim. We're from the Cellar," the man with the bruised face said. "Teach sent us here. I'm De La Pena. It's my real name. This is Green."

"Really. Where's Teach?"

"She's safe."

"Where?"

"I don't know where she's at," he said. "Just that she's safe."

Pilgrim tossed one of Barker's handcuffs to each of them. "Face each other. Hands in front. Put a cuff on your hand and his hand opposite." He kept his surprise that De La Pena offered a real name to him; you never shared your true identity in the Cellar.

So the guy might not be from the Cellar after all. That, or he was desperate to create trust.

The two men faced each other as though they were about to ballroom-dance, slid the cuffs onto their wrists. Green's right hand was cuffed to De La Pena's left, Green's left hand was chained to De La Pena's right.

"Lock them," Pilgrim ordered, and they shut the cuffs. Green looked pissed; he had a small mouth that went to a rosebud. De La Pena was calm. He, Pilgrim suspected, was the more dangerous one.

"These are for girls," Green said peevishly. "They're a little tight."

"Sit down," Pilgrim said. He took their guns from them, one in each pocket. Searched their backs and legs for more weapons, found nothing. He put the guns on the desk, well out of reach.

Paired awkwardly, the two men sank to the floor.

"You shouldn't be here," De La Pena said, no malice in the tone.

"Neither should you," Pilgrim said.

"We're janitors. Cleaning up after a job goes bad."

"Clean up: destroy data, erase Barker's trails, kill anyone who needs killing."

"Crudely put. I haven't killed anyone ever," De La Pena said. "I can't speak for him." He jerked his head at Green, who flexed an enigmatic smile.

"So you say Teach sent you."

"Yes."

"You saw her or she called you?"

"She called Green. I was already here, part of a training exercise."

Pilgrim pointed at De La Pena's black eyes. "Were you training to be a punching bag?"

"She told me to get to Dallas and help this guy clean any Cellar evidence out of the house," Green said.

"She's been kidnapped," Pilgrim said.

"She told us you tried to kidnap her," Green said. "You killed her helper, she escaped. Sell your story down the street, man."

"I killed Barker, yeah, but he turned traitor. Not me. She got grabbed."

The two men stared at him. Not believing him, he saw.

"Who has her?" Pilgrim asked softly. "I think you know. Stop the lies, man." He kicked them hard, nailing De La Pena in the back, and both guys fell over. "She's not operating of her own accord, she's under a thumb."

"She told me what to do," De La Pena said. "She said you'd gone bad and—"

What are you doing, Teach? Pilgrim wondered. "Get up," he ordered them. He could question them in the kitchen; as unappealing as it sounded, a bit of fear at the tip of a knife might loosen their tongues.

De La Pena and Green rose awkwardly, like conjoined twins always facing each other.

Pilgrim gestured them back into the narrow confines of the hallway and they walked sideways, facing each other. De La Pena stood a foot taller than Green, and Green hurried to keep pace. Then Green stumbled, nearly going to one knee. De La Pena stopped and hauled him up, and as Green rose he lashed a sharp, precise kick and caught Pilgrim hard in the gun hand, pinning his weapon back into his chest. Pilgrim backpedaled into the master bedroom.

Pilgrim swung the gun up again, but now they were on top of him, moving as one. De La Pena launched Green again, swinging the smaller man, and Green's feet slammed into Pilgrim's chest. Air whooshed out of Pilgrim's lungs, and as Green fell, De La Pena launched a well-timed kick that smashed Pilgrim's gun out of his hand. The weapon slammed into the far wall.

Pilgrim collapsed against the wall and the two fell on top of him, sliding to the hardwood floor, De La Pena pinioning Pilgrim with his weight, the men's joined hands closing on his throat, strangling him in symphony.

He jammed a finger into Green's eye.

Green howled and twisted away. De La Pena raised and lowered their joined hands, closed a circle around Pilgrim, tried to crush him between himself and Green. Pilgrim punched Green, short and brutally hard, again. Felt lip tear and nose break under his blows. De La Pena pushed all his weight against Pilgrim.

Pilgrim's lungs and his throat were suddenly empty of oxygen. Fresh agony flamed in his shoulder.

Pilgrim's feet lifted off the hardwood, and he shoved them between his opponents and the wall and pushed, knocking them all off balance. The tangle of men collapsed to the floor again and De La Pena's choking hold broke, for just a second. Breath, sudden and sweet. Pilgrim hammered an elbow hard into De La Pena's face, once, twice, pain rocketing up his hurt arm. De La Pena tried to head-butt him, hit the shoulder instead, nearly made Pilgrim faint from the pain. Pilgrim rolled atop De La Pena, pulling Green on top of him.

"Grab his throat!" De La Pena yelled at Green.

Pilgrim's and Green's faces were an inch apart and Pilgrim closed his hands around Green's neck, and Green was trying to squirm away from Pilgrim's reach, panic in his eyes.

"No, no, don't," Green grunted, knowing what the grip meant.

Pilgrim closed his fingers around the jaw, around the head, with precision and care, and the crack was audible. The dying sigh went straight into Pilgrim's face.

Green lolled, a limp weight attached to De La Pena's hands, lying atop them. Pilgrim slid lower, seized Green's dead head, rammed it against De La Pena's face. Pilgrim writhed, ducked from between the bodies, but De La Pena grabbed at his hair and throat.

But Pilgrim twisted free of the clutch of the living man and the weight of the dead man. He clambered to his feet as De La Pena lunged for his legs, delivering a powerhouse kick to De La Pena's jaw, then to the stomach.

De La Pena doubled up, tried to pull Green on him as a shield. Pilgrim let him. Then he grabbed the dead man's head from behind, pounded it again and again into De La Pena's face.

"I'll talk!" De La Pena finally screamed. "I'll talk!"

Pilgrim hit him twice more for measure, then dropped Green's body to the side.

De La Pena stayed still.

"If you move, if you look at me funny, I'll kill you, understand?"

"I understand," De La Pena said through bloodied lips. The blood was not all his own.

"Who sent you?"

"Teach did. But…there's a man. This guy, ex-military, kidnapped me last week. Brought me here. Kept me in a conference room, beat me. Beat me for no reason." He blinked through the blood. "He knew I was ex-CIA. Knew my real name. Said Teach would be here soon to talk to me."

"And she was."

"Last night. She looked like she'd been in a fight. She told me the new guy was a partner, we'd be working with him. I could read the writing on the wall. He's muscled his way into the Cellar and she's letting him."

"You know the guy's name?"

"No. She didn't tell me. He's older but you can tell he's definitely from our line of work. Cold eyes. He smiles like how I think a ghost smiles." He paused. "His house is fancy."

"Describe him."

"Tall, late forties or early fifties, silver-haired, but very fit."

"Anyone else?"

"There's one other guy. Young. Irish accent." He shrugged.

"Dressed in black? Like Johnny Cash?"

"Yeah. This new guy's got Teach deep in his pocket. You may say she's kidnapped but clearly she's working with him."

"Only because he's threatened her or us. She's being coerced; Teach wouldn't ever betray us."

"Doesn't matter if it's voluntary," De La Pena said. "Teach loses control of the Cellar, I go with the flow. Whoever runs the Cellar runs me."

"Tell me where this house is."

"You're entirely missing the point. These guys, they're not keeping her at the point of a gun. They're keeping her because *they found us*. This guy owns us because he can expose us." De La Pena stared up at him through the blood. "What's the CIA going to do when we come to light? Wash their hands of us. You know we can't be acknowledged, we all made the deal when we signed up. We'll get brought up on federal charges." He spat a trickle of blood. "You should just vanish. Give up on trying to get Teach back. It's a new day, man."

"Your loyalty is an inspiration. Teach gets you out of the gutter, gives you a second chance, and you won't fight to help her get free."

"She's not fighting this guy." De La Pena shrugged. "Why should I?"

Pilgrim stood, went to the far side of the room, retrieved his gun.

De La Pena said, "Uncuff me, man; he's dead, uncuff me." He jerked his arm, and Green's dead arm moved in unison. "I told you what you need to know, let me go; I never saw you, and we're square."

Pilgrim stood unsteadily, groped in his pocket for the weight of Barker's passports. "If you move, I'm going to leave him bound to you and lock you out of this house. I can't wait for you to explain to the neighbors why you're walking the streets with a dead guy chained to you." He picked up the phone, hit Redial, listened to the phone beep a number. The number display showed 504. New Orleans area code. After the third ring, a woman briskly answered: "Hotel Marquis de Lafayette, how may I assist you today?"

"I'm trying to locate your hotel but I think I've taken a wrong turn."

"We're near Poydras and St. Charles, sir. Where are you coming from?"

"Oh, I had the address down wrong, I can find it. Thanks so much." Pilgrim hung up the phone. He tried to imagine Barker's last day in this house, preparing for a traitorous operation, one where he had to fool both Teach and Pilgrim, set Pilgrim up for death, isolate Teach for a kidnapping. And the last phone call he makes is to a hotel in New Orleans.

Who was there? Why New Orleans?

"Tell me where she's being held."

"First, unhook me from him, man," De La Pena said.

"Tell me."

"No," De La Pena said. "Uncuff me. You're going to have to trust me, I can help you rescue Teach. But I could tell you and you'll kill me like Green."

"You tried to kill me."

"Orders. But I was told you'd gone bad, and you've talked to me—I see you haven't. I believe you, not the guy who's got Teach. I can help you. He's planning a big job he needs Teach for. I heard them talking. The job is on Sunday."

"What's happening Sunday?"

"I don't know."

Pilgrim watched him. He went to the bedside table,

rummaged in its depths, found the keys. He readied his gun. He wished he'd brought Ben with him, useless as he might be, because this was the moment of greatest risk. He kept the gun on De La Pena, unlocked the first cuff, then the second.

De La Pena slowly stood, hands apart. Fighting in the restraints had scored his wrists raw and bloody. He spat blood again.

"Where's the guy's house?"

"I'm bleeding inside..." De La Pena stumbled, his hand going to the collar of his shirt. Pilgrim hesitated, but then he saw the flash of silver coming from under the collar, De La Pena's arm slashing toward him, felt the bite of the blade into his gun hand as he raised it, and he fired.

The bullet caught De La Pena in the throat. He collapsed, dropping the thin little knife he'd hidden in his collar. His gaze found the ceiling and stayed there.

"You stupid," Pilgrim muttered, both to himself and to De La Pena. The cut wasn't bad but close to his wrist, and he mopped up the blood with a towel. He splashed water on his face, spat into the sink. Everything ached; his wounds were seeping, nausea rocked his stomach.

He finished the search of the house. Nothing. He had a thread—narrow and possibly meaningless—leading to New Orleans and a dirty job in less than forty-eight hours. But Teach was still here in the Dallas area, and he couldn't leave without trying to find her.

He went to the car parked in front of the house, used keys from Green's pocket to open it. A rental; he found the receipt in the glove compartment. The reservation was in the name of Sparta Consulting, the regular Cellar financial front. Nothing to trace back to the new boss. Other than a vague description, and he had no idea if De La Pena had even been honest about that.

He returned to the stolen Volvo and headed down the street. The pregnant lady, still kneeling in her garden with a smile, waved at him again as he drove past, and he waved right back.

21

ON FRIDAY MORNING AFTER THE MAYHEM in Austin, Sam Hector stood, tall and resolute, in front of press microphones at the briefing room at Hector Global's complex northeast of Dallas.

"Nothing can replace the two brave men lost yesterday in Austin. They were working for Homeland Security, as contract guards for an important new office in Austin, in an effort to make all Americans safer." He briefly eulogized the two men and lauded their families. He honored Norman Kidwell, the dedicated Homeland Security officer who had died with his men. "Let me assure you that the three thousand employees and all the worldwide resources of Hector Global will be available to the authorities to bring those responsible to justice." He cleared his throat, and gave the viewing public the benefit of his stern, determined gaze. "All early indicators here point to this heinous attack being the work of a terrorist cell, operating here on American soil. Clearly this is a new danger, a more serious threat to us all that our nation—both government and private business—must work together to respond to with strength and resolve."

He paused to let the drama build; the scratching of

pens against paper stopped; the gathered reporters waited. "Hector Global is and will continue to be an integral part of the War on Terror, especially when terror comes again to our shores. We will give our full cooperation and support to Homeland Security, the FBI, and other governmental agencies."

He took no questions from the press, although they yelled several at him as he left the podium. He heard one inquiring about his business relationship with the missing Ben Forsberg and one asking how much his contracts with Homeland were worth and would he be losing the department's business. Another reporter yelled a question about how much business he'd already lost in the past six months, and it was an effort for Hector not to flinch as he walked away.

He retreated from the conference room to the sanctuary of his own office. Alone. He sat at his desk and pulled from a locked drawer a photo, yellowed with age. The man in the photo was big-built, plain-faced, with brown hair. His name had been Randall Choate. He was supposed to be dead, but he was not.

Sam Hector wanted Choate dead. Soon. The stakes were far too high to let a man like Pilgrim—Choate—interfere with the operation.

Contractors are sometimes each other's most important client—much of the large contracts handed to companies are then subcontracted out to other, more specialized concerns. The resulting network of suppliers and firms made for a considerable intelligence advantage.

Hector started leaning on his network to find Pilgrim. Quietly.

Lockhart Technologies, a fast-growing company based

in Alexandria, Virginia, handled communications and IT support for Hector Global. Sam Hector owned a software engineer inside Lockhart named Gary, whose online gambling addiction required money. Lockhart also provided customized software design and support to the National Security Agency's mainframes for tracking, analyzing, and cataloging millions of phone calls to and from, and now within, the United States. The software was a critical component of the NSA's parabolic satellite listening stations in Yakima, Washington, and Sugar Grove, West Virginia. Gary kept an admin account alive on a mainframe used to analyze the torrents of data—and this morning, at Hector's request, he was secretly loading programs to listen for and identify any phone conversations, happening anywhere in the country, using the word *Choate*. He wanted to know if the CIA knew one of their lost heroes was alive and well.

A financial services contractor—who handled credit card charges for the military and for Hector employees in Baghdad's Green Zone—was told by Sam Hector to alert him to any new credit card accounts opened in the name of Benjamin Forsberg or Randall Choate, or of any new credit card accounts opened with any of the aliases he had identified as used by the Cellar. He also asked for alerts on the use of cards which had been dormant for a month, specifically on charges for hotels, travel, or gasoline, in a five-state area.

The contractor got a number of immediate hits. Hector noticed three from last night in towns between Austin and Dallas, including a charge for James Woodward. That was one of Pilgrim's aliases found by Adam Reynolds. So were they headed for Dallas—or just headed away from Austin? He called the contractor back, told him to call immediately if there were any further charges on the James Woodward card.

Pilgrim must eventually show his head, and Hector wanted to be ready to lop it off.

He slid the old photo of Randall Choate back into his desk. *Soon enough,* he thought, *you scum, you'll be in the coffin you belong in.* He expected that Ben Forsberg—if Choate had not killed him—would be calling for help soon. Both men should be dead within twelve hours, hopefully, if Pilgrim did the expected thing and went to Barker's house. Nice to have people to do the dirtiest work for you; Hector preferred having clean hands.

His phone rang, the cell phone he kept in his pocket, the number that fewer than ten people in the world had. He glanced at the cell's readout. He didn't recognize the number.

"Hello?"

"Uh, yeah. Hi. Mr. Hector? My name is Delia Moon."

He said, "You're Adam's friend." He knew this not because of Adam confiding in him but because he knew all pertinent details about Adam Reynolds's life.

"Oh, yeah. Did he mention me to you?"

"With the warmest regard, Delia. He was so fond of you."

"Oh, um..." A choked sob, controlled with effort.

He waited for her to compose herself.

"I need help, Mr. Hector."

"Of course."

"Adam mentioned that you were going to help him with his project. His software to track illicit banking activities to find terrorists."

Hector squeezed the bridge of his nose and thought:

Idiot couldn't keep a secret. That was unfortunate. "Well, yes, he talked to me about such a project...but I didn't know he was far off the ground with it."

"Well, he is very far along in developing the program. I think that's why he died. And Homeland Security, they've confiscated his computers, and they're going to sit on his software or take it for their own use, and well, it doesn't belong to them. It belongs to...him, to his estate now, I guess."

"And you would be his estate?"

"No," she said, sounding horrified. "His mom. She's sick, she needs money. But it's not the government's. I'm scared they're going to take it and keep it...it's not right. I need your help, Mr. Hector. They won't listen to me but they'll listen to you. Or your lawyers."

"Yes," he said. "We should talk. But privately."

"All right."

He considered. "May I come to your house? I'm afraid the press are all over my place, and I'm constantly interrupted with calls from Homeland Security."

"Yes, that's fine." She gave him directions and he said, "I'll see you shortly then," and he hung up.

He called in his assistant. "I'm going to work from home today."

The assistant—a former army clerk who was not easily rattled—went pale. "Sir. You've gotten another twenty interview requests including CNN and Fox and the *New York Times,* you've got that noon meeting with the lawyers if the guards' families sue, the PR firm wants to give you a strategy update—"

"Cancel it all. I'm not giving further interviews; I've said the words that matter most to me, they can rerun the press conference. I'm simply not available." He knew he didn't have to explain, but he believed so fervently in the power of his own company to do good, he added: "I have to assist the government in its investigation. Are there still a lot of press camped out in front of the gates?"

"Yes, sir."

"Tell the driver to get a car with tinted windows. I don't really want the world knowing where I am right now."

The two men from the Cellar had not returned or reported their progress. Teach sat at the conference table. A laptop, not connected to the Internet, sat before her. She had been typing into a document a detailed history of the Cellar, its agents, and its operations, as ordered that morning by Hector.

He slid into a seat across from her. "Your boys aren't back. Do you think Green and De La Pena abandoned you?"

"No."

"You think Pilgrim intercepted them."

"Maybe." Hate filled her eyes. "Making us your puppets won't work."

"It won't work today," he said, "but it will tomorrow. If I get any inkling that those two took off, I start killing people on the Cellar roll calls."

"You may end up killing us all."

"I may."

"Don't believe for a second that it will be easy."

He leaned over, printed her draft report on the Cellar's activities. As the paper spooled from the printer, he scanned each sheet. At one page his gaze widened slightly; but he felt her gaze on him and he put his poker face back in place.

"What?" she said.

"I'm both impressed and disturbed by the scope of your activities. Would it sound contrary to say I admire you?"

"Yes."

"As you say, this won't be easy, but I know you'll smooth my path. Keep writing." He set the draft on the table and left the room, locking her inside. He leaned for a moment against the door; it was reassuring to know he'd made the right business decision. He felt an inappropriate, insidious urge to laugh, but he choked it down.

Hector found Jackie sitting in a guest room. He'd sent an aide to buy him clothes: black pants and black shirts, as Jackie requested. Jackie kept wearing his pair of black cowboy boots. He looked like a poor man's Johnny Cash. He balanced a wicked knife's handle on the flat of his palm.

The knife glinted in the light as Jackie steadied his hand.

"I need you to put that knife to work on a loose end. Her name is Delia Moon."

Jackie tossed the knife up, caught the handle. "I didn't think Dallas had hippies."

"They can have one less. Be quick and don't get caught."

Jackie put the knife back in its sheath and stood. "I'd like to know why you hate these two guys so much."

"I beg your pardon?"

"Pilgrim and Forsberg. What's your motive?"

"It's not your concern."

"My brother died trying to put Pilgrim down. I'd like to know why he died."

Hector crossed his arms. "Jackie, I wonder if you've thought about your future."

"Yes. Quite a lot. Are you going to answer my question?"

"No. It's irrelevant to your work." He cleared his throat.

"Running a business like yours is dangerous—not just on account of the violence. Trying to bring in the contracts, find clients who will pay, it's almost as dangerous as killing the targets. Every potential client's a cop or a rival who wants you to let your guard down."

"It's not like you can go cold-calling to drum up business."

"So you complete this job, and if you want, you'll work for me. For as long as you like."

"Work for you. Doing what?"

"I'm going to give you Pilgrim's job," Hector said. "His exact same job."

Jackie laughed. "His job's too bloody dangerous."

"But you won't be alone, Jackie." And Hector could tell he'd read the boy right, he'd appealed to his insecurity, because Jackie studied the floor, as though he needed to slip on a mask before he met Hector's stare.

He said, "Sure, I'll give it a solid think, Mr. Hector. Point me toward your hippie chick."

22

TIED TO A TOILET. Ben figured he could holler for help, pound the walls, and the housekeeping staff or another guest would hear him and come to his aid. And then what? At the least he faced a difficult explanation as to how he came to be bound to the pipes, and at the worst he'd be recognized from the news accounts and handed over to the police.

The plastic cuff bit into his skin. He had to loosen it. He lay between the tub and the toilet. A sample shampoo canister sat with its matching bottles of conditioner and soap on the counter. But well out of reach.

Ben yanked the bath towel hanging above his head. He held one end of it and whipped the tail of the towel onto the counter. It knocked over the pyramid of miniature soaps and gels. Ben lashed out again with the towel, caught the plastic bottles under its weight. He slowly dragged the towel and the toiletries tumbled to the floor.

He upended the shampoo bottle over the cuff and greased his skin. He worked the ooze between the plastic and his flesh. Pulling and twisting, he tried to ease his hand through the cuff. Too tight. He worked it for five minutes but made scant progress.

He tried again with the bottle of conditioner, pouring with greater care, making sure he spilled none to the tiles. His heart pounded against the floor and he steeled himself to lose an entire layer of skin. He gritted his teeth and pulled. Agony. He tried to twist his hand through the tough plastic circle but it was simply too tight.

His eyes searched the counter. Nothing else, just a set of sugar packets, plastic cups, foil pouches of bad coffee, and a coffeemaker.

The coffeemaker. The small carafe appeared to be glass. He tried to flick it loose with his towel. Missed. Too far. He pulled himself as close to the counter as he could. The carafe was still beyond his reach. He pulled a second towel down from the rack and awkwardly knotted the two together. He tried again. Missed. Tried again. This time the carafe jarred in its perch in the coffeemaker but didn't buck loose. He heaved the towel in another hard snap, and now the carafe rocked free from the coffeemaker but skittered toward the sink. If it fell into the sink he'd never reach it.

Ben calmed himself before he made another attempt. He aimed the towel, held one corner, tossed it over the carafe. He dragged the carafe slowly past the sink, and then it fell to the tiles, shattering.

Please, he thought, *let there be a piece big enough to cut with.* He pulled the towel off the broken carafe. The handle's metal ring held a jagged rim of glass. He carefully picked up the handle and began to saw at the cuff where it joined to the pipe.

A knock on the door, a voice calling in polite singsong. "Housekeeping...everything all right in there?" The woman had heard the breaking carafe.

"I'm fine," he called. *Please don't let her open the door.*

"Is something broken, sir?" The woman spoke with a Jamaican accent.

"No, everything's fine."

The woman gave no reply. He put the jagged edge back to the cuff and after several more seconds the glass sliced through the plastic. He stood, half the cuff still on his wrist. He stumbled to the door, stepping on an object.

Pilgrim's small sketchbook; Ben must have knocked it out of his pocket during the fight. *Serves him right,* Ben thought, slipping the book into his pocket. He put his eye to the peephole. A housekeeping cart stood on the other side and the woman was speaking into a walkie-talkie and she said, "Yeah, I heard glass breaking in there." She paused, listening for more instructions. "Okay." She pulled her cord of keys from her pocket and stepped toward the door.

He opened the door and walked straight past her. "I dropped and broke the coffee machine," he said over his shoulder. "Sorry, I was trying to pick up the mess." He kept his hand in front of him, the sleeve rolled down to hide the plastic cuff. He reached the elevator and glanced back; the woman was staring at him, *at his face.* He stepped into the open elevator and went down to the lobby.

He hurried past the front desk, stepped out into the cool breeze. The stolen Volvo was gone from its spot. He froze, indecisive, and behind him the hotel doors parted. He glanced back through the glass and saw the hotel clerk standing behind the counter, phone to his ear.

Watching him.

He turned and walked across the lot. Was that what paranoia was, the certainty that everyone was gawking at you, everyone knew who you were, everyone was reaching to stop you and pull you into darkness? It was a worm that turned and chewed and ate at you from inside.

He had to find a car.

The hotel lay along a busy thoroughfare in Plano, one of the largest suburbs near Dallas, and a line of chain restaurants—Cajun, Mexican, seafood, a steakhouse—sat across from it. Behind them stood a strip mall that included a bath supplies shop, a craft shop, a furniture store, a bookstore. Dozens of cars sitting there, and he had no idea how to steal one.

Stop. Think. He stayed calm in negotiating multi-million-dollar business deals; he could stay calm now.

Grabbing keys out of someone's hand—no. He wasn't going to mug an innocent person. And no one left cars unlocked these days.

What had Pilgrim suggested when they were heading for the garage back in Austin, if they'd had to steal a car? Bumper surfing: hunting for key boxes hidden under bumpers. He picked the heaviest row of cars, leaned down low, moving from car to car, skipping the high-end sports numbers. He thought he might have better luck with cars with those stickers announcing kids' activities—wouldn't a mother be more likely to take precautions to keep from being locked out of the car, with kids in tow? He refocused his efforts on those kinds of cars.

Great, he told himself, *you're starting to think like a car thief. Nice.* What did Pilgrim say about his job—*We do the dirty work that's necessary.* Pilgrim was right. You did what was necessary to fight back.

He heard the approaching whine of police sirens.

A woman getting into a car four down from him glared at him as though she knew exactly what he was up to. She put a cell phone to her ear as she backed out of the parking lot.

On the next car he tried—a Ford Explorer—his fingertips touched the square of a key box.

He opened the box, worried it would be a house key but no, it was a Ford key and within ten seconds he was inside the car. He backed out, saw two police cars revving into the motel's parking lot. He drove the Explorer around the back of the shopping center, exited onto a side road, desperate to put distance between him and the police.

Now what? he thought.

He drove west for ten minutes—Plano seemed to be mostly large streets with subdivisions constantly sprouting off the roads, interrupted by shopping centers. He pulled into a branch library.

He could call Sam Hector. Beg his old friend for help. Explain what had happened to his employees down in Austin. Sam had connections of steel into every government branch and agency. He could use his leverage to help Ben clear his name.

Ben put on a pair of sunglasses he found in the Explorer's glove compartment. Scant camouflage, but it was the best he could do. He found a scattering of spare change in the Explorer's CD holder. An old pay phone stood near the door. He fed it quarters and dialed Sam Hector's direct line. The phone rang three times—he could see Sam frowning at an unknown number calling him on a line very few people knew how to reach—then he heard the familiar baritone. "Sam Hector."

A sudden urge inside Ben said, *Just hang up, don't drag Sam into this horror.* But instead he said. "Sam. It's Ben."

"Ben, are you all right? Where are you?"

"I'm okay. I'm in Dallas."

"Where?"

"Sam, I need help."

"Where are you, Ben?"

"I don't want to say; I don't want to put you in a bad situation with the police."

"Ben, I'm already in a bad situation. I have men dead. Why did you leave the scene? You have a lot of explaining to do." In the background Ben could hear a gentle *click-click-click*.

"Help me and I'll explain."

A pained silence. "Ben, come to my house. We can strategize and we'll get you surrendered to the police, get you the best representation. I'll stand by you." *Click-click-click*.

"I can't come to your house. I need information."

Ben glanced over his shoulder, to see if anyone was watching him, recognizing his face from the television. The few library patrons were lost in their reading. He heard more of the clicking—it sounded familiar, though. "Tell me about Homeland's Office of Strategic Initiatives."

"Ben. You know I can't break client confidentiality."

"Please. I need to know who these people at Homeland are, what their job is." *Click-click.* He debated how much to tell Sam. "Listen. I was framed and these people think I'm guilty of being connected to the sniper that killed Adam Reynolds."

"How?"

"Never mind. But I've never heard of this group, and they leaned very hard on me, threatened me, threatened my loved ones, my business. Who runs the group? I need a name."

The silence on the other end of the phone ticked away ten seconds. The clicking stopped.

"Sam, help me. Give me a name."

"Fine. I will tell you if you come to my house." He seemed to spit out every word.

"Just give me a name and a number." Ben hated the begging tug in his voice.

"And watch you do what? Run to Washington and make a fool of yourself? Call the press and undermine an important program? What?"

"Don't lecture me. I'm incredibly sorry your men were killed, but they aimed guns at me and helped Homeland take me from my house and deny me due process. That's not exactly in the normal services your company provides on American soil." He couldn't keep the anger from his voice.

"My men must have been following Strategic Initiatives' orders, not mine," Hector said.

"Sam. You owe me."

A long pause, no clicks. "All right. Strategic Initiatives is a very small and unpublicized group inside Homeland. You won't see them listed on the agency website. They're a think tank on how to slice through bureaucratic procedure and encourage teamwork between the agencies. They contracted with us for security services."

"Why does a think tank need security?"

"Because they represent the cutting edge of counterterrorism thought. The bad guys would love to get their hands on any of the Strategic Initiatives people."

"Who runs it?"

"Ben, come to my house and we can talk."

"No. I'll meet you in a public place."

He heard a solitary click on the other end of the line. "Now you sound paranoid."

"Just tell me who runs Strategic Initiatives." His frustration nearly made him yell.

"I can't. I made a promise to be discreet. That is nonnegotiable."

"I'll tell you what's nonnegotiable. How much money I've made you over the years. How many deals I've helped you win because you weren't particularly good at compromise and negotiation and I was. How much I've contributed to your company's success, and you won't help me in my hour of need."

"Ben. You're hysterical. Just come to my house—"

Ben hung up. He calmed his breathing. The clicks. Sam kept that abacus collection in his home office. He often played with an abacus on his desk, fingering the worn wooden beads back and forth along the rods, when he talked on the phone, when he was bored or nervous.

That might have been the most important conversation he could ever have with Sam Hector, and the man had been playing with an abacus. Like he was doodling on a pad.

He felt sick. Sam Hector, shying away from him. So much for loyalty. Every mooring of his life seemed undone. He drew a deep breath.

He remembered the phone number Vochek last called on her cell phone when Pilgrim went through the call log. Delia Moon, who'd left a message. She might be the woman whom Reynolds had called four times, a partner, a confidante, someone who could be of help to Ben in clearing his name—saying, *That's not the Ben Forsberg that Adam Reynolds knew.* Or who could tell him how Adam had found Pilgrim and the Cellar, and could help him find them again.

The library was not busy; a few retirees reading magazines,

a few people surfing the Web. He saw his own face on the front page of the paper, held up as a man read the inside of the section. On the library's reference shelves, he found a phone directory. He looked up her name. Not in Plano. He worked his way through the suburbs' directories and found her address in Frisco. He consulted a map, sketched out directions, and headed back to his car.

Delia Moon's house stood in a tidy section of grand but cookie-cutter homes, all with fancy stone exteriors and oversized garages. Hers was one of the few finished ones; construction seemed to sprout from the Dallas prairie as fast as weeds and wildflowers. He drove twice past the house; he could see a kitchen light gleaming. It was nearly one in the afternoon. He saw a dark Mercedes parked down the street, in front of two finished houses that still had dirt instead of sodded grass and with For Sale signs the only sprouting growth, a guy in dark glasses holding a newspaper open, probably house hunting.

He parked down the street, in front of a just-finished house that still had a For Sale sign in front, and walked back three houses to Delia Moon's home.

He had an idea of what to say, but no clue if it would work. His throat locked.

He rang the doorbell. No answer, but he could hear the distant whine of a television. He rang the doorbell again. "Ms. Moon?" he called.

The door cracked open. Before him stood a tall young woman, dark-haired. She opened the door barely an inch. He saw a green eye and a cheek scattered with light freckles.

"I'm not talking to anyone today."

"My name is Ben Forsberg," he said. "You and I were the last people Adam tried to call before he died. We need to talk."

"How did you know where I lived?" Through the inch of space the green eye peered at him.

Ben swallowed. He was unused to lying; but then, he was unused to removing bullets from flesh and forging signatures and stealing cars, and right now a lie was necessary. He cleared his throat. "Homeland Security brought me in for questioning. The person who killed Adam had my business card in his pocket. They think I might be the next target." He paused. "I saw your number on one of the Homeland agents' phones when they were trying to reach you."

"You were going to help him get his software business off the ground," she said, and he realized, *She bought it, she thinks I'm Pilgrim's pretend version of me.*

"I wanted to help him," he lied. "Can we talk?"

"I don't know…" She bit her lip, and now he had to convince her, lie if he had to, or she would shut him out, probably phone the police.

"Listen. Whoever hired that sniper to kill Adam, they could come after you if they suspect he confided in you."

The door stopped. Now she frowned. "I'm a nobody."

"Still. If you knew what he knew…"

"All I know is, all his ideas, his software he'd developed, Homeland Security took it all. But…"

"But what?"

"I don't know what they're going to do with his research. I don't want them to steal his work. I want to protect it."

He needed to know what this research was as well. He pressed his advantage. "That's exactly what this group at

Homeland might do. Access to his software is going to save them millions." He hoped his bluff made sense. "But maybe I can help you get his property back."

"Just a minute." She shut the door and he stood, waiting, for thirty seconds until she opened it again. She was out of breath, as though she'd been running. "Come in."

Ben stepped inside the house. The rich smell of cinnamon coffee hung like a perfume. Delia Moon gestured at Ben to walk first into the kitchen and he did, realizing she did not want her back turned to him. *No sudden moves,* he thought, *don't scare her.*

She was pretty but her face seemed careworn, as though life had made her suspicious and cautious. "You want coffee?"

"Sure. I really am sorry to intrude upon your grief," he said, and he was. He remembered how awkward people seemed toward him after Emily's death. Murder paralyzed everything in your life.

She went to the cabinet and reached for an extra cup. She poured him a cup and refilled her own.

"I hope you don't mind black," she said. "I'm out of cream and sugar."

"Black's fine." He took a sip of coffee. The taste sent a surge of heat racing along his bones. It was a moment of calmness, of normalcy, good coffee drunk in a sunny, bright kitchen.

She pulled a gun from the back of her jeans, from under her untucked batik blouse. "Please put your hands on your head."

He thought: *She shouldn't have given me a hot beverage, I could throw it on her, get the gun from her.* Funny how your mind started to work when you were afraid all the time. But he set the coffee down. "I'm not a threat to you." Slowly he put his hands above his head.

She glanced at the remnant of the plastic handcuff on his wrist. "Lay down on the floor."

He obeyed. "I don't have a gun," he said.

"I never thought I'd use this one. Adam insisted. Me living here alone." She prodded at him with her foot, along his legs, along the small of his back.

"Delia, please listen to me. There was a man who stole my identity. He pretended to be me. He's the one who approached Adam. He works for a secret group in the government. Adam found his false identities, the ones used in undercover work, and this man and this secret group came looking for Adam. To discover how he found them, when no one was supposed to be able to identify them."

She stepped back from him, kept the gun leveled at him. "False identities—" she started to say and then stopped. And he saw the dawn of belief in her eyes.

"You believe me," he said in shock, and she nodded.

The sense of relief—after two days of not being believed—was vast. Someone believing him. He shivered, put his face in his hands. "Finally. Thank you, Delia."

She slowly lowered the gun, two sudden tears inching down her face.

Ben slowly sat up from the floor. "These people he discovered are sort of spies, but they're not part of the CIA. They do the dirty jobs that the government can't own. I need to know exactly how Adam found them."

"He was stupid and brilliant." She wiped away a tear. "He told me he had created a set of programs that would help track patterns used by people who are using fraudulent identities. He thought it would be useful in tracking terrorists. He wanted to do good. He kept saying we had to find them before they strike."

"But terrorists aren't the only ones who try to hide behind false identities and accounts," Ben said. "It could also apply in finding covert operatives."

She wiped at her nose with the back of her hand. "He talked about stuff like 'common behavioral patterns'—false names, quickly established and deactivated credit and banking accounts, large cash withdrawals from those kinds of accounts."

"Brew all the data together and it sounds like a Google to find bad guys." Ben frowned. "But that wouldn't work unless you could have access to a very wide array of unrelated databases. Financial, law enforcement, governmental, travel, corporate. The trail any of us leave in our lives is across a quilt of databases that aren't sewn together."

"Couldn't the government get him permission for that?"

"Not without tons of warrants. But he did it. Someone got him the access."

"Adam wouldn't try to expose undercover cops or CIA agents or anybody working for good." She shook her head. "Never. Not on purpose."

"I don't believe he knew he was searching for covert government agents. Maybe he was told they were bad guys. Did he ever mention to you that someone wanted to fund this software?"

"He mentioned one, a guy named Sam Hector—that Mr. Hector might fund his research. But this was months ago. I called him today when I realized the government had taken all of Adam's ideas. I thought he could help me. He said he'd come talk to me about how we could get Adam's research back from the government."

"I know Sam."

"Oh, good."

"Not really. He dragged his heels on helping me. It wasn't like him." He wondered if Sam was feeling his own set of pressures from the government. Maybe Sam knew much more than what he was saying.

"Well, Mr. Hector's coming here and he's going to help me."

And he would do nothing for me that wasn't under his own terms. What was wrong with Sam? Bitterness rose into Ben's throat. "Then he must see more value in helping you than helping me. Delia, this is huge. Have you told anyone, the police, about what Adam was doing?"

She made a face. "There was a Homeland woman here, but she acted like I was mud on her shoe."

"Joanna Vochek."

"You know her?"

"Yes. She might believe me."

"She didn't believe a word I said," Delia said. "I'm supposed to call her if I remember anything else." She pushed Vochek's number at him; he opened the paper, memorized the number. He might need it soon.

He handed her back the paper. "But you believe me."

She nodded. "Yes. I do."

The doorbell rang.

"Is Sam on his way over here now?" Ben asked. Delia hurried to the front door.

"Yeah," she said. She put her eye to the peephole.

Jackie had been sitting in the Mercedes, puzzling over how to get into Delia Moon's house without a fuss when Ben Forsberg—the civilian from the parking garage last night—pulled up in a white Explorer.

He waited, watched Ben talk his way into the woman's house. Interesting. He called Hector's number. No answer. He left a message. Waited a few minutes and Hector called back.

"Her and Forsberg are here together."

"Then why are you calling me? Kill them."

"I'm calling because you're pretty freaking particular about how things are done," Jackie said. He ended the call and walked out to the house. Rang the doorbell, bold in the daylight. Saw the peephole's flick of light get eclipsed by whoever was answering the door.

Jackie fired his Glock through the peephole.

23

<figure>◆━━●○●━━◆</figure>

Indonesia, Ten Years Ago

RANDALL CHOATE HAD READ through the Dragon's files on Blood of Fire: a new group, disorganized, usually crippled by internal squabbling. Suspicion linked them to several murders in the Muslim community in Sydney, to two killings in Lebanon, to a bombing in Cairo. Very bad guys.

Clearly the man had done his research, thought out the possibilities, analyzed the risks and minimized them.

But the Dragon's network of informants was gone, destroyed in less than a day. Which meant…what? A single source had betrayed the whole network? One informant knew about the rest? That did not seem likely to him. The Dragon, the legend, had made a mistake along the line, and now Choate was stuck with him as a partner.

But he liked the plan; he would do the dangerous work with a computer and a keyboard; the Dragon could do the dirtier work of killing Gumalar and his terrorist liaison, once located.

Four hours after Agency hackers in a small lab in Gdansk, Poland, launched a 3 A.M. cyber attack on Gumalar's bank,

Randall Choate sat down at a bank computer wearing a suit, a tie, and a visitor's pass. His ID indicated he was with Tellar Data.

"You can clean up from the attack?" The bank's information technology manager stood behind him, arms crossed. The thin sheen of a sweat mustache shone on his lip. It had been a most stressful morning.

"Yes. Since you can't." Choate was supposed to be abrasive.

"I would like actionable insight, please," the manager said.

Choate began a long, technical run-on sentence about repairing the databases, with atomic-level detail about checking field integrity before repopulating the records, operating seamlessly with front-end enterprise transactions, and other murmurings of reassurance. All would be well and they could restore any damaged records from the backups. The IT manager asked pointed questions and Choate gave correct responses. When he was done (the manager had begun to fidget), Choate jerked his arms, so the cuffs of his shirt and his sleeves went up, a maestro ready to work.

The IT manager left him to his labors.

Choate started the search, loading a program that would not leave a trace of its passing, hiding behind a series of protocols to check the database integrity. In addition to searching for corrupted records, the program hunted for the five aliases Gumalar used to funnel money to the suspected Blood of Fire terror cell.

He found four of them; the fifth returned a null result. He funneled the aliases' financial transactions and addresses to a log file. The IT manager came in halfway through the operation and watched the screen as millions of transactions in the database were inspected.

"Hacker scumbags," Choate said conversationally.

The IT manager agreed and inspected a network problem on another terminal, talking softly into a phone. The program finished its run, and as Choate removed a program CD from the system, he surreptitiously slid a blank CD into the drive, burned the file of suspect transactions to the CD. When the IT manager went to take a phone call, he slid the CD into a pocket in the back of his suit jacket.

Done. Gumalar's financial trail that could expose the Blood of Fire cell in Jakarta was now within reach.

The IT manager brought him tea, and it would have been noticeably rude not to accept. He sipped the hot beverage and his cell phone rang. He expected it was the Dragon, calling to check if all was well. He was two minutes past his deadline.

"Daddy?"

"Sweet pea." He loved the sound of Tamara's voice. He didn't even know what time it was back in Virginia. Twelve- or thirteen-hour difference. It was ten in the morning now in Indonesia; she was up late.

"Are you coming home by next week? Because I'm going to cook you a birthday cake."

"It's your birthday, hon, not mine."

" 'S okay. I'm cooking two. Vanilla for me, chocolate for you."

"Perfect, Tam. I already got you your present."

"Really, what?"

"Gonna be a surprise." He'd bought her and her mother matching red silk jackets.

"Not a doll. Jenny's dad went to Europe and brought her back a doll, it's ugly."

"No dolls for my doll." He finished the tea, spoke softly. "I got to go, sweet pea, but I'll call you tomorrow when it's morning there, okay?"

"Okay, don't forget to get on the plane."

"Never in a million, baby doll. Can I talk to Mommy?"

"No, she's busy."

"Um. All right. I love you and I'll talk to you soon."

"Bye, Daddy." Tamara hung up. Well. Kimberly didn't want to talk to him. Probably because the rates were so high. Yeah, sure.

Tamara's voice made him ache, made him ready to go home. He did dirty work but she was his treasure of all that was good. Strange how a kid could make you conscious of the innate need to be a better person.

"I need to double-check this data before we do the data restore," he told the IT manager. "I'll go to our office, review this with my analysts, and I should have a report for you within a couple of hours."

"I am pleased," the manager said. He followed Choate into the elevator; two other men in suits stood there. His skin prickled, but they were thin and slight, dressed like midlevel managers hoping to make a solid impression. Choate reached for the ground floor button but it was already lit. He turned to make small talk with the IT manager. Strong hands grabbed his arms. He slammed his head backward, felt a nose break against his skull, heard a scream of pain. Hands jammed his head against the elevator wall, a needle slid into his neck.

The lit buttons of numbers whirled and danced, grew smeary as though he viewed them through rain. He was instantly drowsy and happy. The strong arms tightened their grip, hustled him toward a door.

He laughed and told them about Tamara's red jacket before the darkness shuttered his eyes.

Randall Choate still had both his hands.

They were bruised and beaten, his knuckles purpled. He had lost two teeth in the back of his mouth. Every rattling breath told him two ribs were broken. One earlobe was torn and he had not slept in two days—every time he began to drowse, Gumalar's thug threw icy water in his face.

He woke up in a room of plain cinder block, with a high window letting in a soft, cloudy gleam of light. He was tied to a wooden chair; his interrogators had a table and a lamp and a chair. The room had nothing else but the rubber hose, the pliers, the bucket, a trash can, and a leaky faucet; its slow drip played a maddening tune.

He had started to doze again; the ice water slapped his face. He opened his eyes to see Gumalar sitting across from him, eating a banana, frowning.

"Let us try again. I am an optimist." Gumalar chewed, gestured with the half-eaten banana. "I have a contact who tells me that you are CIA."

Choate's stomach was as empty as a waterless well, but the smell of the banana made bile rise in his throat. "No . . . please, mister . . . I work for a database consulting firm . . ."

"Your work for Tellar Data is a lie." Gumalar held up the CD that held the financial transactions of the aliases. "Why did you have this CD?"

"Please let me go." The words were out of his mouth before he realized it, and a curl of shame unfolded in his chest.

"Your name is Randall Choate. You live in Manassas, Virginia. You have a wife and a daughter." Gumalar lowered his voice. "My reach is long, Mr. Choate. If I want to reach out and touch your family"—he tossed the banana peel into the trash can—"I will. Now. You are CIA, sent here to spy on me."

"No, no, no." It was no struggle to put fear into his voice; they were threatening his family. The terror he'd felt for himself faded like the dusk, replaced by a darkness that thrummed in his chest. Kim and Tamara, no. How did they know so much about him?

"Tellar is a CIA front."

"No. No, sir. Please, whatever this misunderstanding is, you got to let me go. My company will pay you, is that the problem? They'll pay to get me back."

"I'm not going to give you back. You're going to tell me what sort of operation is being mounted against me."

"I don't know anything—"

"This Englishman they call the Dragon," Gumalar said. "Where do I find him?"

"I don't know—"

More water, more torture, more ripples of pain shuddering under his skin. Gumalar's thug clicked a pair of pliers in front of Choate's face and made a grand show of removing his sock and his shoe.

Choate stayed silent, gritted his teeth, told himself not to scream.

With a deft yank the thug wrenched out one of Choate's toenails. The thunderbolt of pain made Choate dry-heave and piss himself. He screamed and the thug hit him with the pliers, cracking his cheek. The thug kicked the chair over in a rage and beat him senseless.

Time passed, he did not know how long. The slant of light through the high window was different when he awoke. He was alone.

Suddenly from the next room, voices drifted through the wood: *Let us see if this Dragon breathes fire.*

Then Choate heard a scream. A man. *No, no, you got the wrong guy, man...* A voice with a soft rural English accent. The voice revved to a scream. *Bloodyhellbloody hellahhhhhh—no no no...*

They'd found the Dragon. Someone had betrayed them both.

Are you the one they call the Dragon?

I, oh, please don't...

And then a horror, the sound of a sharp object chunking into wood and a scream that would have unsettled the demons in hell. The scream lasted half of forever and then devolved into sobs and a moan. Slaps, mumbled questions about CIA operations in Indonesia. More screams. More.

The door clanged open, Choate opened his eyes. Men dragged what was left of the Dragon into the room. His wrists were bloodied stumps loosely wrapped in pillowcases, sodden red, his eyes wide with terror, his chin smeared with vomit.

"Who is this man?" Gumalar yelled, and for a moment Choate didn't know if he was yelling at him or the Dragon.

"I never saw him before in my life," Choate said, and the Dragon hung his head.

"We will kill him if you do not talk."

"You've already done half the job," Choate said, and he spat at Gumalar. A fist started hitting him in the head, and after the seventh blow and a brutal kick, the chair he was tied to toppled to the floor and he fell with it. The world went hazy and gray.

Time meant nothing. He jerked his head up at the roar of a gunshot. Men mumbling, arguing, one saying in Indonesian, *We can't learn anything from him now, you moron.* For a moment he thought he'd been shot; but he wasn't, he was alone.

He heard doors opening and closing. But his stayed shut. They would come for him now, kill him now. Voices grew louder, arguing in Indonesian. He heard the distinctive, soft grind of a body being dragged across concrete.

"Hey. We talk again in a few days. When you very thirsty, you very hungry, we talk some more." The thug's voice was thin through the heavy door.

Leaving him here. Leaving him here to die. To starve to death or die of dehydration in the middle of a huge, teeming city.

Footsteps walking away, a door shutting.

The Dragon must have given them what they wanted; if not, the torture would have started on him. Maybe they were going to negotiate for his release. No. He had seen Gumalar's face. He choked down the hope that he was going to get out of here. They had no reason to keep him alive.

Choate barely dared to move. The ropes binding him to the chair were as tight as they ever were...but the chair felt strange. The back of its frame moved as he struggled. Wood grated against wood. He closed his eyes and collected his thoughts. Slowly he began to move his bound hands. Thinking of nothing else, ignoring the agony in his foot, in his face.

Crack. The back of the chair, already damaged from one of his attacker's kicks, parted from the seat. He tried to pull loose from the ropes but they remained too tight. Still tied, now just to two broken chunks of furniture, his arms to the chair's back, his legs to its seat.

Nothing to do but wait for them to come back and kill him.

When he woke up, the room was still in darkness, the tall window that had provided gray light was black with night.

I will touch your family.

He tugged on the ropes. Tight. He scooted the damaged chair against the concrete wall and began to pound his back against the hardness. Again. Again. Again.

The chair's back splintered further. He pulled with his fingertips, wriggled his back, and eased out the damaged wood. The ropes loosened as more pieces of chair slipped free. Finally, after what felt like hours, he wrenched his left hand free from the coils. Then, slowly, his right hand. Pain throbbed up both arms as he tried to move them for the first time in two days. After a while he pulled his feet clear from the ropes.

He stood on unsteady feet. Stumbled until he reached a wall. Felt along for the door. Locked. He tried the light switch. It flickered on.

In the distance, he heard a door opening. They were coming back. Lied about staying away for days; they'd probably just left to dump the Dragon's body.

He glanced around the room. A table, a high window just to let in light. He pulled the table under the window. He picked up the chair the thug had sat in while interrogating him. He put it on the table and grabbed one of the chair legs. It was the only weapon he had. He stuck it down the back of his filthy shirt, and he jumped up and grabbed the window's ledge. He held tight and used his other hand

to unlock and raise the window. He fell back down to the
table, then climbed back on the chair and jumped up again.
He swung a leg up to force himself through the window and
dropped into an alleyway. The night sounds of Jakarta—
the purr of endless traffic, honking, the wind carrying the
wail of music—hummed in his ear.

He ran for the road.

"I don't understand," Choate said. The bedsheets were
scratchy, and despite his exhaustion he had little interest in
rest now.

"You're going home," the station chief, Raines, said. He
was a scarecrow of a man, as though the heat and humidity
of Indonesia had winnowed away much of him. He smoked
kreteks, clove cigarettes, and the sweet smell knotted Choate's
guts.

"But Gumalar..."

"Never mind Gumalar. Our investigation is shut down."

"But the Dragon...they killed him, they, they chopped
off his hands. Someone inside betrayed us."

"Yes. One of his informants."

"No. His informants didn't know about me. They
grabbed him *after* they grabbed me. The only people who
knew the Dragon and me were working together were
the CIA."

Raines frowned, as though personally insulted. "Listen,
then the Dragon talked after you came to town. He was a
black ops dirty job guy, he didn't exist even before he died.
He was a free wheel, he wasn't an actual agent."

"I'm telling you we have a leak inside the Agency. Gumalar knew about my family, they knew my name...I never
mentioned any personal details to the Dragon."

"Then we'll seal the leak. But you're blown. You're going home. Gumalar's family knows about the investigation. We're being asked to back out by Indonesian intelligence. They will handle it."

"Gumalar owns someone inside Indonesian intel." Choate put his face in his hands. "He's dumping money to terrorists. He kidnapped us because we got close and he wanted to scare the Agency off."

"What part of *go home* do you not understand? It's not your problem anymore. Your flight leaves tomorrow morning. Be grateful and happy you're alive, Randall."

The nurse brought his dinner and Randall Choate thought, *No, I'm not leaving tomorrow. I'm not leaving until the people who threatened my family are dead.* And he felt a debt to the Dragon, a need to see justice done. He nearly laughed. He had not wanted a partner; now he was going to avenge the only one he'd ever had.

24

———◦◉◦———

THE BULLET SHATTERED THE GLASS, tunneled through the door, and plunged bent and misshapen into Delia Moon's right eye.

Ben caught her as she fell, dead. A second shot splintered the lock, the bullet passing above his neck as he knelt, lowering her. He flinched.

A third bullet boomed and the lock shattered.

Delia's gun; he remembered she'd set it down on the kitchen counter.

Ben retreated to the kitchen. He grabbed the gun. Heard the front door kicked open.

The back door off the kitchen was a French door, studded with glass panes, painted a cheery yellow. The back door was visible from the front foyer, and for a few seconds when he rushed the door, he would be in the line of fire. But he hesitated, telling himself, *Stop overthinking, just do; stop overthinking, just do,* and over the rattle of his panicked breathing he heard a footstep on the tile.

He'd waited too long, let himself be cornered. Stupid. Now he couldn't reach the back door. Not for sure, not without shooting the gunman.

So shoot him.

I can't shoot another human being, he'd said, and meant it, but he also couldn't stand there and allow Delia to die unavenged and himself to be killed. Pilgrim's taunt—*You don't have what it takes*—ran hard in his ears. Ben put both hands on the gun. He didn't know what he was doing. But he would have to do it.

The house was suddenly as hushed as an empty church. The noise of his own breathing seemed loud as a drumbeat. He tried to swallow but couldn't.

Ben aimed the gun at the opening in the far corner of the kitchen, which faced out onto the foyer. Where would the shooter think he would stand or hide? He had no idea. He hunkered behind the kitchen island, watching around the corner. He could retreat entirely behind the island, but then he wouldn't see from which way the shooter would come.

A rush of movement past the corner and Ben fired the gun; he didn't anticipate the kick, and plaster flew from the corner where his bullet struck, well wide of the mark.

He pivoted farther around the kitchen island's corner, extending the gun again, and Jackie, the kid from the parking garage with the elfin dark Irish face, fired at Ben.

Ben felt a tug in his flesh through the jacket, then heat, and with horror he realized his arm was hit. *Shot.* He felt more shock than pain and he hesitated and tried to fire again and missed, the bullet plowing into the tile.

Jackie kicked Ben in his wounded arm. He gasped and Jackie shoved the barrel of his gun onto Ben's forehead.

"Drop it!"

Ben obeyed, letting go of Delia's gun. Ben closed his hand around his arm and blood pulsed between his skin and his cheap jacket.

"You're Forsberg."

Ben nodded.

Jackie yanked him to his feet. Dizziness washed over him. "Pilgrim. Where is he?"

"I don't...know. He...took off." *I'm shot,* he thought crazily.

"I don't believe you." He shoved Ben back with the gun, caught him off balance. "Tell me where Pilgrim is."

"No." Ben collapsed against the granite counter.

Jackie put the gun in his pocket and slipped out a large knife. Steel gleamed in the fluorescents and he seized Ben's hair with one hand, put the knife close to Ben's throat. He watched Ben's eyes widen as the blade drew near to skin. "You ever hear of a pound of flesh? I'll carve a pound off you. Then I'll carve off another. Whittle you to the bone."

Ben closed his eyes. If he convinced Jackie he was truly ignorant about where Pilgrim was, he was instantly useless. And therefore dead. "I won't tell you."

The tip of the knife twirled and Ben felt its edge pressing into his flesh. He opened his eyes.

Jackie gritted his teeth into a smile. The knife moved to Ben's chest, sliced through his shirt, poked at a nipple. Ben felt flesh part under the steel. Then the tip danced along his stomach, downward toward his groin. Stopped.

"You're holding your breath now. Wondering where I'm gonna stick it. Depends on you. Pilgrim killed my brother, you useless waste. You're gonna tell me where to find him."

"I...I..." In the quiet, they heard the rumble of a passing car from the shattered front door.

"Let's go where we can have a nice productive chat. You help me, you live. I want Pilgrim dead more than I want you dead." Jackie put the knife back against the side of

Ben's neck and hurried him toward the door, past Delia's crumpled body.

"I'm sorry," Ben said to her. He thought he was going to vomit from fear and pain. The knife felt sturdy and sharp enough to decapitate him.

"What are you sorry for?" Jackie said. "*I* killed her."

Blood splashed out of the meat of Ben's arm; sudden, bone-deep pain bloomed bright in his flesh. They hurried through the front door. Jackie shoved Ben across the yard. He staggered, kept his balance. He had to get away. But Jackie was as tall as he was, heavier with muscle, and several years younger. Ben was sure he could not straight-out beat him in a physical fight, especially with a wounded arm, and Jackie had the knife and a gun.

So rattle him. Get him off guard. He became aware of resolve settling into his skin. Odd—a day ago he would have been frozen in panic; now fear was a luxury. "My arm…"

"Shut up your whining."

"My arm…" Ben faltered again, falling into the turned earth of the unsodded lot next door to Delia's house. A For Sale sign stood in front of him, sporting a stylized logo of a rose. The real estate agent's name was Rosie. Cute.

"On your feet," Jackie said and Ben closed his fingers into the loose dirt. Jackie grabbed his hair again and yanked, baring Ben's throat.

Ben threw the dirt over his head, dusting Jackie's face and eyes. He pushed hard back into Jackie, catching the knife between them. Jackie yelled, his hands going to his eyes, staggering at the push.

The cloud of grit caught Ben's eyes, too, but Jackie got the worst of it. Ben yanked on the Rosie sign. It pulled free from the soil, and he swung it hard into the blur of Jackie's face. The flat of the sign connected with Jackie's jaw and cheek with a satisfying *thrum*. He swung again and knocked Jackie to the ground.

Ben already had one bullet wound; down from loss of blood, he couldn't risk losing to Jackie in a fight. So he dropped the sign and ran, clawing the dirt from his eyes.

Jackie spat in rage and frustration. He swung the knife hard where he thought Ben was, the razor-sharp edge hissing through the empty air. He pawed one-handed at the blinding grit, trying to clear his vision.

Ben stayed low, running for his car. He shoved his bloody hand into his pants, fingers finding his keys.

Jackie's hand closed around the weight of his pistol. He fired, aiming at the sound of retreating footsteps, and Ben heard the crack of the shot pressing just wide of his shoulder.

Ben reached his car, got in, hunkered low as he started the engine.

In the rearview he could see Jackie running toward him, wiping his eyes, vision clearing. Jackie paused to sheathe the knife under his pants leg and then, blinking, fired the gun at the purr of the engine's ignition. The bullet dinged the Explorer's bumper.

Ben floored the car in a peal of rubber. He veered away from the curb, and Jackie's next shot almost got lucky, starring the rearview mirror on the driver's side.

Ben pressed the accelerator hard against the floor. The Explorer—graceless, then finding its speed—roared down the street. A stop sign stood at the end of the street but Ben accelerated, took the turn hard, a police car honking at him as it slammed on its brakes. The development was all new, curving streets and cul-de-sacs and circles, and the wrong turn would leave him no place to go.

Wiping grime from his eye and steering with his elbow—his right arm hurt as though a lit match had been jammed under the skin—Ben saw, in the rearview, the police car closing in on him. Perhaps someone had heard the sounds of shots inside Delia's house. He weighed stopping, telling the officer everything, and started to slow down. The police car came close behind him.

But then, revving up behind the cop, came a black Mercedes, sleek as night.

He couldn't stop now; Jackie would kill both him and the officer. He gunned the engine and arced away from the curb as the Mercedes revved, accelerating with its much more powerful engine.

The Mercedes caught up with the police cruiser and Jackie poured gunfire. He still couldn't see well, and the spray mercifully hit tires instead of flesh. The police car screeched to a stop. The officer fumbled for a weapon, got out, and aimed at the Mercedes.

I'm not sure I can outrace him, Ben thought, and he slammed hard into a left turn. Jackie stayed close. Ben thought of all the car chases he'd ever seen in movies. Always on highways, or in urban cores, with lots of options to turn and nip and evade, the cars dancing with the cameras to delight the audience. But this terrain was gently rolling prairie shaped into newborn suburbia. He had no place to hide. There were new houses and half-built houses and empty lots. He was going to die on these newly minted streets.

The road curved, dead ending, and Ben took the turn hard enough that he felt the Explorer's wheels lift and crash back to ground.

He faced a cul-de-sac of new houses, one finished, the other four in various stages of completion, one bricked, two more framed, the other just foundation waiting for wooden bones. Ben floored the car into the circle and didn't stop.

The back window exploded, shot out. Glass peppered the back of his head, sharpened confetti, nipping at his neck and ears.

He couldn't win on pavement. The Mercedes was too fast. Ben peeled past one of the houses being framed— a driveway had already been poured, circling back into a side-entry garage that was nothing but concrete and lumber. He drove off the driveway to flat dirt, veered hard past the skeletal house, tore into the empty, matted ground around the unfinished shells.

The Mercedes closed on him.

Ben leaned into a hard turn, pluming up dust and dirt, praying the tires wouldn't puncture on a stray nail. A flat tire meant the end. He saw the Mercedes drop back, unable to handle the ridges of dirt at the same speed. Ben roared back onto the main road.

Beyond the edge of the road was flatland, cleared and fenced for future lots, rolling slightly downward to a dip that he guessed was a creek. But beyond that would be another road.

He could make the creek—maybe—but the Mercedes couldn't.

Ben powered onto the flatland. The Explorer jostled and bounced.

In the rearview the Mercedes rocketed onto the cleared land.

What would Pilgrim do? The thought nearly made him

laugh past the nausea of loss of blood and pain. Then he knew: *He would think more than one step ahead.*

The land began to slope down; there was no creek as he'd imagined but a fence of strung wire. He hit the fence at seventy miles an hour.

The Explorer tore through the wire, pulling posts from the earth, and one of them rammed against the passenger door like a fist. Wire scoured the paint off the hood. A post clobbered the front windshield into a web of shattered glass. The Explorer spun out, and he floored it again, trying to regain speed.

In the rearview the Mercedes glided through the gap in the fencing he'd made.

The land now rose in a gentle incline. Ahead of him he could see a large, heavily trafficked road, two lanes divided by a thick no-man's-land of construction.

On the road, traffic hummed at a fifty-mile-per-hour clip. He laid on the horn, tried to time the cut across the highway. He swerved a bit to the right, trying to give a minivan room to get ahead of him and open a small break in the traffic.

He nearly made it.

The Explorer exploded across the two westbound lanes, aiming for the no-man's-land, just ahead of a Lexus SUV. But Ben didn't see the pickup truck powering past the Lexus on the outside lane, and as he made it across, the pickup clipped the Explorer's back right bumper.

The Explorer spun; Ben fought for control to keep from spinning back out onto the highway, back into the path of traffic. He wrenched the wheel with both hands, his wounded arm lighting up in agony despite the adrenaline, and managed to right his track, barrel forward. His heart jammed in his mouth; he looked back, saw the pickup complete its own spin, traffic slowing, cars braking. The pickup driver was a fortyish guy and Ben could see his face, frightened but unhurt.

He glanced behind him again. Jackie's Mercedes had dodged the traffic—well, most of it, he spotted a bad dent on the passenger rear side—and the German sedan tried to regain its speed.

The Explorer rattled like it was shaking apart as he hurtled past the construction markers and barriers. The land here lay rougher and not planed smooth. The rearview showed him the Mercedes wasn't chasing him in a straight line; Jackie bulleted along the road's shoulder, then cut across at an angle. Drawing closer, cutting off Ben's options. Now Ben could only go to the right.

Half a mile shot by, then another mile. He wheeled past idle cranes and two men on a pickup truck bed, staring up from construction plans, at an interloper in their space. He saw a large mall to his right, on the other side of three lanes of traffic.

The construction zone was coming to an end, nothing but turned earth and huge concrete cylinders, machinery jammed into parking slots. Nowhere to run.

The mall was his last hope.

The Mercedes, moving like an express train now, surged toward him.

He veered out onto the road, narrowly missing an Escalade with a silver-haired lady driving—she shot him a diamond-studded finger. He straightened the car, could see the Mercedes swerving, looking for an opening, a few car lengths behind him. He punched the accelerator and the worn, beaten Explorer tried to respond, but the car began to grind and jerk, like a runner hobbling from injuries.

Now the entrance to the mall: a Nordstrom's, a twenty-screen movie theater, a massive bookstore chain, a Macy's, a Home Depot, a couple of other department stores—all the features of the comfortable marketplace of suburbia. Ben shoved his way onto the shoulder, honking a clear path to the right, seeing the Mercedes trying to cut over to nail him, two cars behind the Mercedes colliding and sliding into each other.

He saw Jackie's face, etched with fury, hatred, determination.

Ben wrenched a right into the mall's road system, and Jackie overshot the turn, standing on brakes, then powering the car into reverse on the shoulder. The Explorer limped up an incline and Ben zoomed through a stop sign, drove over a curb divider. He jetted up a parking row for the front entrance. Suddenly a front tire gave, the rim started to work toward the pavement, and he urged another thirty feet out of the crippled car.

He'd have to lose Jackie in the mall. He nosed into a vacant slot and got out of the car, scanning the lot for a sign of Jackie's Mercedes. He saw Jackie, four rows over. Driving toward the mall entrance. Hunting him.

Ben stayed low to the ground, wrapping the jacket around his bullet wound. Blood dotted his shirt, the top of his pants, but he thought he could hide most of the stains and damage by holding the jacket close to him. He spotted the Mercedes hovering near the entrance, then turning, three rows over. Jackie would spot the shot-out windows of the Explorer within seconds.

Ben ran, bent close to the ground, ignoring the curious stares of shoppers. He reached the end of the row and then bolted across the open pavement toward the entrance.

Down the row he saw the battered Mercedes cruise to a stop and Jackie abandon the car in the middle of the right-of-way.

Ben stumbled inside the mall. The new mall was high-end. Ornately tiled floors, leather chairs and couches artfully arranged so people could relax and sip lattes and wait for shopping relatives in comfort. Friday afternoon had brought a good-sized crowd, mostly teenagers and young mothers.

Ben walked fast, trying not to draw attention to himself. He risked a look back to see if he was leaving a trail of blood. He wasn't, but he saw Jackie, following with purpose, not running.

And Jackie smiled. The cat closing in on the mouse. Hand in his jacket pocket. That would be where the gun was. Jackie's gaze locked on Ben's.

Ben reached an intersection in the promenade, a left and right that each led to an anchor store. Across from him was a home electronics store and suddenly a dozen images of his own face looked back at him from the displayed TVs, tuned to CNN.

He stumbled away, wedged his hand into his hair as though lost in thought, shaded his face with his palm. Think. He realized that he needed a big store, a place with short sight lines where he could lose Jackie. He hurried through the thickening crowds—a pair of jugglers performed in one of the intersections, and people stopped to watch—and veered toward one of the less expensive department stores. He had a sudden hope that the store would be more crowded, both with shoppers and merchandise, than the pricier options. More places to hide.

"Mister, you're bleeding," an older woman said to Ben.

She carried Pottery Barn and Macy's bags, and she gestured at his bloodied shirt. Then at his face. Her mouth pursed. He gave her a half smile and a nod. He hurried past her.

"Mister? Hey, wait," the woman called.

She might be grabbing a security guard. Ben risked a backward look. Jackie kept pace, not closing in on him in front of witnesses but keeping a constant distance. He couldn't see where the woman had gone.

Ben went into the department store, past a young woman handing out perfume samples, past silver-draped tables covered with brightly boxed gifts, past red-inked banners announcing 15 percent discounts. He dodged mothers pushing strollers, couples walking hand in hand, a trio of women hunting for the bridal department.

Mistake. Too many people, and if Jackie started shooting...Ben got on the escalator. He hurried past the standing riders. He turned, saw Jackie in unhurried pursuit, and he had a horrible sense that the boy would simply pull his gun, fire a head shot at Ben, and take his chances with escaping from the crowd. Second mistake, Ben thought. If he made another error an innocent bystander might get killed, and the thought burned his chest.

Jackie boarded the escalator behind him.

Ben stepped off and around, taking the next escalator to the third floor, where he booked a hard left through housewares and furniture.

Here the merchandise stood closer together, with false walls creating bedrooms, living rooms, and dens, fewer open lines for Jackie to catch sight of him. A labyrinth of staged décor. Fewer customers; he thought more furniture might move at night or on weekends, families and couples browsing together. But not on a Friday afternoon.

One of the alcoves was a den, done in an Asian motif: a low-standing teak coffee table, a minimalist sofa with red silk pillows, Chinese characters sewn on them in black thread, a jade sculpture, a large vase with cranes and flowers painted on its surface. He grabbed the vase with both hands. His arm cramped in agony. The vase was heavy and reached from his waist to his head.

Ben ducked back against the alcove and waited.

Jackie ran past, intent on catching sight of Ben, and Ben rushed him in six steps, swinging the vase hard as Jackie turned and dipped his hand in his jacket pocket. The vase slammed into Jackie's face like a ceramic baseball bat, shattering.

Jackie reeled back, and Ben swung at him again with the remnant of the vase, the heavy bottom. He socked Jackie in the mouth and the young man went down, face bloodied, lip cut, in a half-conscious sprawl.

Ben leaned down, took Jackie's gun and keys from his jacket pocket, dropped them down the front of his own shirt. Where was the knife?

Jackie tried to focus on him through a bloodied mask. Ben leaned down and, with his good hand, hit Jackie as hard as he could in the jaw. Twice. Jackie tried to make a fist and Ben pounded Jackie's head three times against the floor.

Jackie stopped fighting, his eyes unfocused.

"Hey!" a woman started screaming. Ben looked up. The woman was a sales associate, manicured hand at mouth.

"He has a gun. I saw it in his pocket. Call the police," Ben said. "He followed me from a house on Nottingham Street. He hurt a woman there."

The woman retreated toward the sales desk's phone. She

pointed a finger at him as though it would freeze him in place. "Don't move."

Choose. Stay and explain to the cops that Jackie had killed Delia. But then he was in jail and maybe funneled back to another Kidwell. He stumbled to his feet and ran. He heard the woman yell, "Stop!" He didn't.

She'd have security on him in a minute. He headed for a door marked "Associates Only." It wasn't locked and he went through, hearing the woman yelling behind him. He rushed down a corridor leading off to an empty break room and a much larger back stock area.

And a freight elevator. He hit the button.

Get out to the parking lot. This was an anchor store, it would have a lot of exits. Find Jackie's car, take it.

He waited for the elevator to arrive; it cranked up sluggishly from the ground floor. It boomed as though it hadn't been serviced in years, a noisy throat-clearing rise up the elevator shaft.

He pressed himself against the wall. The elevator chimed its arrival, the cargo-wide doors slid open like a slowly drawn curtain. The elevator stood empty. He rushed inside and jabbed the first-floor button and the Close Door button.

He heard the door to the employee area open. Feet running, stumbling. "I'm...gonna cut you...to shreds."

No. The doors began to close, sliding on their own ancient schedule. Ben yanked out his shirttail, groped for the gun and the car keys.

Jackie raced toward the closing door, his forehead a blood smear, eyes raging, nose bent. The knife low, tight in his hand, ready to strike.

The doors started to close. Ben raised the gun and fired;

Jackie saw the gun, his expression of rage shifted into surprise; Jackie dodged to the left; Ben pivoted to follow Jackie's lunge and fired just before the doors slid shut; the elevator began its arthritic descent.

Did I hit him? Did I kill him?

Ben stood motionless in the elevator, the gun warm in his hand. *What's wrong with you, you could have stopped the doors, idiot, you had the gun,* he thought.

The elevator settled; the doors inched open. He hid the gun awkwardly under his shirttail, listening for pursuing footsteps. Only silence.

He turned and hurried out of the cargo bay exit, jumped down to the parking lot.

Ben ran now. Pain drove him like an engine. He reached the stretch of parking lot where he'd abandoned the Explorer. The black Mercedes still stood where Jackie had left it, an angry man standing by the sedan, blocked in.

Ben hurried to the driver's door.

"Seriously, learn to park," the man said.

"I will," Ben said.

The man gawked at him, the blood on him, the sweat. "Hey, do you need help?"

"I'm fine, thanks." Ben slid into the Mercedes.

"Wait a minute, wait..." A note of recognition in his voice. He pulled a cell phone from his pocket.

Of course it was a stick shift, since his arm wasn't working right. But he was alive. No complaints. He gunned the Mercedes into a lurching motion, found a rhythm. Every time he changed gear the dull agony pulsed.

Ben powered out of the lot. *You had a gun, he only had a knife. You could have hit the button, opened the doors, you could have shot him dead. You cannot run, you have to take the fight back to these people. They will never stop chasing you.*

Through the pain he thought of Delia, lying broken on the floor, gone in a second, like his Emily. He'd shot twice at Jackie and missed both times. Pilgrim was right; he was no good at this war. He prayed as he pulled back onto the main road through Frisco that the man in the parking lot didn't get the license number, wasn't calling the police, that sirens wouldn't rise in pursuit of him in the next minute.

A rage filled him, eclipsed the pain in his arm and along his body from Jackie's toying cuts. It was a hot and fierce anger he'd tamped down hard into his heart, kept at a simmer. Seeing Delia die gave it energy, fueled it like long-dry tinder exploding into flame.

You ran and you should have killed him. You should have killed him for what he did.

Jackie Lynch trembled. More from fury than pain. Ben's final shot had missed him, because he'd gotten out of the line of fire, stumbling against the wall.

And not had the guts to leap and jab the elevator button, reopen the doors, confront Ben. The thought of being shot with his own gun had slowed him, made him hesitate. Not caution, but cowardice. Stupid—he could have gutted the amateur with one sweep of the blade.

"You're worthless," he said to himself, mumbling through his broken nose and cut lips. The heat of shame warmed his bones like a fever. He had hesitated as Ben cut into the mall crowd, when he should have taken the shot then run. A terrible mistake, a sorry excuse for a Lynch.

He suddenly fought back tears. He was the son of one of the most feared men in the IRA. He remembered the dark basement in Belfast where men who were suspected of whispering into British ears were brought; he could still see the terror in their eyes as they were placed in the chair across from his father. He was brother to a man revered for his ability to kill and not be seen. But he was a sorry legacy of their blood, taken down by an amateur he'd badly underestimated. He didn't even have his car keys now. His face was a bloody fright; anyone who saw him would remember him. And if the police found him, started questioning him, found his ties to his brother and hence to his brother's clients in the Mideast—then all was ended. He would never see the outside of a prison again.

He reached the store's loading docks, hung back in the shadows for a moment. He kept the knife up his shirtsleeve, ready to drop into his hand. A young man wheeled an armoire into a delivery truck, came back out onto the dock, and then steered his dolly through another door. Now the back of the truck was empty, the driver conferring off to the side with a coworker holding a tablet PC, tapping at the screen and shaking his head at his companion, then laughing good-naturedly.

Jackie stepped into the back of the truck, squeezed through the narrow maze toward the cab, hid between a refrigerator and an armoire. He took off his shirt and pressed it against his cut and battered face. Would he have awful scars? Would his face be ugly now?

Thirty seconds later, the truck door slid shut, plunging him into darkness.

He heard footsteps on the loading dock, security men asking questions about two men running through the store, the truck driver saying he'd been standing here the whole time, he'd seen nothing.

Jackie waited, to see if the doors would open or if the truck would take him.

After another minute, the truck's engine roared to life, moved forward out of the bay.

Escape was escape. But this was humiliation, running, losing to a nobody like Ben Forsberg. As he bounced in the darkness, he imagined Ben's face gaping in terror, dying slow on his knife's point, screaming like the cowards in the Belfast basement. The bloodied smile seemed tattooed on Jackie's face.

25

BOB TAGGART'S DEN APPEARED to be a bizarre hybrid of a gun show and a used bookstore. Tall bookshelves covered one wall, jammed full with tattered paperbacks and battered hardcovers. Another wall featured a collection of antique firearms mixed in with newer guns. Bright yellow squares of Post-it notes lay beneath several of the mounted guns. Vochek could see notes penciled on the squares of color. The handwriting was as precise as the characters of a typewriter. Stacks of books towered from the floor, volumes on history and weaponry and guns.

"I'm working on a book on firearms," Bob Taggart said. "I'm on the ninth draft of my outline. I'm being very methodical in how I approach my work."

"I admire that," she said. She leaned closer, looked at the guns. A French pistol from 1878. A German revolver from 1915. A police special from Prohibition-era Chicago.

"If they could talk," he said. "Other than spitting bullets."

"We'd be out of our jobs."

He laughed, a rich, warm sound. Taggart was a short man, heavyset, with a silver burr of hair cut into a retro flattop. He had a warm and ingratiating smile. He had his hands behind his back and he rocked on the balls of his feet, beaming at his guns. Vochek gave his fingers a quick inspection as he pointed out the beauty of an antique firearm from Prussia: no wedding ring. She wondered if maybe Mom would like Taggart, wondered if he ever made his way to Houston.

"You truly have quite a collection," Vochek said.

"I'm mindful about my purchases. I research them. I'm careful and methodical."

She wondered if he was preemptively defending his work on the Emily Forsberg case before she asked a single question. He offered her iced tea, she accepted, and he got them their drinks. He settled into a recliner; she sat on the couch across from him.

"I'm not sure how I can help you," he said. "The lead investigators were in Maui. I only did questioning here of people in Dallas in support of the Hawaiian investigation. Everything on the murder was in the file. The case remains open."

"But cold."

"Yes."

"Well, you're the closest, so I'm talking to you first, but I'm sure we'll be talking with the investigators in Maui as well. I read the file. You were, indeed, very methodical and careful."

Taggart shrugged. "Not that I made much of a difference for Emily Forsberg."

She heard bitterness under his words. "I'd just like your impressions on the case. You can get so much more from talking to an investigating officer than simply reading the file."

"You get all my prejudices and theories." He smiled.

"I'll take those," she said.

"And this is because you want to find Ben Forsberg."

"Yes. We found a link between Forsberg and a known hired killer. I want to find out how strong the link is and how long ago it was forged."

"You mean, did he use a hired killer to get rid of his wife?"

"Yes."

Taggart frowned. "I suppose anything is possible."

"What did you think of Ben?"

"As a suspect or a person?"

"Both."

"I did not talk with him until he returned to Dallas. So, you understand, I did not see him in the immediate aftermath of his wife's death, which is when you can learn the most about a suspect's emotional reaction to the crime. He'd had a few days to compose himself, to deal with the shock of her death. He was... There's a phrase I used in my career. Devastated but dignified."

"He does have a reserve about him," she said.

"The more calculating murderers often do. But from what we found, he and Emily were very much in love, very happy. They'd met through their work, dated for two years, gotten engaged. Nothing to indicate trouble. No signs of abuse, or infidelity, no money worries. He carried no life insurance policy on her. They'd only been married a week." He shrugged. "Plus—killing her on their honeymoon? If he didn't want to marry her, he could have backed out a few days before. Usually people with doubts immediately after a wedding resign themselves to the marriage or start thinking annulment. But..."

"But."

"They didn't stay in a hotel. They rented a house in Lahaina. That was a bit unusual, and if he wanted her dead, then it was certainly easier to kill her in a house than in a crowded hotel. But she handled the arrangements; apparently renting the house was her idea—her mother confirmed that with me. Ben and Emily were together most of the time, obviously, it being a honeymoon. Their last morning there, he went to play golf with another honeymooning husband they'd met down on the beach—which gave him a good alibi—but he only played nine holes, not the eighteen he originally told Emily he would. If he planned the shooting and he didn't want to be there when she was shot, he should have played the whole course." He cleared his throat. "Of course, he could have taken a gun, gone up the hill, shot her dead. But he has no experience with firearms, and there was zero forensic evidence that he'd handled or fired a gun, or managed to acquire one while on Maui."

"The police thought it was random."

"Yes. Windows were shot out in two empty rental houses a half mile away, some empty car windows shot out near the airport. Bullets all matched. The shot into the Forsberg house was the final one. Ben had just left the golf course when the first shots were heard and reported—not enough time to get to the first scene. The timing weighed the inquest in his favor."

"So several random shots and Emily Forsberg was just unlucky."

Taggart shrugged. "An idiot kid drinking beer, probably, taking potshots. But the bullet nailed her square in the forehead."

"A precise kill." The kind of shot that a Nicky Lynch could make.

"Or an incredibly unlucky shot."

"And no trace found of gun or gunman."

"None."

"What about Ben's business? If he was involved in shady dealings, and she found out about it…"

Taggart shrugged. "Too much government contracting is shady—just my opinion—but we found no history of questionable business."

"She worked for Hector Global."

"Yes, she was a very senior accountant. Being groomed to be Sam Hector's chief financial officer." Taggart tented his fingers over his whiskey-barrel stomach. "Sam Hector delivered a eulogy at her service." He stopped, opened his mouth again as if to speak, closed his jaw as though reconsidering. He tapped his fingers on his chair's arm.

Vochek raised her eyebrows.

He spoke slowly. "Maybe Ben wasn't the shady dealer; maybe Sam Hector was."

"You suspected him?"

"Careful and methodical, remember." He risked a smile. "He was in Los Angeles and two contractors backed him up. But you know, he has his own plane. A Learjet Delta-5." He paused again, gave her an enigmatic look. "It has the range to fly to Hawaii."

"You think Hector could have flown to Maui, killed Emily, and come back? But there would be records of the flight."

"This is a man who moves hired soldiers and equipment all over the world, sometimes in secret. If he wanted to get to Maui without attracting attention, I believe he could." Taggart shrugged. "But he had no motive we could discern and he had an alibi."

"Back to a dead end."

"Tell me about this hired killer you mentioned."

She took a photo from her purse and slid it to him. Taggart dug bifocals from his pocket, studied Nicky Lynch's face.

"He looks like a barkeep."

"He was a trained sniper."

Taggart raised an eyebrow. He handed her back the photo of Nicky Lynch. "A sniper. I guess that explains it, then."

"You don't think Ben Forsberg hiring a killer is the tidy solution."

"I . . ." He stopped and glanced at his watch. "It's five o'clock somewhere. I would like a small glass of bourbon. Would you care for a drop?"

The sudden shift in his tone surprised her. His ruddy skin paled. She didn't want one, but she sensed accepting his offer might loosen his tongue as much as the bourbon. "Yes, please, just a finger's worth."

He stood and fetched them each a measure of bourbon, handed her one of the crystal glasses, and sat back down in the recliner. "We're miles off the record. You tell anyone I said this, and I'll deny it."

She allowed herself a tiny sip of bourbon. "Sure."

He took a long, savoring sip of his drink. "Have you met Sam Hector yet?"

She shook her head.

He stood up and splashed more bourbon in his glass. "This is the part I won't repeat. When I started digging at Sam Hector, I got leaned on hard. Avalanche hard. By my supervisor and by a suit from Washington. I was told Sam Hector was not a suspect, could not be a suspect, and did not merit further scrutiny. I asked why, because I do not like getting leaned on and I thought, he's got big government connections, he's just throwing his dic—pardon, his weight around. I mean, could you do something that looked more guilty?" He touched the fresh bourbon to his lips. "I got into police work for two reasons. My dad was a cop and I admired him more than anyone I ever knew. Second was, I have a basic problem with unfairness. I know that sounds naïve, but it's the way God made me."

She offered him an awkward smile. "I'm the same way." She thought of the dead Afghan kids, cut down in their pajamas. She understood Taggart and thought he understood her. He would have made a far better partner in work than Kidwell. "But we live in an inherently unfair world."

He shrugged. "I felt Sam Hector wasn't making my corner of the world more fair. So I dug a bit and found that the suit from Washington who warned me off was a senior CIA official."

She set down her glass. "Why would the CIA care about Sam Hector?"

"At first, I thought, well, maybe the CIA's a big client of Hector's, he seems to do work for every government agency. But the CIA protecting him is an inverse in the power relationship. If he's in trouble because of a crime he committed, and they've hired him, they're going to cut him loose."

"But instead they back him."

"So they warned me off, and I let myself be warned off. But I always wondered, why did the CIA not want me to dig at Hector? Why would the CIA be shielding him?"

She drove from Cedar Hill back into the heart of Dallas, headed north on Central Expressway, cut across Plano to the private air park, and let herself into the safe house. The pilot who'd flown her up from Austin had thoughtfully stocked the refrigerator with basics, and she made herself a salad and a sandwich. She hadn't realized until the bourbon inched into her stomach that she was starving.

The phone rang. "Vochek," she said.

"Delia Moon is dead," Pritchard said.

The words hit like a hammer to her chest. "What? How?"

"A man matching Ben Forsberg's description was seen driving at high speed from her neighborhood. A man in a Mercedes who was either chasing him or fleeing with him shot at a police officer who responded to a report of shots fired. A woman was checking out a house being built down the street and heard the shots and called the police."

"Ben...killed Delia?"

"We don't know yet. What is going on, Vochek?"

She didn't like the chiding tone in Pritchard's voice. "This software that Adam Reynolds was developing, about searching financial databases—what has the team found on it?"

"Why do you ask?"

It was not the response she expected. "Because Delia was dodgy about a project he was working on, said it was a prototype. She didn't want to describe it to me. She was worried we wouldn't return his property."

Silence for a moment. "He was working on a way to identify and track people using false identities via combining information from lots of different databases. At least that's what an encoded prototype on the system appears to be. But he didn't save any queries or results from the program—I'm not sure this program would even work. And we can't test it; we don't have access to all those different databases."

Vochek said, "False identity. One you invent, or one you steal." The competing charges on Ben's credit card made more sense to her now—especially if someone had stolen Ben's identity. "I want to know why you told me to stay away from Sam Hector."

"He's just a contractor. We're under the gun to produce results here, Joanna. He has nothing to do with—"

"He knows Ben Forsberg. He might be of help in finding him."

"He's not going to give shelter or help to a fugitive. It would be career suicide."

Vochek couldn't keep the anger out of her voice. "You're the second government agency to be shielding Hector during a criminal investigation. Why?"

"I am hardly shielding him; I am keeping you focused on what matters, Joanna."

"I want you to find out for me if Sam Hector is ex-CIA."

"You want."

"Please."

"Well, he's not. There's an extensive government file on him. He's ex-army. Not CIA."

"Never mind what his file says." She tempered her tone.

"Joanna. Leave it alone. Just find Randall Choate. That's all that matters. Don't get distracted."

"If Hector is ex-CIA, don't you think we should know that little fact?"

"Sleeping dogs," Pritchard said. "But I can tell you won't give this up, so fine. I'll see what I can find."

"Thank you, Margaret." Vochek hung up. She had a sinking feeling that she'd opened a box best left sealed. Sam Hector was a powerful and respected man, but too many of the threads seemed to loop back toward him.

Vochek clicked on the television, found a twenty-four-hour Texas news channel, waited for an account of Delia's murder to run.

Dead. Adam Reynolds, who had called Kidwell for help. Kidwell and the guards. Now Delia. The same awful sense of helplessness that she'd felt seeing the dead Afghan boys, cut down by a covert group, clenched her chest. No more, no more, no more.

She dug through the phone book and called Hector Global, argued her way up the chain to Sam Hector's assistant.

"I'm very sorry, Agent Vochek," the assistant said, "he's not in today, and I doubt he'll be in this weekend. We've had a real tragedy here—"

"I know. Tell him I was at the hotel when his men were killed. Ask Mr. Hector to call me at this number. I need to talk to him about Ben Forsberg." She thanked the assistant for his help.

She went back to her unfinished dinner, ate the rest of the food without tasting it.

Leave it alone. Just find Randall Choate.

She was suddenly afraid of what else she might find.

26

PILGRIM PULLED THE STOLEN VOLVO, now on its third set of license plates, into the parking lot of the apartment complex in east Dallas. In the backseat were two sacks of groceries. Food and sleep sounded like heaven.

He got out of the car. He had been careful in approaching the lot, trying to make sure he wasn't being followed, making sure no hunter lurked in a car. No one in the Cellar knew about the apartment, the same as no one knew about the storage unit he'd loaded with guns and cash. It was his escape hatch, his hideaway. He spent most of his time in the wonderful constant anonymity of New York City, but this dump was his secret base for any job that brought him to the Southwest or Mexico or beyond. He paid for the apartment once a year, sent cash for the utilities. The complex was seedy, and the landlord was only too happy to have a unit that he didn't need to worry about dunning for rent.

He had not been here in months. Another large apartment complex next door had been razed, a bigger shopping center rising in its wake, just the shell of the building—steel beams and concrete floors—in place so far.

Pilgrim headed up the stairs. Sitting in front of his door was Ben. He held a gun between his raised knees, loosely, not aimed at Pilgrim. On his wrist Pilgrim could see the remnant of the plastic cuff. He was pale, shivering in pain, and Pilgrim saw dried blood on his hand. He could probably take him in three steps, knock the gun from his hand. But he wanted to hear what Ben had to say.

"Hello," Pilgrim said. "I'm really surprised."

"I'll take that as an insult."

Pilgrim shifted the bags in his grip.

"I do what I put my mind to," Ben said.

"You didn't bring the police with you."

"Are you scared that I'm here?" A challenge rose in his voice.

"Scared. Of you." Pilgrim set down the grocery bags. "How did you find me, Ben?"

"I got shot in the arm. You patch me up and I'll tell you how I found you. And I'll tell you exactly how Adam found you."

"I'm suspicious you would trust me again."

"I don't trust you for a second. You screw me over, you screw yourself over." A hard edge touched Ben's gaze. "When Emily died, I was so frozen...it took me two minutes to call the police. Because her being dead couldn't be true. I refused to see what was right before my eyes."

"It's called shock."

"It's called how I live. I saw a woman—completely innocent—die today. I can't see that again, not after my wife. I can't keep running. I want to take the fight back to these people. Whatever it takes."

Pilgrim picked up the bags. "Come in and let's get you cleaned up."

Pilgrim disinfected and bandaged Ben's arm as Ben gritted his teeth. "An expert shot Jackie made, to wound you."

"Don't compliment him." Ben dry-swallowed four ibu-profen tablets. He sat still and then started to shake, the adrenaline easing out of him.

"So, Sherlock. How did you find me?"

"Bugs you, doesn't it?"

"I don't like security holes."

"Your storage unit-slash-army depot. I figured if you had a storage unit near a major airport hub, you might also have an apartment close by. In case you needed to hide before you got on a plane, or you wanted to vanish for a few days without having to travel. It made sense to be close to your resources, as you call them. You didn't want me to know about any resi-dence you had, since you were planning to dump me as soon as you were recovered enough from your injuries. So I went back to the storage facility office, and they remembered I'd been there this morning, moving out boxes with you. I was asking about renting a unit myself, prices and such, and the very nice clerk was looking up units on their system to see what was available. She got a phone call, and when she turned to take it, I snuck a peek at their computer screen and typed in your unit number. It gave this address."

"You're lucky they didn't recognize you from TV."

"I wore a cap and I talked in a thick fake Boston accent. I didn't even use the Sneeze and Hide."

Pilgrim went into the narrow, compact kitchen. "Tell me how Adam found the Cellar."

"No," Ben said. "First you tell me what you found at Barker's."

"Ben, in your case, ignorance truly is bliss."

"Wrong. Because if I know too much, you can't aban-don me again. Which means you'd have to kill me, and you won't."

"I killed seven people yesterday. I killed two more today. You'd make it an even number." But he gave a crooked smile.

Ben pulled the small black sketchbook from his pocket. He tossed it to Pilgrim, who caught it one-handed and tucked it close to his chest. He then slid the sketchbook into his pocket.

"Thanks." He turned back to the counter, started empty-ing the grocery sacks, heating the oven for frozen pizzas.

"You didn't realize you'd lost your sketches."

"I hope you like pepperoni." Pilgrim checked the oven setting he'd fiddled with twenty seconds earlier.

"You dropped it when we fought in the bathroom."

"I said thank you."

"Who's the kid in the drawings?" Ben asked.

Pilgrim slid two frozen pizzas into the oven.

"I know what it is to lose someone, Pilgrim. My wife was funny, and sharp-tongued, and brilliant, and loving, and hardworking. She drove me crazy, both good and bad. I've never been the same since she died. Not for a second."

"Don't give me that 'she completed you' garbage." Pil-grim slammed the oven door shut.

"Completed me? No. She would have laughed at sen-timentality. But she made me a better man, in every way. And when she died...I can't be better again. I don't even know how to start. No one can fix it; I have to figure it out on my own."

Pilgrim stood away from the oven; for a moment he thought of a little girl's voice on a tinny cell phone call in a Jakarta bank, urging him home for her birthday. "You said you knew how Adam found the Cellar."

"I said you first."

Pilgrim told him about the attack at Barker's house; that his own colleagues were now hunting him. He described Teach's kidnapper, using the vague terms that De La Pena had provided. That Teach was being held in a house but that he did not know where the house was. That Barker had last called a hotel in New Orleans. "I spent this afternoon trying to track De La Pena and Green back to where they came from. There wasn't a GPS in their rental car I could use to see where they'd come from. The rental car was in Green's name, paid for by Sparta—"

"Your front company."

"Yes. So it was paid for with Cellar funds. I made no headway. Does his description of the guy who's giving Teach orders sound familiar?"

"He sounds like any number of guys who might be in this line of work," Ben said slowly. The man did sound vaguely like Sam Hector—but fit older men would be a description for practically every suspect with a military background.

Pilgrim shrugged. "De La Pena was desperate not to betray the guy, which tells me he had major motive to behave, either through reward or threat. I'm not sure I can trust anything De La Pena told me. Tell me what you learned."

Ben told him how he escaped from the hotel, stole the Explorer, made it to Delia's house, and about his desperate flight through and from the mall in Frisco. Pilgrim listened, chin on steepled fingertips.

"You're lucky to be alive." Pilgrim got up, pulled the cooked pepperoni pizzas from the oven, put them on plates, and sliced them. "Considering you made about a dozen stupid mistakes."

"I missed a chance to kill him."

"You didn't give him an equal chance to kill you.

Sometimes the smartest move in a fight is to retreat." A look crossed his face, regret of the bone-deep sort, and he turned away from Ben. "You're alive to fight tomorrow, and it sounds like he came out of it far worse than you did."

"Now what?"

"There is no what. Ben, do yourself a favor. Turn yourself in to the police. I know you think I'm rotten, but leaving you in the hotel was a way to keep you safe."

"No." He stood and got their drinks, took his plate of pizza. His arm ached but the nausea had passed, and now his stomach rumbled and clenched, a raw pang of hunger. "Discussion over."

Pilgrim started wolfing his food down. "Fine. We stick together, then." It was such a simple assertion that Ben knew Pilgrim would not go back on his word this time.

"Barker called New Orleans," Ben said. "Delia Moon mentioned New Orleans, said Adam wouldn't go anywhere near New Orleans right now. And he told Kidwell when he called him that there was a major threat brewing. Those two statements have to be connected."

"There are lots of government contractors in New Orleans. Lots of fat deals."

"Yes," Ben said. "FEMA contractors, hundreds of them. Companies with contracts to rebuild and for relief efforts. For a while there were a large number of private security contractors to maintain order in the city right after the hurricane, but not so many now, and they are mostly tied to private businesses."

"We have three contractors connected to this case—Adam and Hector. And you. It's not coincidence. You said Delia calls Sam Hector. And a killer then shows up at her door."

"We still have no connection between Sam and Jackie. He was putting his business before our friendship today, but I can't believe he'd be involved in murder."

"You can't or you won't. Sam Hector is your blind spot, Ben."

"Let's consider this from another angle. This software Adam was building. To unearth and connect illicit activities across databases. He needed funding presumably to have time to write a massive amount of code or to hire out parts of the work. It's stuff the government would love to have."

"True."

"And let's say Adam was originally not working for the government, but was working for Bad Guys who want to find and destroy the Cellar. But if you want to kill a group of people—especially a group of skilled operatives like the Cellar—you don't let them wander freely. You kill them dead before they can kill you." He paused, let the words sink in. "So if said Bad Guys found Green and De La Pena, why not simply kill them? What's the purpose of finding the Cellar if you don't destroy it?"

Pilgrim said, "Exposure."

"Think corporate. Takeover. You force them to do your bidding."

Pilgrim stood, fists clenched. "I am so going to end these people."

"What do you know about this Office of Strategic Initiatives that Vochek and Kidwell work for?"

"Zero."

"Could Strategic Initiatives simply be trying to take over the Cellar?" Ben crossed his arms. "Remember, a few years back, when the Department of Defense didn't like

the intel it was getting from the CIA, they started forming their own intelligence agency. The Cellar would be a
premade CIA."

"And they're willing to kill their own people like Kidwell
and Hector's guards?"

"They're willing to hire the Lynch brothers."

"It's very dangerous to come after us."

"Maybe you have an enemy in a high place," Ben said.

Pilgrim stood. "Let's see what we can find in Jackie's
Mercedes."

The Mercedes sat parked a block away, in another apartment lot. The dented door and scraped sides gave it an air
of belonging in the neighborhood that otherwise it would
have lacked.

They drove the Mercedes back to Pilgrim's apartment,
parked it in a pool of light. Ben opened the glove compartment, began to search the papers stuffed into it. A map of
Texas, a map of Dallas, a registration receipt, and proof of
insurance. "Car owned by McKeen Property Company,"
Ben said.

"McKeen. That's the same company that owned Homeland's office in Austin."

They searched the rest of the car but found nothing else,
so they went back to the apartment. "We need to find who
owns McKeen," Ben said. "And if we don't or can't, then
we go to Sam Hector. He provided staff to Kidwell. And
he balked at giving me any information on this Office of
Strategic Initiatives."

"Ben, I understand he's your friend, but his name is
cropping up here way too much for me. I don't know anything about him—"

"He urged me to come see him. Said he'd get me a

good lawyer. The best money could buy. But he absolutely refused to tell me who was behind the Office of Strategic Initiatives."

"So do you trust him?"

"I don't know. I'm not sure. A real friend would have told me everything I needed to know. Maybe we never know people as well as we think we do."

Pilgrim finished his pizza, wiped his mouth with a paper napkin. "And here you are with me. Instead of your old friend."

"Because you need help. You can't stop these people alone. I'm just doing what's right and necessary. Same as you."

"It might be necessary, but it's not right."

"Are the people you killed bad or not?"

Pilgrim shook his head. "I'm not going to tell you campfire stories."

"Spare me the gory details."

Pilgrim sat at the table, drank from his water bottle. "I killed three terrorism financiers in Pakistan. One was a Pakistani government official. So no way our government could own that one. A couple of times I killed people selling secrets to the Chinese." He took another sip from the bottle. "I killed a British gun runner in Colombia who was trying to cut a deal between UK extremist groups and the Cali narcotics rings for financing, to kill British judges. The guy was supposed to be alone; his girlfriend was with him. I had to kill her, too. A single shot to the heart. She started to scream and never finished it." His mouth narrowed into a thin line.

"Did she know he was with the extremists?"

"I assume. Her brother was the head of the ring."

"Then she made her choice in her associates."

"But I *assume*. Maybe she was clean, just getting a nice vacation in South America. Maybe she didn't know her brother and her boyfriend were very bad guys."

"Odds are she did know. People have to bear responsibility for their choices and their actions, Pilgrim."

"Then I'm doomed." He looked at Ben. "Ben, you don't ever get used to it. Ever."

"But you're fighting the good fight."

"So you approve of what I do."

"I understand the need for it," Ben said.

"But do you understand the price?" Pilgrim was silent for several seconds. "Once, I made my biggest mistake. I tried to destroy a terror cell in Indonesia. Years ago. I failed miserably. I lost…everything."

For the first time Ben saw a tremble touch Pilgrim's hands.

"I guess you don't want to talk about it," Ben said.

Pilgrim didn't answer; Ben heard only the passing of traffic on the nearby road, the soft hiss of the tires on pavement.

"I don't need a friend, Ben. I just need your help to stop these people."

"All right."

"I'm thinking…we're missing the obvious. Adam is hunting terrorists and the sniper who takes him down has terrorist ties. What if the reason Adam died is because the terrorists found out about what he was doing? Maybe they were watching him and they saw me and they learned what Teach and I are. Maybe this mess is way more about Adam than you and me."

Ben was silent.

"Terrorists operating on American soil, with serious

resources, targeting the people who could expose them or bring them down. This fight could be much more important than getting Teach back, or saving the Cellar, or clearing your name," Pilgrim said. "Do you understand that?"

Ben nodded. "Maybe he really found terrorists here, and the Arabs in Austin were part of it..."

Pilgrim stood. "We have to find who's behind this McKeen company."

"Wait. You said you lost everything. Did you lose the kid in your drawings?"

Pilgrim shuffled feet on the grimy carpet. "Don't, Ben."

"Is she your daughter?"

"Please. Do I look like a family man?"

"Not now. Maybe before you were a guy like you."

"Leave it alone, Ben. You don't hear me asking you about your wife." He took a deep breath. "All right, business consultant, what do you need to find out about McKeen as a company?"

"A laptop and an Internet connection."

Pilgrim pulled a red matchbook from his pocket and tossed it on the table. Ben picked it up. Blarney's Steakhouse.

"Very popular with the imported gunman crowd," Pilgrim said. "And look there." He pointed at a line below the phone number: "FREE WI-FI 24/7."

"A crowded restaurant? Absolutely not. My face is all over television," Ben said.

"Not the face I'm going to give you."

Ben barely recognized himself. He wore a fake dental front to make his teeth seem bigger; and slightly tinted glasses from Pilgrim's cache of goodies that made his blue eyes appear brown. His blond hair went under a baseball cap.

Blarney's Steakhouse—the original of the regional chain—sat in the prime corner of a major thoroughfare in Frisco. Behind its giant shamrock sign was a glass building, where the shamrock was reproduced again, albeit smaller. The restaurant, when it had gone chain and started a slow expansion across the South, had needed an actual headquarters and had moved to the building behind it.

Blarney's had taken everything good about Ireland and made it cheap. Badly produced Irish folk tunes warbled from speakers, the singing muffled so that patrons wouldn't be distracted by the poetry of the lyrics. The entrees were given names such as Dubliner Chicken and Leprechaun Lamb Chops and Erin Go Blossom, a huge fried onion appetizer. Walls were covered with obscure faux Irish sporting memorabilia, framed pages from Joyce and Yeats, reproduction street signs from towns all around Ireland.

The large bar (made to resemble an American's ideal of the interior of an Irish castle) attached to the main restaurant was full of people watching basketball, the Dallas Mavericks rallying from behind, a win nearly in their grasp.

Ben took Pilgrim's laptop and sat at a corner booth. He felt incredibly nervous about being out in public again—but Pilgrim said, "Hide in plain sight, you'd be surprised how few people notice anything going on around them." Most of the bar's patrons seemed entirely focused on their own conversations or on the close game being waged on the hardwood. "Who's gonna look at you? They got *American Idol* to watch, and basketball brackets to bet on, and cell phones pressed to their ears."

Pilgrim ordered martinis made with expensive vodka and two hefty appetizers, to keep the waitress happy, so she wouldn't care about them staying a while.

Ben started digging. McKeen's website simply showed a banner apologizing for technical difficulties; the website was down. Odd. But perhaps McKeen might be suffering from media shyness after the Austin gun battle on its property. He jumped to a series of business intelligence sites where he maintained subscriptions. It was a risk to enter his password, in case people who knew his habits were hunting for him, but he had to take the chance.

McKeen was privately held, so there was scant financial data to be found other than analyst projections.

The martinis and the badly named Casey quesadillas and the Armagh artichoke dip arrived. Ben drank a hard sip of his martini. Pilgrim ate, watched the data spill across Ben's screen in silence.

Ben read and clicked through a long march of analyst reports, news releases, and forum discussions on McKeen. Not a lot. McKeen started off as a construction company, divested into retail and office properties about ten years ago, mostly in the South. They started doing specialized construction for the government, restoring facilities in Afghanistan after the fall of the Taliban.

"More contractors," Pilgrim said.

The expansion continued: McKeen landed a large reconstruction contract in Tikrit, but had to pull out due to the insurgency; bought out a few regional construction companies in Texas and New England; bought Blarney's Steakhouse.

"Wow. McKeen owns Blarney's," Ben said.

"I'm going to go scout out the corporate headquarters behind the restaurant," Pilgrim said.

"Don't do anything stupid."

"Just sit here and keep getting smart," Pilgrim said. He got up and left.

Ben read further: McKeen was bought by a private equity group, MLS Limited, two years ago June 15. Two months after Emily died.

How different would life be if she had not died? They might be planning to have a child. They might be sitting on the couch at home, watching this same basketball game. She would be full of the energy and love and life that had so defined her personality, and he wouldn't be wearing a disguise in a bar, trying to find out who was trying to kill him.

He started tapping again, buying and reading and mining through analyst reports, now hunting for information on MLS Limited. It was in turn owned by another three-initial firm, headquartered in Bermuda. That company, in turn, was a subsidiary of another practically invisible company, one Ben couldn't find a detail on. He'd hit a roadblock. Ben's head began to spin. Someone was hiding behind an entire, meaningless maze of names.

He wasn't going to be able to find the name behind McKeen, not with what was available on the Web. Frustration made him feel sick. He drank the martini, ate the olive. He ate half of the too-chewy quesadilla and nibbled at the clover-green artichoke dip.

He had another idea. There was a discussion board devoted to security contractors. He surfed to it, wanted to see if he could find anyone who had done contracts for the Office of Strategic Initiatives. He started paging through the "threads," the discussions of topics. There was one called "Missing Contractor." He clicked on it.

It was about him. A few executives at his smaller clients had ventured to his defense, but a number of others were gutting him. Ben Forsberg was no longer considered a kidnapping victim. According to news reports, he had been identified by the housekeeper and the manager of the motel near the LBJ Freeway, and he'd been identified by a sales associate at a department store. He scanned the words:

Two contractors died and this piece of trash ran—he better hope the cops find him before one of us does...
It had to be a crooked deal he was setting up...He probably screwed the dead guy on a contract and had him killed...

The venom and the conjecture went on. Each poster used a fake name on the board, so he could not know who was savaging his reputation, but the momentum was on their side. His few defenders were shouted down by the righteous. He had an account on the board and wanted to post, *You idiots don't have a clue as to what you're talking about.* It was a business that based much of its appeal on loyalty, but little loyalty was being shown to him. He went to the site's search bar and entered "Office of Strategic Initiatives."

No results. If someone had done a contract with Kidwell's group, it was not being broadcast or discussed.

The basketball game went into its final minutes and still Pilgrim did not return. He watched the Mavericks win, then the screen switched to a West Coast game. He drank Pilgrim's martini. His bullet wound began to throb, his head felt fuzzy. Bad idea. They were making scant progress, and getting drunk was not an option.

Pilgrim walked into the bar and Ben could see his face was ashen. He sat across from Ben, noticed the two empty martini glasses at Ben's elbow, gestured to the waitress for another round. He gritted his jaw in cold fury.

"What?" Ben said. "What's wrong?"

Pilgrim said nothing until the waitress brought two more martinis. He watched her leave, then drank one down and chewed the olives. "I broke into the offices."

"How?"

"Ben, it doesn't matter. I have my ways. I wanted to access the CEO's computer, see if there was any data relating to McKeen. But much more interesting was this picture hanging on the CEO's wall." Pilgrim pulled a newspaper clipping from his pocket. It looked like it had been cut from a picture frame, a newspaper article celebrating the original launch of Blarney's. The caption under the picture listed the people at the ribbon-cutting: the owner, a couple of his investors, the mayor of Frisco.

"Is this Sam Hector? Is this your wonderful friend?" Pilgrim tapped the man at the far side of the photo, smiling thinly, with his intense eyes. Pilgrim's finger trembled as he pointed at the man's face.

"Yeah, that's Sam. I didn't know he was an original investor in Blarney's."

"There's quite a lot you don't know about your friend. His name's not Sam Hector, at least to me."

"What?"

"That man destroyed my life ten years ago," Pilgrim said.

27

Indonesia, Ten Years Ago

THE HUNT FOR THE DRAGON's killers took Choate into the rain-slick streets, into trash-reeking alleys, smoke-clouded restaurants, a gritty airport hangar. Information flowed at the point of a gun or with the folding of bills into a grimy palm. The info he'd found in the bank was next to useless; those aliases and accounts vanished. But he found people who were family and friends of the Dragon's murdered informants; they gave him slim threads of hope and rumor to follow. He stayed out of sight; the CIA and the BIN knew he hadn't bothered to set foot on the plane back to Virginia. His colleagues were searching for him.

Three days of careful and constant tracking brought him to the end; he stood in a darkened upstairs hallway, gun in hand. Waiting to kill. Gumalar would be arriving at this house within a few minutes. Then the score would be settled, his family's safety assured.

The house was a grand mansion in Jakarta's wealthy Pondok Indah neighborhood. Outside, distant traffic hummed like a swarm of insects. The breeze smelled of the soft jasmine blossoms of melati. On the floor below him, Choate heard the terrorist leader complain to the drug lord: "Inconsiderate man, always running late."

Yes, Mr. Gumalar, please hurry up and get here, Choate thought. Tonight Gumalar was coming to deliver a laundered two million dollars to the Blood of Fire cell that wished to undermine the Indonesian government. The house belonged to a drug lord who had a vested interest in a weakened government and was providing a neutral, secure location for his two friends to conduct their business.

The men chatted like a pair of old widows, gossiping about television and mutual friends, as though their business was not the devastation of human lives.

Choate checked his watch. Gumalar was late; there had been a change of plans, one of Choate's new contacts told him in a whispered phone call, moving the meeting to here from the city of Bandung, a hundred miles away. Choate had raced back to Jakarta, driving like a madman, frantic he'd gotten bad information—but here the terrorist leader and the drug lord waited. Choate wondered if the men were simply being cautious in altering their plans, or if they suspected they were being hunted since his escape from his prison.

Because someone—perhaps even someone in the CIA—had betrayed him and the Dragon to Gumalar. Someone might have also told his prey that he hadn't left the country.

Choate glanced at his watch and prayed for Gumalar to keep the meeting. Tamara was having her birthday party in three days, and if he did the kill tonight and walked back into the Agency, he'd be back home in Virginia in plenty of time to help decorate the house, help Tamara bake her own cake. He knew if he got this impossible job done so that neither he nor the CIA could be blamed, he'd be forgiven for leaving the hospital and continuing the operation.

A downstairs door opened. He caught his breath. He heard a chorus of greetings, the drug lord speaking in Indonesian, saying "Hello" and "Well, all right, if you had to bring him," sounding a bit surprised. Men's voices, speaking quietly. An answering murmur from Gumalar. Then the drug lord said, "Yes, well, upstairs and to your right."

Someone was getting directions to the bathroom.

Perfect, Choate thought, if it was Gumalar's bodyguard— he could take the man out immediately, charge down the steps, kill the other guard, kill the drug lord. The drug lord was a heavyset man of sixty; Choate did not think he would be a problem. Gumalar was in his forties and had no fighting skills. The guards were the main threat, and if he could eliminate them separately the job would be smooth.

Maybe he could even catch an earlier flight back to the States.

He heard the soft tread of footsteps on the marbled stairs. Approaching him.

Choate aimed the gun with a leisurely, practiced stretch of his arm. A single shot to the throat. He was ten feet from the stairs, and as the man stepped up the flight Choate would wait for the guard to turn, his eyes adjusting to the darkness of the landing, lit only by the faint glow of lamps from downstairs, not seeing Choate.

He waited.

A child stepped onto the landing from the stairs.

Choate froze. The boy was maybe ten, thin, dressed in jeans and a T-shirt that celebrated a Japanese trading card game, and wore high-top red sneakers. He glanced over at the corner where Choate stood and he froze.

Choate held the gun and his finger lay ready on the trigger and the boy's throat was in his sight. The boy's gaze locked on Choate's face, as though looking at the gun was too horrible.

Decision. Kill the boy so he could kill everyone in the house.

Choate froze. Unable to fire. Unwilling to fire.

The boy screamed.

Choate ran into a bedroom and went through the open window. He hit the roof. He skidded down its sharp slant, grabbed at the roof's edge, seized it, slowed his fall, dropped off the overhang. He landed on the first-floor roof, jumped from it to a metal patio table by the mansion's pool.

He hit the ground, drawing both guns, and he saw an armed man—Gumalar's thug, the one who'd tortured him—rounding the corner, firing, and Choate blasted rounds. The man went down, his chest a bloody ruin.

Choate turned and, through the window, saw four men standing in a room: the drug lord. The terrorist leader. Gumalar.

And the Dragon.

Alive, wearing dark-rimmed glasses and a suit, his shaved head covered by a dark wig. He still had both his hands. One of them quickly raised a Glock, centered its aim on Choate.

Choate emptied his clip, the window shattering, the drug lord and the terrorist leader each taking a round in the throat, Gumalar collapsing, clutching torn guts. The Dragon dove behind the heavy desk, one of Choate's bullets announcing its accuracy with a spray of his blood against the wallpaper.

Choate ran. He scraped through the thick bamboo privacy thatch at the edge of the estate, plunged into the street. He dodged a BMW that was barreling down the road, ran north. The homes on the street were large and well lit; he had few places to hide. He had a motorcycle stashed a block away, in a darkened part of the driveway in an unoccupied house that was for sale.

He sprinted into the house's yard. Tried to kick the motorcycle into life. It wouldn't start.

He heard police sirens rising. He ran to the next house; an older but well-maintained Audi sat in the driveway. He broke the driver's window, opened the door, cracked open the console underside, hot-wired the car. He revved the car hard into the street just as three police cruisers tore into the road, closing in on him. He floored the car, took a hard right, putting a map of central Jakarta in his head. *I can lose them if I can get to Menteng, get to the Agency safe house.*

They chased him for a half mile, enough time for him to think, *Dragon was the traitor,* and then another police car barreled right in front of him and he swerved to miss it, crashing the car into a storefront. He hit the steering wheel hard and his last thought was *I'm going to miss my baby's party.*

When he woke up he was in the infirmary in an Indonesian jail. The CIA said they had never heard of him.

28

"YOU'RE TELLING ME MY BEST friend is your worst enemy." Ben turned the Mercedes into the parking lot of the apartment. Pilgrim leaned against the window of the passenger seat. He had just finished telling his story of Indonesia to Ben.

"I think he's your worst enemy, too, Ben."

"Sam Hector and the Dragon can't be the same man." Ben parked the car, turned off the engine. "Sam isn't British and he was never bald. He never worked for the CIA. He has an entire life history. I know it."

"Accents and hair can be changed. Did you know him ten years ago?"

Ben was silent. They went inside the apartment.

"Ever meet any of his college friends? People he worked with before he started his company?"

"No. He worked overseas for the army. He was a military liaison to allied armed forces." Ben muttered the words as if he were reading them aloud from a résumé he knew by heart. Sam, taking him on a fishing trip to Florida to celebrate a big contract. Sam, introducing him to Emily, then two years later, toasting him and Emily at their wedding. Sam, voice breaking, paying tribute to Emily at her funeral.

Sam, an assassin? No.

"Ah. That was his cover, then. Being a liaison officer allowed him to move around easily. Kill wherever he was needed." Pilgrim turned to him. "This is why I wasn't going to be offered a job with the rest of the Cellar. He knew I'd recognize him."

Ben turned off the engine.

"He wanted people to think that the Dragon was dead; that was his execution I was supposed to hear in the next room. He walked away from his cover in the CIA to set up his company. Maybe with the CIA's help. Maybe on his own."

Ben felt his stomach sink. His mouth went dry. "Sam's first big contract with Hector Global was in Indonesia. With the foreign ministry, consulting work to their security service. Because there had been an attempted assassination against a prominent government family..."

"He played both sides. As the Dragon, he set up the attack on Gumalar that the CIA wanted done. He must have even killed his own informants, put their hands in that bag—if he was vanishing as the Dragon, he didn't want any locals who could name him or ID him. The Indonesian intel guys in the park were there because he told them I would be there, doing a job on their own soil. Then he switched sides, told the Indonesians he could get the CIA to back off if they gave him a security contract. He launched his company with the blood of innocent people...He profits from ruining a perfect CIA operation. He makes it look like he's lost his cover and even his buddies at the CIA buy it; they stay in bed with him. Maybe he paid them off. He profits from protecting people who were funding terrorists." Pilgrim shook his head. "He destroyed my life..."

Ben reached for Pilgrim, touched his shoulder. Pilgrim flinched, pressed his fist against his mouth.

"I told them the Dragon was alive; they told me I'd killed him with that shot before I ran. They covered for him and sold me out." He sank to the floor, cupping his hands in his head. "I'm going to kill him."

"No wonder you preferred not to have a partner all these years," Ben said. "What was your family told?"

"I looked up the news accounts later...They were fed a story that I was smuggling drugs on the side. I'm sure they were told that I died in the jailbreak Teach staged."

"I'm sorry, Pilgrim." He thought of the drawings of the girl, her imagined transition from toddler to teen, Pilgrim's only connection to his daughter.

"So he gets you out of the way and uses my name." Ben was quiet. "That means—" He stopped.

"Finish the sentence, Ben. It means the Lynch brothers worked for him. It means the gunmen were in Hector's pocket, too, and he sent the gunmen into the Homeland office to kill us all. Including his own people. Just like back in Indonesia."

Ben's temples began a slow drumbeat pound. "You understand this goes against everything I've ever known about this man. He puts loyalty and country ahead of all. He kept me going when Emily died...he was there for me..."

"You understand he spent years living a double life. Fooling you, or anyone else, is going to be easy for him. He pulled the double frame on us. It's no coincidence Barker gave me your identity. Hector knows I'm a threat to his takeover of the Cellar. You're somehow a threat to him, too."

"No."

"Those dates you showed me. You said Emily died two years ago. Same time McKeen gets bought by a mystery company. She was an accountant. Maybe she found money being used she wasn't supposed to know about."

"Now you're reaching too far. Sam adored Emily." He thought of Emily, laughing on the phone with Sam, in the minutes before the bullet ended her life. No.

"Get it through your head. You don't truly know this guy. He's a trained killer, Ben, and the most manipulative man I've ever known. Jackie is driving a car registered to a company he once had dealings with. He's connected."

Ben was silent for a long minute, thinking of Sam's insistence on not meeting him in a public place, of the soft, bored click of the abacus while Ben had begged Sam for help. "Okay," he finally said.

"We're going to his house," Pilgrim said. "Force him to tell us where Teach is."

"No, we're not. That's suicide right now. His house will be a fortress. It's also exactly what he would expect," Ben said. "We're going to beat him by doing what he doesn't expect."

29

FIVE PAST MIDNIGHT, a quiet Saturday. Jackie sat and drank the shot of vodka neat. The alcohol stung the cuts in his lip, but he didn't care. He closed his eyes and let them water, then blinked.

He'd escaped from the delivery van, easing out at the first stop when the deliveryman busied himself loading an oven onto the dolly. Jackie had crawled out of the truck, unseen. He spotted a busy thoroughfare a block away, which saved the trucker's life—Jackie didn't need to kill him to get away, and disposing of a full furniture truck would have been a hassle. Jackie walked a quarter mile, until he reached a gas station and called Hector to come pick him up.

Hector wasn't happy that Ben was free and Jackie had lost a car. Jackie didn't care.

He peered out the window, bored, restless, ready to hurt someone. Hector had well over a dozen security personnel—as arrogant as the British Army had been, he thought, in the Belfast of his youth—wandering the property. The men made Jackie feel safer, but their presence was a pain; he and Teach had to be kept out of sight. Hector did not want to explain to his squad of respectable former policemen and ex-military why a woman was being held against her will. No one was allowed in the main house but Hector.

Jackie downed a second shot of vodka. He got up and went downstairs to the conference room. Teach and Hector sat at the table, scribbling on a chart drawn on a plain map of the United States and Europe. It showed names connected by colored lines, notes penciled in, and Hector had taped pictures to some of the names.

"That the whole Cellar, then?" Jackie asked. "All your little spies?"

They both looked up at him.

"I have ears," Jackie said.

"If only you were as good at the rest of your job," Hector said. To Teach, he pointed at six names. "These six, they'll do fine. Call them, tell them to get to New Orleans by this afternoon, come to your safe house there tonight"—he tapped an address written on a notepad—"and await further orders."

"You said you wanted to kill people in New Orleans," Jackie said.

"The Cellar's going to continue its good work, Jackie. I've found a cell of young Arabs in New Orleans who have all snuck into the country under false ID. They're terrorists planning to launch an attack here. You and me and our friends in the Cellar are going to kill them."

Jackie laughed. "I'm surprised by the altruism. I don't figure you do nothing without getting paid for it." He smirked at Teach, who had been mostly silent, speaking only to answer questions.

"Believe me that when I say killing this group of guys is the right thing for our country." He pushed the phone toward Teach. "Make the calls."

He listened while she did, following his orders to the letter. She hung up.

"Very good, Teach."

"If you know of a terrorist cell, why not simply call Homeland and tell them, let them take the risk of taking the cell down? You'd be a hero," Teach said.

"I don't need acclaim to be a good citizen." He stood. "Jackie, put Teach back in her room." He walked down to his office, closed the door. The day had not gone perfectly—nothing had since Nicky Lynch, damn him to a thousand hells, missed his shot—but the situation was salvageable. He was going to win.

He checked his messages. One from his assistant, saying an Agent Vochek with Homeland was very eager to speak with him. He deleted the message.

An array of photos stood on his walls: Hector shaking the hand of the president of the United States, posing with his contractors in the Green Zone, touring a mountain stronghold in Afghanistan. Now he would truly make his business grow again.

Hector's cell phone buzzed. "Yes?"

"Mr. Hector? This is Fred Espinoza." Fred was a Hector Global employee who handled the security account for Blarney's Steakhouse.

"I'm busy, Fred, this isn't a good time."

"I know, sir, what with our men dying in Austin... I'm real sorry about that, sir...but given what happened in Austin I figured you might want to know about any breaches at any client companies. We had a break-in at Blarney's corporate headquarters tonight."

"Details. Now."

"Sir, well, I'm not sure how he did it. At 9:30 this evening we had a guy deactivate the alarms. Caught him on the videotape system. He broke into a keypad and hooked a PDA into the system; it read the codes and gave him access." Espinoza stopped. "Not a typical burglar."

"No." He ran his fingers along the abacus's beads. "What did he do?"

"I have the video footage, sir, posted on our internal website."

Hector found the page with the video. *Randall Choate, now known as Pilgrim, the major annoyance that must die,* he thought. Pilgrim hurried through the darkened halls into the CEO's office. He flicked on a penlight, scouring the room. The scene was then picked up by a hidden camera in the CEO's office. Pilgrim tested the file cabinets, found them locked, stopped and stared at the wall. The video showed Pilgrim bending close, shining his pool of light on a framed photo. The ribbon-cutting of the first Blarney's—Hector remembered it, a happy day.

Pilgrim removed the picture from the frame, tucked it into his pocket. Then put the flashlight's glowing circle on his hand and raised his middle finger for a good five seconds. The rest of the video showed his exit from the building.

"Have you informed the client yet?" Hector asked.

"Yes, sir. It's bizarre—the intruder doesn't take anything of value."

"Given the one-fingered salute, it must be a prank."

"A rather elaborate prank, sir." Espinoza sounded doubtful.

"Well, like computer hackers wasting their intellect on defacing a company's website." He slid all the abacus beads to one side with a clatter. "We need not report this to the police."

"Sir?"

"This might be a gentleman hungry for attention, to hurt the Hector Global name. We've already had one facility attacked and now this intrusion. The last thing we need is the police getting ahold of this video, and a joker leaking it and putting it on YouTube. This guy's just trying to show that Hector Global's not doing its proper job, and he's gone to great lengths to prove it."

"Yes, sir," Espinoza said.

"We cannot handle more bad publicity regarding our security services. Cut a deal with Blarney, tell them we'll give them six months of free work. Just keep them calm and keep the police uninvolved."

"Yes, sir."

"And, Fred? Thanks for alerting me to the situation. You've done me a huge favor."

"Yes, sir. Good night."

He watched the video again. Choate, stealing an old picture of him.

He didn't know me as Sam Hector. Now, for sure, he does. He had not assumed that Choate knew of his rise to the pinnacle of contracting work; he'd thought Choate was dead. Only a few days ago he had learned that Choate was alive. *So...now he knows me by my real name.*

The next time I see that finger, I'll shoot it off, he thought. So Pilgrim was still in Dallas. Maybe he had cut Ben Forsberg loose, maybe they were working together. That last thought did not appeal; but he was smarter than both of them. There was little they could do to him, hiding like the rats they were, but they needed to be stopped. Put down.

The phone rang. It was the contractor he'd asked to

notify him of any charges on the James Woodward credit card. "A charge came through at a Blarney's Steakhouse. I called the restaurant. Four martinis, two appetizers. The server said there were two men in the party."

"Thank you." So they were together. Ben and Pilgrim, drinking and snacking and breaking into offices. Weren't they extra confident? He would end their arrogance.

He slid a fingertip along the abacus on his desk, moving beads from one side, whittling the top rod's value. Ben. Stupid—he slid the last bead to zero. He'd been an economic soldier of value, helping with the business deals, putting money into Hector's pocket, a workaholic easy to exploit because he had no life of his own to live since Emily died. He'd been useful until he wasn't. Just like every other person.

He hurried to the room where Teach slept, handcuffed to a bed. He kicked the side of the bed and she awoke with a jolt.

"Up," he said. "I want to know where they're hiding."

"Who?"

"Pilgrim."

"I gave you every Cellar account, every safe house we have . . . I gave you everything . . ."

"You kept Barker near an airport hub in Dallas, same with De La Pena in Chicago, with Green in Denver. It's your pattern, your method. Pilgrim would copy it here if he wanted a hidey-hole."

"Then it's his and not mine, and I don't know about it."

He put his face close to her. Her breath was sour; he hadn't permitted her the dignity of a toothbrush. "Dallas is close to his kid."

Teach didn't flinch. "He doesn't have a kid."

"Yes, he does. Tamara Choate. Her name's Tamara

Dawson now. Her new stepdad adopted her. No reason not to, what with her good old dad dead and all. She's fourteen. She lives in Tyler, eighty miles east of Dallas. That's why you give old Pilgrim all the jobs in this corner of the country. Lets him swing by and goggle his kid from a distance. I don't wonder if he might have a place nearby so spying on her is easier, gives him a pillow to lay his head after a job."

She shook her head. "He had no children."

He slapped her hard. "Tell me where he's hiding. Or I'm going to have Jackie pay Miss Tamara and her mommy a call." He leaned down to her. "Don't make the man's daughter pay."

Her lip bled. "I can't tell you what I don't know." She gave him a look he didn't like, the fear ebbing, pure hatred firing into her soft, pale eyes.

"Give me his address or I'll encourage Jackie to spend quality time with his daughter." He stroked her chin with his fingertip. "I like kids. Don't want to hurt them. But if you don't help me, I'll hurt her and she'll never, ever be the same. I won't kill her. I'll leave her alive. It will be the worse of the two fates."

She gave no answer, her bowed head hanging over her lap, as though lost in prayer.

"Are you holding out hope that Pilgrim's going to rescue you? Give it up."

She raised her head. "How many dead men you got?"

He went to the door, favoring her with a remorseful sigh. "Jackie, come in here for a minute, please."

Jackie stepped inside. His face was terrible: the bruising from his broken nose, the bandages crossing his face. Hector touched Jackie's jaw.

"If you're a fourteen-year-old girl, and you wake up in

the middle of the night to find that face above you—no offense, Jackie—you're going to piss yourself in sheer terror." He turned to Jackie. "Pilgrim's got a fourteen-year-old sweetie pie of a daughter. I'm going to give her to you. Tell Teach here what you'd do to her. Don't leave out any details."

Jackie glanced at him, reading the other man's need for calculated savagery, then smiled and sat on the edge of Teach's bed. "I don't normally contemplate hurting girls, but Pilgrim's daughter, wow, okay, I'd have to get inventive. I'd start with giving her a fierce poking. I'd let her feel a bit of good before she felt no more pleasure, ever again."

Teach didn't flinch.

Jackie pulled the knife from its leg sheath. "Let me tell you some of the ways my da got the Proddy bastards and the traitors in Belfast to talk when they were sure they wouldn't. See, they'd get brought down to his basement for a cup of tea and a nice long chat. If the chat went bad, Da would get out the knives."

Teach didn't move. Jackie thought if he leaned forward and kissed her he'd feel the fear in her lips.

"But see, it'd be worse for Pilgrim's girl. Back in Belfast, when the stupid men started talking, my da stopped cutting their faces and their privates. The knife's work was done. But I don't want her to talk. There's nothing she can tell me to save herself." He turned the knife and its glint caught the dim light above her bed. "I only want her to hurt."

Jackie began a recitation that chilled Teach's blood, painted horrors in her mind so that she flinched from his soft whisper. But still she shook her head.

So Jackie started to demonstrate.

KHALED'S REPORT— NEW ORLEANS

On Sunday, we start our work. If I have not ruined everything.

I am terrified because I fear I have jeopardized all my training, all my sacrifice. I was unprepared for random chance. Today I walked through the French Quarter on one of my exercises, trying to determine who is following me and how I can lose them in the crowds. I am sure that the crowds are smaller than normal, since Katrina, but the streets still throng here with happy Americans, hazed on their crimson hurricanes of liquor and fruit juice or their canned beers.

I entered my own haze today. Halfway through my exercise with my trainers, I saw someone I know, from home in Beirut. A girl, named Roula, a cousin of a good friend. I remember hearing that she was studying architecture at Rice University in Houston. One would hope she would be hard at her studies. But no, here she is, walking with a trio of blond American girls, looking very American herself in jeans and a sky-blue polo shirt and a set of bangle bracelets.

She is lovely, walking with these American beauties, tucking a lock of her dark hair behind her ear. I glance at her twice, once in shock and the second time to be sure it is her. I turn my head but she has sensed my stare and she turns.

She won't recognize me, I hope, and I duck my head and turn away abruptly to study a display of junky T-shirts for tourists in a store window.

"Khaled?" I hear her voice call, rising in surprise at the end.

No.

I turn and start to walk away and then she says it again, loudly, so I stop. Glance back at her. She smiles at me in recognition.

"Khaled, hello, how are you?"

"Fine," I say. "How are you, Roula, what are you doing here?" The words all feel woolly in my mouth.

"I'm visiting for the weekend with school friends." She gestures back at the American beauties, who look at me and through me, a skinny Arab boy with the awkwardness of an engineering student and therefore of minimal interest to them.

"Ah," I say. My watchers—I can see them now, they don't even try to hide from me—are watching me talk to this girl. I wonder what that will mean for her. I have an urge to run.

"What are you doing here?"

I am supposed to be in Switzerland, studying finance. "Ah, well, my adviser at my school—I'm at the University of Geneva—is giving a speech at Tulane, and I came with him." The explanation rings hollow to me, but I force a smile behind it and gesture at the window full of junky T-shirts. "You caught me in an unacademic moment."

Roula laughs. "Well, how long are you in town?"

"I leave Sunday."

"So do we." And then, of course, in the manner of my people, she begins to inquire about my mother, my cousins—she knows my brothers and my father are dead and she says nothing of them.

I answer quickly, ask after her own family, then take refuge in consulting my watch. "Well, this was a lovely surprise, Roula, but I must get back to the campus. I didn't give myself enough time to explore." I tender an awkward grin.

She gives me a bright smile. "Well, it was nice to see you, Khaled."

"Good to see you, too." I turn and walk away and I don't look back. My outing, my training run, is ruined. Two blocks farther I risk a glance. There were two trackers following me, and now there is only the one. The other tracker is, of course, now shadowing Roula.

I am brought back to the house, questioned thoroughly. I explain she is a friend from home, studying architecture in America. That she is harmless.

"But you are not supposed to be here," the masters say to me. "What if she mentions to her family, to her friends, that she saw you here?"

"I gave her a story consistent with my cover," I said, and they laugh, not because it is funny. I keep hoping they will tell me this is a test, that Roula is part of the organization. But they give no such reassurance.

"What should I have done?" I say, miserable.

"You don't talk to her. You walk away, you get away from her."

"But she knew it was me. To run would increase her suspicion—"

"But she would never be sure it was you. You spoke with her. She knows too much."

Coldness touches my heart. This is not how it is supposed to be. I have come here to learn how to do good work, how to kill those who must die, not innocents like Roula. "What will happen?" I finally say.

My masters exchange a glance. "Her family's phones in Beirut will be tapped; their e-mail and physical mail will be monitored. We will listen and see if she mentions seeing you here. If she does not...fine. If she does...well. Then we shall see. This is on your head, though—let it be a lesson you never forget." As though I was a prankster schoolboy, fresh from a whipping.

I am not sure I believe them. I am sick with fear for Roula. I return, at their orders, to my room. I lie on my bed and study the ceiling. I feel they are watching me; this is a test, and I am failing.

The door opens. I sit up. One of the masters, the one called Mr. Night, enters and closes the door behind me.

"Are you going to hurt her?" I ask in a rush.

"Of course not," he says. "You must think us rather impulsive. Or cruel."

"I'm a realist about our work."

Mr. Night nods at me. "But, if necessary, someone will speak to her. Impress upon her, forcefully, the need for silence. Your presence here must be kept secret."

I swallow. *Forcefully* can cover many options. But if he says she will not be harmed, I believe him. My life is in the hands of these people; I have to trust them. "I understand."

"If she is unable to keep her silence..." He shrugs.

"She will," I assure him. "She is a very sensible girl

from a good family. Perhaps someone in her family could be recruited as well."

"Perhaps." He clears his throat. "I need to know if you're truly ready for the job, Khaled." (It is painful for me to record his words, but in fairness I must.)

"I am. I am. Please." I have a sudden fear that I might now be expendable. But they need us…there are so few of us willing to do the work, to take the enormous risks. I had already risked so much in coming forward, in making it here.

He studies me for a long while, saying nothing, and I compose myself and don't plead my case further. I have to be strong now.

"You are still one of us. Here is your assignment."

I nearly collapse in relief, but I do not let emotion cross my face. I read the file they hand me, see what my first battle in the war will be.

I am more eager than ever to do my job. They release me from my room. I drive over to the shooting range and start putting bullets into the targets, each squeeze of the trigger a relief.

30

DAWN CREPT IN THROUGH THE HEAVY, yellowed curtains, as though reluctant to bring brightness to the darkened rooms. Ben awoke on the futon; he could feel the hump of the gun under his pillow, and he pulled his hand back from it with a jolt. His arm ached. He'd slept far heavier than he'd thought possible.

Pilgrim was awake and brewing coffee, standing over the sink, staring into space.

"Hey," Ben said.

No answer.

"You're not a morning person," Ben said.

"We should have gone after Hector last night. Sleep was the last thing…"

"Unclench the fist. Hector knows I am questioning his loyalty since I didn't call him back, and I'm betting he knows about your visit to the McKeen office now. Not hearing from us is keeping him off balance."

"I can't just abandon Teach."

"You abandon her if you get killed in a pointless attempt to save her." Ben stood up from the futon. "We take the fight back to him, but we act like subtle knives. Not cannons that roar and attract a lot of noise."

"This isn't how I roll," Pilgrim said, "You don't know what we're up against—"

"You wouldn't even know who your enemy is if it wasn't for me. So maybe you can permanently shelve the talking-down-to-me act, because it's gotten really old."

Pilgrim set his coffee cup down. "Fine. What do you suggest?"

"Hector's strength and his weakness are his business. It's what gives him power, but it's also what he's most fearful of losing. I helped him build it up; I can tear it down."

"You mean you can expose his dirty laundry."

"It's not as much dirty as it is questionable. What I can do is get in touch with every one of his contacts at the various agencies and imply that he's going to be under investigation very soon."

"You're a fugitive and lacking in the credibility department," Pilgrim said.

"I say I'm hiding from his security forces." Ben helped himself to coffee, black and strong. "We launch a two-pronged attack. Start smearing Hector with the people in government who matter. Politicians run from a stink. We put the stink on him. Second, we contact Agent Vochek. Delia Moon gave me her number. We cut a deal with her."

"Useless if they want us dead."

"I don't believe she wants you dead. Leashed, maybe. What will help us is that you did necessary work, ordered by the government."

"Correction. Necessary as decided by a small and secret group."

"And that group might be her target far more than you. Vochek might cut you a really good offer to come in. You know more dirty laundry about the government than I ever will about Hector."

"I still say we face Hector down."

"You've already hurt him badly, you've made him desperate. You wiped out Hector's teams, you killed his sniper. He'll have beefed up compound security just because he lost two men to supposed terrorists. He'll virtually have an army on his property. No way will you get to his house. We don't even know that's where he has Teach."

"Fine. I see your point." Pilgrim said this as though it caused physical pain. "So what do we say to Vochek?"

"Don't freak at my idea." Ben took a deep breath. "The Cellar's done. Adam Reynolds already found you; it's just a matter of time before Homeland finds the other Cellar agents. You just have to decide whether you surrender peacefully and cooperate, or not. Give them details about your jobs. Your results. They'll go easier on you."

"I joined the Cellar to avoid jail. I can't go back into a prison." He parted the curtain slightly, surveyed the lot. "You understand that Strategic Initiatives' cure for us might be a bullet in the head."

"I don't believe Vochek would be party to murder."

"You've been fooled by Sam Hector for years, so pardon me if I question your judgment of character."

"She wasn't comfortable with Kidwell leaning so hard on me. Says something about her as a person."

"She was playing the good-cop role."

"Fine. We play good cop by giving them something. We can't fight Hector, not on his own turf. We can't go to the police. Whatever is going down tomorrow in New Orleans, if it's bad, if we step forward now with the information, get it to Homeland, we can cut a deal."

"But we have no idea what's happening."

"Help Vochek put all the pieces together and then you're a good guy."

"She'll just arrest us."

"I know this is a different approach for you. But please, let's try it. We give Vochek ammunition. Everything you know about the Cellar. Everything we both know about Hector, both in his business and in his days in the CIA. There's a relationship there and if—"

Pilgrim shook his head. "Vochek's group hired Hector… Someone in that group could smother the information."

"Yes. It's a risk. But we're going to have to meet with her face-to-face, see if we can convince her. You did save her life."

"Not on purpose."

"Take the credit, we need it."

"Ben. This course of action sounds sane to you. It sounds crazy to me. I just want to get a gun and kill Hector. Problem solved."

"Doing it my way makes it a lot more likely that we survive." Ben stepped forward, leaned on the cracked Formica bar that divided that kitchen from the tiny dining space. "Jackie Lynch was in league with the people that killed Kidwell. Homeland's going to want Jackie's head on a plate, and he's driving a car that ties him to Hector. They therefore will want Hector's head on a plate. If there's an alliance between them, we destroy it. Isolate him."

"You should call Vochek."

"No." Ben shook his head. "You will."

"I have poor phone manners."

"You're the one with the information she wants. But you're going to meet her by yourself. Because she may set a trap and she can't catch us both. One of us has to stay free if the meeting goes bad."

Pilgrim nodded. "She's not catching me, don't worry." He rubbed his forehead. "I'll call her." He shook his head at Ben. "No offense, but I really am not getting used to having a partner."

"Hopefully it's not for much longer," Ben said.

31

VOCHEK GLANCED AT THE CLOCK—just past nine on Saturday morning—and studied the photos of the dead men. The investigators on Kidwell's murder, operating out of the Homeland Security office in Houston, sent her the latest on the dead Arab gunmen.

The men had been identified; they were all from the southern suburbs of Beirut. Two of the men were brothers, two more were their cousins, and all were tied to a gang that ran drugs into Beirut and did muscle work when hired.

She remembered a truism she'd read about the Middle East in a book by former CIA agent Robert Baer: you don't recruit individuals; you recruit families, tribes, clans. Here was a perfect example. But the one with dyed blond hair, the other with two piercings in his ear—these men did not strike her as typical fundamentalists.

She called one of the Homeland investigators in Houston, let him complain about working with the FBI for three minutes, then she said: "But these guys don't seem like religious extremist types."

"Oh, I don't think the Murads are prayerful boys. They've always been hired help." She heard a shuffle of paper on the investigator's desk. "The Murads all flew in via Paris then Miami, staggered over five days. Tickets paid for in cash in Beirut. But they all stayed together at a hotel in Miami before they flew into Austin, the morning of the attack." He coughed a smoker's hack. "Here's the sticky part. Back in the 1980s, Papa Murad, the head of the clan, was eyes and ears for the CIA."

"Interesting."

"Yeah. When we were hunting the embassy bombers, he was an informant. Not a great one, but he was willing to point a few fingers for a price. He dropped off the Agency payroll about a decade ago. One of his sons got tangled up with a Blood of Fire cell in Lebanon, did some for-hire bombing work for them, got murdered a few months back."

"So the Murads have played both sides."

"Yes, but you wouldn't know it to hear the CIA. They say they don't have a file on the Murads, which beggars belief; they've been part of the Beirut underworld for two generations. My sources are two retired CIA field officers. And Mrs. Murad."

"You talked with her."

"She's not speaking publicly, of course. And she could be trying to defend her family's honor, say they're not terrorists. But frankly, it's more dangerous for her to link her family to the CIA than to Hezbollah. She said her husband mentioned he'd gotten a call from an old friend, big money for a favor."

"Who's the old friend?"

"She says he was an Englishman her husband knew years ago called the Dragon. Of course the CIA denies that they know, or have known, anyone by that code name. In fact, the CIA is no longer talking to me."

The Dragon. She said, "Of course they're putting distance and denying they know anything. Former hirelings of theirs attacking a Homeland office on American soil? It's a PR nightmare. They won't touch it."

Former CIA informants, and now a mysterious Englishman from the Murads' CIA days. "Why does someone hire a gang from Lebanon? You could just as easily find gunmen closer to home."

"Quit asking hard-to-answer questions."

She tapped her finger on the table. "They attacked an office that wasn't even open yet. Very low payback for the effort put forth. Let's say they get caught or killed. Arab gunmen attacking a Homeland office, it creates a different image in the media. That sounds like a terrorism attack. But this wasn't."

"Probably not." She heard the investigator shuffling another file.

"So what were they after? They could have taken Kidwell if they wanted a Homeland officer. And if they wanted Ben Forsberg…why? What does he know, why is he valuable to them?"

"I don't know. I'll keep digging."

"Maybe the only *want* was wanting everyone dead."

It still didn't tell her why. She thanked him and hung up. She wanted to sleep—she had gotten precious little of it last night—but she couldn't shut her mind down.

She called Margaret Pritchard. "Did you find out about Sam Hector, if he was CIA?" she asked.

"I've got feelers out. Don't get your hopes up for a speedy answer." She sounded uninterested.

"Feelers?" Impatience churned in her chest. "Pardon me, Margaret, but can't you just call the CIA director and ask?"

"Please. If he was CIA deep cover, they aren't going to tell me."

"They will if you tell them he's a suspect in a Homeland agent's death."

"Sam Hector is hardly a suspect."

She told Pritchard about the Murad/CIA connection, what Mrs. Murad had said about a man called the Dragon.

"I don't care about an idiot called the Dragon. He sounds like an extra from a Bruce Lee film. I care about Randall Choate."

"Choate and this Dragon are both ex-CIA. Hector is allegedly ex-CIA. We need to see if they're connected."

"You would make me proud if you would follow a straight line, Joanna."

It sounded like a compliment she'd wish her mother would make instead of complaining. "You hired Hector to give us logistical and security support in hunting down the off-the-book operations. But could he have his own agenda in finding these groups? He could be using us to piggyback for his own purposes."

Pritchard made a dismissive huff. "He could hardly plan for me hiring him."

"Maybe he didn't plan, until you hired him."

Tick. Tick. Tick. The clock on the wall measured the wrath of Pritchard building. *Maybe she knows she made a mistake in hiring Hector and she doesn't want to admit it. It could be fatal for her career,* Vochek thought.

Pritchard said, "He would hardly risk a lucrative business screwing up a government operation."

"A businessman will do anything if he thinks the risk is worth the payoff. Who told you we had to go after the off-the-books groups?"

"That's classified, but my directions came from a very senior person."

"And Hector has millions in contracts with the government. He knows every senior person."

"You're making a presumptive jump."

"Then test my theory. Find out about Hector. What are you afraid of?"

"Remember we work in a hierarchy, Agent Vochek," Pritchard said coldly. "But if it will be of help to you, I'll tug a bit harder on my fishing lines." Pritchard hung up.

You're stalling, Vochek thought. She could hear it in Pritchard's tone. So either Pritchard knew more about Hector than she admitted, and didn't want Vochek to know; or—far more frightening—Pritchard didn't know about Hector's background, and she had been played by him, and was refusing to see that she'd been played.

The phone rang. Ah, Hector hopefully. She answered her cell, frowning at the number-blocked readout on the screen.

"This is Vochek."

"I hope you didn't have a headache."

Shock raced through her like steam through a pipe. She knew the voice instantly. The man at the hotel who had knocked her out, locked her in the closet.

"Yes. Hello."

"I hope the headache's past."

"Nearly. I'd like to talk to you, Randall." Her own voice sounded thin to her in the stillness of the room.

"Randall Choate is still dead. At least until you and I come to an agreement."

"What are your terms?"

"Sam Hector goes down."

Silence for ten long seconds. "Excuse me?"

"Hector hired the gunmen that killed your partner. One of his people killed Delia Moon and tried to kill Ben yesterday. We stole the guy's car from him, and it's registered to a shadow company that's connected to Hector."

"I need details."

"You'll get them. When we meet. You come alone. Anyone else is there, I run, I don't look back. Homeland gets nothing and you're still hooked at the hip to a killer like Sam Hector."

"I'm not sure I feel comfortable coming alone. You hit me in the head."

"You tried to break my neck with a baton. Let's forgive and forget." She could almost hear the smile in his voice. "If I wanted you dead, you'd've been dead in Austin. I'm still waiting for the thank-you for saving your life by sticking you in that closet."

She swallowed. "Thank you, Randall."

"Soccer fields off Plano Parkway. Noon. Come alone. If I get a sense that you've brought company, I'm smoke."

"Ben Forsberg. Is he all right?"

"Ben is okay." Then she heard regret tinge Pilgrim's words. "So you know—Ben is entirely innocent. He did not hire Nicky Lynch. I used his identity without his knowledge. But Hector's tried to kill Ben multiple times in the past two days, so Ben's shy right now. One more thing for you."

"Yes?"

"I don't have details, but if you've got any hot leads about a threat in New Orleans, take it seriously. That's my Boy Scout moment."

"New Orleans."

"Yes."

"Okay. Randall?"

"Yes?"

"I want to help you come in. I don't want you or Ben hurt."

"Words are cheap. See you at noon." He hung up.

Well. Pilgrim's offer could be genuine or it could be a trap. Protocol demanded that she inform her superior.

She hesitated. She was not by nature a rule bender. But . . . she knew Pritchard. Pritchard would demand backup for Vochek and the immediate capture of Pilgrim. They would have an actual rogue CIA agent—tied to an actual dirty dog group—in their custody. Of course she might talk him into surrendering, but capture would guarantee he would be in their grasp.

And New Orleans—what did that mean? She had no idea if a threat had been identified against the city. It was a lead she couldn't keep to herself, it would be grossly irresponsible. Decision made. She called Pritchard and explained the conversation.

"I'll contact the New Orleans office, see if they have a hot situation working," Pritchard said. "Of course it will be a bit difficult to attribute this warning to a man who's been presumed dead for a decade. Are you willing to meet with him alone?"

"Yes."

"I'm not willing to risk it. If he won't surrender to you, then I want him followed."

"He'll spot a tail."

"Not our people. I'm calling Secret Service in Dallas."

"Not their jurisdiction."

"Ah. But he said he stole Ben Forsberg's good name.

Identity theft and financial fraud are under Secret Service's purview."

"Please. Let me handle this. Alone."

"We already lost Kidwell. We have no idea of what this man is capable of."

"And the things he said about Sam Hector?"

The long silence returned. "I want to see the evidence that he has."

"Should we put working with Hector on hold?"

"On this man's word? Please." On the phone, Vochek could hear the tap of Pritchard's nail against the desk. "Evidence, Joanna. Let's find the meat on the bone first."

32

———◈———

TEACH BROKE AT TEN THIRTY Saturday morning. She gave them the name of the street and the apartment number—she had known about them for years, shortly after Pilgrim got the property under a false name, and let him think she knew nothing.

Jackie cleaned off the knife—not too much blood, the cuts had been shallow and strategic—and patted her on the cheek. "Lovely help you've given us. You've saved that girl a bad few hours. Now she can die an old lady."

Hector gave her a cloth to sponge her face, her mouth, her legs. She trembled and he wondered if it was more from rage than fear.

"Let's go. She's coming with us," Hector said.

"Us?" Jackie asked.

"You and me. We're taking Pilgrim out."

"I can handle it. Without help." Jackie felt reinvigorated from the night; he'd gotten Teach to talk, a necessary job done right. His father would have been proud of him.

"I need to get back into the field."

"I thought you just supervised."

"Every manager should get his hands dirty now and then," Hector said.

"Why bring Teach with us? Lock her up here."

"I have a lot of guards here, and I don't want to leave her behind. Where she might be discovered by my people." A pause.

"Sure," Jackie said with a nod and a half smile.

"I'll pull the car up close to the house. Get her ready. I just need to get one thing before we go. In case Ben is there."

Ben tapped the keys on Pilgrim's laptop. He wrote a detailed report of every contract he'd helped Sam Hector win. As far as he knew, nothing in the deals was illegal—but certainly, elements of the contracts might raise watchdog eyebrows, in terms of timing, lack of competition, or inexact wording that might favor Hector more than other vendors. Most businesses in the real world hoped to make a profit; Hector Global worked a guaranteed profit, sometimes up to 15 percent, into every deal with the government. Charges that cost the company eighteen dollars were billed to the government at eighty. A number of contracts had been virtually no-bid; Hector's only invited competitors were firms that were too small actually to do the work, rendering the competition moot. There had been delays in services rendered, with no delay in payment.

Ben put his face in his hands and took a long breath. He'd helped create this monster. And now—with contracts imperiled, with funding drying up—what would the monster do to survive? His work and smart counsel had helped Sam Hector win deals, made Hector richer and more powerful, with a grasping reach into every agency surpassing that of senior elected officials.

Pilgrim came into the room, loading a clip into his gun. "I'm leaving. I want to scope out the site thoroughly before I meet her."

"I hope you come back," Ben said.

"If I don't..."

"Then I'll find a way to bring him down."

"I would rather eliminate him with a bullet than a spreadsheet."

"Whatever works." Ben stood. "Good luck." He offered Pilgrim his hand. Pilgrim shook it, then left without another word.

Ben sat down to finish his brain dump on the laptop. He wrote every conversation he could remember having with Hector regarding work for Homeland. Writing was peace, a return to normalcy, from the chaos of the past two days. But his shot arm began to ache with the typing. Now he just needed to compile a group of people to send it to—representatives and senators and State and Defense officials who didn't much care for the contracting business—and convince them to take him seriously.

Since he was currently a fugitive, that would be difficult.

He got up, went to the kitchen, got a glass of water, needing to stretch his legs. He wanted to think.

Pilgrim's sketchbook lay on the counter; a clear sign that he expected to return.

Ben picked it up. He was tempted to page through the drawings again, but it felt like a violation. But he didn't like leaving it where it might be forgotten if he had to leave quickly. He stuck the small black book in his shirt pocket.

He took his water and went to the window. The day had grown cloudy, gray skies the color of worn chains. He scanned the parking lot. Nothing odd. The construction crews weren't working this Saturday on the massive construction next door; he heard the soft calming whisper of the wind.

As he closed the curtain and turned away from the window, a Lincoln Navigator turned into the lot.

He glanced at his watch. Pilgrim should be at the soccer fields by now. He decided to write down the list of people who were Hector's political enemies and then find Internet access so he could start e-mailing them. He finished his water, refilled the cup.

A sound from the front door. A scrape. The lock clicked, being forced, and then the door was open, Jackie entering, gun out in front of him, sweeping the room, finding Ben.

"Hands on head and get down!" Jackie ordered. "Oh, this is going to be good, man. Seriously."

Ben obeyed. His gun was still under his pillow on the futon. No way to get to it.

The door slammed closed. He kept his face to the gritty kitchen tile. He heard rapid movement through the apartment: Jackie seeing if Pilgrim lay in wait in the bedroom. He started to crawl for the futon and then Jackie was back in the bedroom doorway, gun aimed at him.

"I don't get to rough your face up," Jackie said. "But I'm still going to hurt you." He leaned down and pulled the cell phone from Ben's pants pocket, tucked it into his dark jacket. He was dressed in black, with black cowboy boots. His face was braced with a nose guard and bandages.

"Clear," Jackie called to the other side of the door.

Sam Hector stepped inside, holding a woman in front of him. She was fiftyish, graying hair, a generous mouth, haunted blue eyes.

"Sam..." Ben started.

Sam's smile was a crooked slash of arrogance.

Jackie hauled Ben up by his shirt, shoved him to the living room floor. Now the futon was four feet away from him; the pillow, hiding the gun, was at the opposite end. The woman—Teach, he presumed—sat on a chair, pushed there by Hector.

Hector stepped between him and the futon. He held a gun, aimed at the floor.

"It would have been easier if you came to my house, like I asked. The customer's always right, Ben."

"I hate being wrong," Ben said, "and I was wrong about you."

Hector gave a twitch of a shrug. "You've been wrong about a great deal, old friend."

"I'm not your friend," Ben said.

"True. And you're not going to grow old."

"Like Adam and Delia and your own guards down in Austin. You're a murderer."

Hector raised a hand, waved his fingers. "My hands are clean. Where's your new friend?"

"Gone for good."

"Give him his answers." Jackie yanked Ben up from the floor, delivered a savage blow to the face that slammed Ben's head into the wall. Ben felt a tooth loosen; blood oozed from his nose. The tip of the knife skimmed down to his stomach. "Or I'm playing cut-it-off with you."

A trickle of blood from his nose tickled Ben's lip. "What did I ever do to you, Sam, except make you *richer*..."

"You know I loathe people who delay. Where is Pilgrim, when's he coming back?"

"He's not coming back."

"Jackie, check the laptop, see what he was doing," Hector said.

Jackie went to the laptop, opened the recent documents menu item. "Writing a report about you and your contracts. Not very nice one. Paints real unkindly, it does."

"Delete it. See if there's anything else interesting on the hard drive, then wipe it clean." Hector tried the smile again. "You have been an unpleasant surprise, Ben. Seriously. I knew you had a brain, but I didn't suspect the spine." He eased down in front of Ben. "Where did Pilgrim go, Ben? I won't let Jackie play with his knife on you if you tell me."

Every time death loomed in the past two days, Ben had felt terror touch his bones, adrenaline igniting his blood. But now—the knowledge of death, no escape here—an odd calm gripped him. He had to protect Pilgrim, no matter what they did to him with knife or gun. The realization settled him. The lie was easy: "He went to your house to find Teach."

Hector's face—the mask that had fooled Ben for years—betrayed no reaction. Then Ben saw the barest twitch at the corner of Sam Hector's mouth, a whisper of rage. "He's not that stupid. Neither are you."

Delay him. "How do you pretend to be a normal human being when you're so clearly not, Sam? I trusted you, I was your friend—"

"Basic math: People are either help or hindrance." He slid a sealed envelope from his jacket, tossed it on Ben's lap. "If you don't want to cooperate, Ben, so be it. I'll show my cards."

"I'm not interested."

"You are. Open it."

Ben tore open the envelope, pulled a set of photos free. The images hit him like a giant's fist, crushing his lungs, flattening every thought in his brain.

Emily. Photographed with a telescopic lens, standing in the kitchen window in the Maui house in the moments before she died. Next photo. The same. Next photo, her clicking off the phone, looking pensive, almost looking up at the camera, a frown on her face. Then a photo of the kitchen window, a bullet hole marring the glass, Emily sprawled on the tiles.

The photos spilled from his hands onto the floor. His throat thickened, his chest tightened. "Why?"

Hector laughed.

"Why did you...Why?"

"You mean who?" Hector laughed, the cat batting the dying mouse.

"You murderer—" Ben yelled, but then Teach bolted from the floor, threw herself at Hector. She closed a hard grip on his throat—Ben saw the astonishment in Hector's eyes—and Ben jumped up, grabbing for Hector's gun. Hector wrenched free from them both, kicked Ben in the face, sent him sprawling. Hector powered his pistol into Teach's stomach and fired.

Teach collapsed, eyes open, mouth clenched. Ben got up again, and Hector slammed the pistol into Ben's face, kicked him in the stomach, to the carpet.

Lying on the floor, Ben's eyes locked on Teach's. She blinked once, twice, stopped, tried to speak.

"Jackie." Hector watched Teach, the gun steady on Ben. When she stopped breathing he prodded her with the foot. "Dump her in the bedroom."

Jackie picked up Teach's body and carried her into the bedroom.

Ben crawled to the futon. He could hardly breathe. The gun. The pillow. His only chance to get away and to kill this man.

"I suppose it's rude to point out I've taken everything from you," Hector said. "Your wife. Your good name, your business. Your dignity."

"Why . . . why?" Make the smug murdering freak believe he'd broken Ben. He got a hand under the pillow, crouching as though he feared a kick or a blow from Hector. He shivered, spat blood. Emily. She had changed him in life, and now that he knew the truth of her death he felt changed again. Determination filled him like an ache in his bones. Not a moment's hesitation.

"You're going to tell me where Pilgrim is, Ben, because I know you. You're weak. You'll trade me the information for an easy death. You want to look under Teach's clothes, see the cuts?"

His fingers touched the gun. Hector would shoot him as soon as he drew it, and even if he stood his ground and managed to kill or wound Hector, Jackie would attack him from the other room. The odds were dismal.

But otherwise, they would kill him and wait for Pilgrim to return. Death was doing nothing. He thought of Pilgrim's words: *Sometimes the smartest move in a fight is to retreat.*

"Delia told me all about New Orleans," Ben said plainly, and for a moment surprise slackened the clench in Hector's face. Ben flung the pillow straight at Hector's head and swung up the gun that lay underneath it. The feathers exploded from the pillow as Hector fired a shot through its center. But Ben emptied the clip in Hector's direction as he ran for the window. Hector threw himself backward and behind the kitchen counter for cover. Ben's spray of shots pocked the counter, the wall, punctured the refrigerator, as he ran the ten feet.

Hector rose to return fire but Ben hit the window.

The closed, dusty curtains caught Ben as he jumped through the glass, the heavy fabric protecting him from the jagged shards. His momentum carried him onto the landing.

Stopping or taking the time for the stairs meant death, and he rolled without hesitation, slid himself under the metal railing of the walkway, dropped one floor to the grass below.

The apartment stood at a corner, and if he ran to his right he'd be wide open, they could shoot him from the second floor. So he ducked under the walkway, ran in the opposite direction, hit the corner. He could hear their footsteps starting to barrel down the stairs.

Try to do what they don't expect. He turned a second corner; the chain link dividing the complex from the neighboring construction was just ahead. If he was lucky they'd decide he was still running north, when he was backtracking south on the opposite side of the building. Ben went over the fence, ignoring the barbed wire that tore at his arms, his khakis.

"There!" Jackie's voice, from the parking lot to his right. He'd been spotted.

Ben hit the sand and ran into the maze of the construction. The building was U-shaped, as it faced the street, its unfinished sides open to the elements.

Now he looked back. Hector was at the Navigator's wheel, plowing through a gate on the side of the fence, Jackie running behind the SUV. Drawing his pistol.

Ben dodged wheelbarrows, stacks of drywall, an idle forklift. The Navigator roared behind him. He dodged to the left, and Jackie, behind the Navigator, fired.

It was either get shot or be run down. He kept going straight, the SUV always between him and Jackie, and running through piled debris where the Navigator couldn't go. Supposedly. He glanced behind him, and the Navigator plowed through the construction junk, sawhorses and broken drywall flying, ten feet behind him.

Ben jumped up onto the foundation and headed for an interior wall that was already erected; he needed cover. He went around the wall as gunfire hit it with a low, vicious whistle.

He heard the Navigator screech to a buckling stop, then boot heels hitting the concrete. He exited the other side of the shell—a clear path all the way to the next chain-link fence on the opposite side of the lot.

More than enough room for Hector or Jackie to shoot him. But there was nowhere else to go. *You can't outrun him forever and your gun is empty.* He'd counted the bullets, like Pilgrim taught him, and the news wasn't good.

He ran, and louder than his own panting he heard the pounding of footsteps behind him.

Several yards beyond the chain link, he saw a knot of men and women waiting in the shelter of a Dallas Area Rapid Transit bus station. He launched himself onto the fence, using a pole to haul himself upward. Now he spotted a ditch breaking the land between the site and the bus stop.

He scrabbled over the fence, went head over heels, and the shots boomed, one hitting his shoe—a violent jerk rocked his foot—another shot hitting his chest like a hard kick. A third shot nailed the metal pole that lay against his stomach; it thrummed from the force as though an invisible man kicked it. Ben fell, headfirst, stayed low and rolled, went into the ditch. Water and mud, runoff from the site, smeared the bottom.

Ben sucked breath into his lungs, staggered to his feet, heard a man saying, "What the hell?" A woman screamed, and yelled in Spanish, "Gunshots, I heard gunshots." Ben ran down the ditch, staying low, bending low to crawl through a drainage section that barreled under the street.

The crowd—someone would be calling the police. He hoped. He eased out of the opposite end of the drain and clambered up the side of the gulley. He found himself in a vacant lot, with a large sign announcing more office space soon to come.

No sign of Hector. They might have fled as soon as they saw witnesses. Hector would not want anyone identifying him. Hector would be running.

Ben groped for his cell phone. Gone. He remembered Jackie had taken it.

Blood welled from the laces of his running shoes. The pain in his chest throbbed and he probed his flesh, half afraid to find a bullet hole. His chest ached to the bone, as though it had taken a hammer's blow. A tear in his shirt pocket. He found a hard rectangle beneath the hole. Pilgrim's small sketchbook, with the drawings of the young girl, wore a bullet embedded in the leather cover.

He had to find Pilgrim, but he had to get off the streets. He was bloodied and muddied and memorable.

He ran toward a convenience store and the alley behind it.

It was a surprise to learn that homeless people had cell phones. A group of three men stood behind the store. They stopped talking, giving Ben a suspicious glare as he approached them.

"Excuse me," Ben said, "is there a pay phone nearby?"

"Naw," one of the men said. "What happened to you?"

"I fell into a ditch. Hurt my foot." All three men looked down and inspected his foot; blood oozed from the sock.

"Church down the street, they give you some ice for that," one man said.

"Ice and a prayer," a second man laughed. "Who you need to call?"

"Friend. He'll come get me." Ben glanced over his shoulder. No sign of pursuit. They'd have risked being seen if they'd lingered, with the crowd at the bus station looking for them. It didn't mean that they wouldn't be combing the area looking for him.

"You're the man on the front page," the first man said.

Ben froze. The three men studied him.

"Yeah," the second man said.

"We stay informed. Ain't got much else to do but look at the paper," the third man said.

"Is there a reward?" the first man asked. The other two moved in a circle, cutting off Ben's lines of retreat.

"Please. Please don't report me." He was begging for a break from people who'd either never had one or never made the most of one they'd gotten. "I'm innocent. Please. I'm trying to stop the people who killed my wife."

The three men looked at each other. "Like on *The Fugitive*?" one asked. Ben nodded.

"If there's a reward, cops'll figure out a way not to pay us, that's for sure," the first man said. "I don't want to be on TV, either. Family's always looking for me."

"Here." The second man dipped in his pocket, pulled out a bulky phone. "You can use mine, but no more than one minute. Prepaid. Got mine at Walmart. And nothing personal, but I hold the phone so you don't run off."

"His foot's bleeding, he runs, it's a short race," the first man said, and laughed at his own wit.

The man held the phone and, stunned, Ben dialed the number. Then the man moved the phone to Ben's ear. "Speak up clear, Mr. Fugitive. It's not the best-quality sound."

33

───◉───

THE THREAT OF RAIN HADN'T kept the soccer fields empty; dozens of families and kids, in varying shades of uniforms and ranging from ages four to ten, wandered between the rectangles of green. Mothers, fathers, and siblings stood on the sidelines, chatting among themselves or calling out sweetened encouragement to the players. Coaches clapped and frowned; high school kids serving as referees blew whistles and acted supremely bored.

Dads cheered their daughters. Pilgrim knew Tamara played soccer, but he'd never worked up the nerve to watch a game from a distance; the risk was too great. Why did he choose this place, filled with fathers and daughters? Salt in the wound, rubbed there himself.

Pilgrim moved through the crowd. He was dressed in a phone repairman's shirt and baseball cap, a treasure from his cache, and he stayed on the edge of the crowd.

He spotted two people watching him in the first five minutes: a soccer mom who didn't seem to know the other moms on her side of the field, standing a bit apart, arms crossed, her eyes not fixed on the glorious play of a child but instead scanning the crowd a bit too often. There was another, a compactly built young man in a referee's shirt, but the shirt was untucked and hanging loose over long pants. Might be a gun there. He was no bigger than the teen-aged refs, but his face was that of an older man. He kept glancing around at the other games.

Neither approached him. They wanted him to talk to Vochek. Probably they would try to take him after they talked, when he left.

But she had broken her promise, or a superior had over-ruled her. Stupid.

A group of six-year-old boys had finished their game and their obligatory juice box and snack, and they and their parents walked as a herd. He stayed close among them, a cell phone at his ear, pretending to be deep in conversation.

He walked into the parking lot with them and glanced back. The watchers were still in place and he didn't make anyone else following him. He ducked into his car and didn't bother backing up. He barreled forward, over the curb and into the grass, and shot out onto the road. He had preprogrammed Vochek's cell number into his phone. He pressed the button.

"I said come alone," he said.

A sigh. "I wanted to," she said. "Got vetoed."

At least she was smart enough not to deny the obvious. "I'm sorry," he said, "but I can't deal if you break agree-ments."

"I can offer you a deal. How about if you come and talk to me and my boss."

"I must decline your kind invitation. I'm sorry, you've bruised my trust."

She was quiet for a moment and her voice softened. "Randall. I know you have a daughter. Tamara. I could make it so you can see Tamara again."

A chill slipped into his chest like a knife. "You stay away from my kid. And my ex-wife."

"I don't mean them harm, I'm trying to give you what you want."

"You don't know what I want, Vochek."

"Then you tell me what you want."

"To talk with someone with the actual power to negotiate with me. Good-bye."

"Wait, please—I need to know what's going down in New Orleans."

"I need to know, too. Good-bye, Vochek." He hung up and did an immediate U-turn, pulled into a Jack in the Box parking lot, and waited.

Five minutes later, he saw her pull past in a Ford sedan. Two other cars, both Fords, stayed close to her.

He pulled out after them. Tailing in Plano was both easy and challenging; the roads tended to be straight shots, but traffic was heavy—it was a suburb of a quarter million people—and drivers wove in and out of lanes for every inch of advantage. The trick was to stay close, not too close, and not lose them in the quickly changing lights. Without showing yourself.

The three cars headed back toward a shopping mall, then turned into a neighborhood across the street. Pilgrim was surprised to see a runway bisecting the neighborhood, a series of hangars with an array of private planes sheltering under the tin roofs. He U-turned hard, saw the cars stop in front of one of the houses.

Found you, he thought. What an interesting place for a safe house, with an airport built right in.

At the shopping center he located a place to perch where he could still see the house. She and her colleagues would go inside, she would call her boss, report failure, perhaps plead for another chance.

Interesting they didn't go back to an office. Vochek, Ben had said, was based in Houston. He wondered if her colleagues were local. If they were, and they left soon...

His phone buzzed. He didn't recognize the number calling. He clicked it on. "Yes."

"It's Ben."

"Yes."

"I need help."

"Explain."

"I'm six blocks from the apartment. Slight accident. Hurt my foot. Hector came over, and he got wild, you know how he is."

"Are you okay? Does he have you?"

"I'm fine and no he doesn't."

He knew Ben wouldn't betray him, even if Hector was holding a gun to his head right now. He knew it with a clarity that cut through a momentary doubt. "I'm at the Plano Palisades shopping center, across from the Plano Air Ranch Park. Do you have money in your wallet?"

"Yes."

"Get a cab."

"In Dallas? They don't exactly wander the streets looking for fares."

"Ben. Give me your address, I'll call a cab for you, I'll cover the fare. I'm north of the Nordstrom's, edge of the lot."

"Okay." Ben sounded like he might faint. He gave Pilgrim the address.

"You all right?"

"I am beyond sorry." Dread colored Ben's voice. "You were entirely right."

"About what?"

"I have to go, my time's—"

And the phone went dead.

Well. If he was wrong about Ben, and Hector had just found his location, let Hector come. He'd just wait, shoot Hector and Jackie in the knees, drag them to Vochek's safe house like a cat bringing torn, dead birds as trophies.

An hour later, the cab pulled up. Pilgrim got out of the Volvo and unfolded bills for the cabbie. Ben got in the passenger side, eased his shoe off. Not looking at Pilgrim.

"Tell me what happened." Pilgrim leaned down, inspecting the foot.

"I have bad news," Ben said. Pilgrim leaned back. "Teach is dead."

Pilgrim said, "Tell me." His expression stayed like stone as Ben explained.

"She died trying to help me."

Pilgrim's mouth contorted. He got out of the car, stood by the door, leaned his head against his arm on the car's roof. Ben got out on the opposite side of the car, faced him over the car's roof.

"Pilgrim . . . man, I'm sorry."

The traffic hummed by and kept them in companionable silence for a few moments. Pilgrim lifted his head. "He killed her because he doesn't need her anymore. He has complete control of the Cellar. He's won."

"No. We're still alive, we can fight him. We have to. He killed Emily. He had photos of her. Photos taken of her right before and after she was killed."

Pilgrim's face paled; he shook his head. He seemed to wait a few moments for his voice to return. "Ah, Ben."

"I was an idiot—I defended him—I made him a fortune...and he killed my wife."

"Where are the pictures?"

"I don't know. They were on the floor...I doubt Hector headed back to the apartment to collect them."

Pilgrim ran a hand along his mouth. "So the photos are still there. With Teach's body."

"What does that matter?"

"It may mislead the police." Pilgrim took a deep breath. "We got to keep moving forward. Let me see your foot."

"I'm okay."

"Give me a job to freaking do, all right?"

He used the first-aid kit in the car to doctor Ben's foot—the bullet had slowed considerably in moving through the fake leather and the dense mesh, leaving a wicked track, parting a chunk of flesh from the foot's top. The bullet was stuck in the bloody sock, between foot and shoe. Pilgrim thumbed the bullet onto the floorboards.

"Here's another one." Ben handed him the damaged sketchbook. "I put it in my pocket, I didn't want you to lose it."

Pilgrim plucked the bullet from the pages, put the book in his pocket without a word, without inspecting the damage to the pictures. "I don't have anything for the pain, Ben."

"I don't need anything. Now what?"

"We talk with Vochek." He nodded toward the house. "Only one car there now; her sidekicks are gone. Let's go."

34

―――•◦•―――

THE SAFE HOUSE FEATURED a porch camera, and after the doorbell rang, Vochek frowned at the face on the screen. She held a gun in her hand as she opened the door.

Ben raised his hands and said, "I'm unarmed."

Vochek gestured him inside and said, "Where's Randall Choate?"

Ben shrugged and stepped inside. They heard a stifled cry and the sound of weight hitting the floor. "We mean you no harm, but he wants to talk to you alone."

She hurried to the kitchen. The Homeland pilot who had been assigned to the safe house lay unconscious on the floor. Pilgrim craned his neck into the refrigerator. He found a Coke and popped the tab. On the stove tomato soup bubbled; ham sandwiches lay half-assembled on a cutting block. Pilgrim killed the heat under the soup.

"Messy boil-over," he said.

She aimed her gun. "On the floor. You just assaulted a federal officer."

"You all think a great deal of yourselves," Pilgrim said. "If he's such a federal wunderkind I shouldn't be able to take him down with two love taps. Kindly point your firepower elsewhere. You wanted to talk, well, here I am. We're even on your turf."

"Get on the ground!" she yelled.

"By the end of tonight either your career will be in the toilet or you'll be running Strategic Initiatives. Your call."

She kept the gun aimed on him.

"Please listen to him," Ben said. "We're on your side. We have the information you need to do your job and we're willing to share it. But you have to help us in return. You already know Pilgrim is good at vanishing. Don't test him."

"He told me you were innocent." She didn't move her focus from Pilgrim. "But I'm not sure I should believe someone who's been lying about being dead for ten years."

"Sam Hector is the reason Pilgrim had to vanish. Interested yet?" Ben said.

After several more seconds, she lowered the gun. She knelt by the unconscious pilot, checked his pulse, ran a hand over his head.

"He'll have a headache, nothing more, he's out for another hour or so," Pilgrim said. "Here, we'll put him on the couch." He and Ben carried the pilot into the den, set him on the cushions, propped a pillow under his head. Ben waited for Vochek to go back to the kitchen; he dug in the pilot's pocket, removed the man's cell phone, stuck it in his own pocket as he returned to the kitchen.

"Talk." She stood again.

Pilgrim poked a spoon in the tomato soup, made a face. "I'll tell you every dirty job I've done in the past ten years. Every job I know the Cellar's done."

"The Cellar."

"That's the code name of the group of CIA misfits and outcasts you've been chasing."

"The Cellar." She sounded slightly dazed, as though she'd just woken from a dream. Ben guessed she hadn't even known the name of the group she'd been hunting. "Okay. I spoke with my boss and I'm authorized to deal with you if you're willing to surrender."

Pilgrim frowned at the word *surrender,* as though it carried an unpleasant odor. "Fine. First, Ben gets granted total immunity. He's innocent."

"Okay, I'll do my best."

"Your best will be outstanding, Agent Vochek, or I will shut up tighter than a miser's fist." Pilgrim gave her a condensed version of the past days, with special details about their escape from the Homeland office in Austin. Ben noticed Pilgrim left out one critical bit of information—the name of the hotel in New Orleans that Barker had phoned. He figured that Pilgrim thought it best to have a card to play in future negotiations, so he said nothing.

Vochek did not interrupt or ask questions—she frowned, shook her head a few times.

Finally she said: "You can confirm Sam Hector was a CIA assassin known as the Dragon?"

"It will be my word against his, unless the CIA opens up about him."

"The CIA will face enormous political pressure to keep their mouths shut about Hector. He's made a lot of powerful friends," Ben said. "But that's not our first worry. Our first worry is New Orleans."

"I still don't understand what the threat is."

Pilgrim leaned against the counter, took a long drink of soda. "He's hijacked the Cellar to do a dirty job. Work he couldn't use his regular security contractors to do, either because they lack the training or because they're decent

guys and they would balk or ask too many questions. The
Cellar agents believe that they're taking orders from Teach.
But we don't know what the job is. I'm just going to bet
it's huge, because he's taken huge risks to make it happen."
He cleared his throat. "I'll help you stop the Cellar from
executing the job."

"That means you stay free for now," she said slowly.

Ben said, "But we stick with you. And we need your plane."

"Plane." She blinked once, as though she'd seen his lips
move but no word reached her ear.

"This house sits on a runway," Ben said.

"Useless now," she said. "You knocked out the pilot."

"I can pilot," Pilgrim said. "We leave immediately.
Before this guy wakes up."

"Just go to New Orleans?" She shook her head. "No. We
need to call the CIA, call Homeland…"

Ben shook his head. "Hector's a contractor. He does this
for money. Your secret office at Homeland paid him to find
the Cellar. He did that but he didn't share the information
with you, did he?"

"No. If he has… my boss hasn't told me."

"But now he's gone beyond that job, he's taking the Cellar over, taking control of its missions. He has control of a
team of highly trained agents who think they're doing good
by doing what they're told. And if he's seized control of
the Cellar, it's possible"—and he paused to let the words
penetrate—"another client has paid him to. Not your boss.
Someone else has bought their own private CIA."

The words hung between them like a curse.

"And he has bought it by killing my friend and mentor,"
Pilgrim said. "He killed Ben's wife. He's going to die. Not
pay. Die."

Vochek's face paled in the flicker of the kitchen fluorescents. Ben reached out and gently touched her arm. "Hector just decided to use me and Pilgrim because he needed to eliminate Pilgrim—who knew him from his assassin days—and me because I would be an easy frame to be tied to a hired killer because of how my wife died. He kills Adam and Pilgrim, and because Pilgrim's been working with Adam using my name, I then look like I'm connected to them both. It would come out after he was dead that Pilgrim was an ex-CIA assassin; Hector would have made sure that information leaked. Then I take the fall for my wife's death—and maybe for Adam's and Pilgrim's deaths. His plan got an unexpected boost when Pilgrim left my business card on the sniper's body."

"I still don't understand why he targeted you, Ben, if you were his friend."

"Two birds, one stone. He must have wanted me out of the way as he was taking over the Cellar, because I know his business so well, and the frame gives a solution to my wife's murder," Ben said.

"And we've given him business." Vochek closed her eyes for a moment. "My boss is Hector's client. Margaret Pritchard. She's been running interference for Hector all week."

"Then we can't trust her," Pilgrim said. "You can't trust her, either."

"I can't just let you take a Homeland plane and go to New Orleans."

"Agent Vochek," Pilgrim said. "You want our cooperation, that's what we've got to do. Decide. Or we'll decide for you, with all due respect."

35

Sᴀᴍ Hᴇᴄᴛᴏʀ ᴀɪᴍᴇᴅ ʜɪꜱ Lᴇᴀʀᴊᴇᴛ down his private runway. The compound fell away below him. He set the plane's course, radioed into Dallas airspace. Then he went silent, slipped off the headphones, and called a number on the plane's phone. He said, "I hope you're leaving some gumbo for me."

"Hardly. I expected to hear from you before now," Margaret Pritchard said.

"Listen. There's been a break in the project."

"I'm listening."

"Early this afternoon Dallas police found a body in an apartment. I have a source inside the department. The body is that of a woman who, I believe, is connected to Randall Choate."

"How do you know she is—"

"I don't. But it might be worth it if your agent flashes Choate's picture to the landlord, see if anyone recognizes him. See if you can match the woman's photo to any known ex-CIA, including those missing in action. My source at the force will send you complete info." He cleared his throat; he didn't need to go into detail about the additional findings in the police report: the scattered photos of Emily

Forsberg in the moments before her death and the description of Ben Forsberg given by the bus station witnesses. Better for her to hear it from an impartial source. The only thing he'd taken from the apartment was the laptop; no reason to let the cops recover Ben's deleted report from the hard drive.

"Too many deaths," she said. "We can't keep this under wraps."

"Wrong. They've been in hiding for years, and thanks to Adam's work and my digging, I've rooted out three of them in the past few days; this woman could be the fourth. This group is imploding under the pressure I'm putting on them," he lied. "They know they're close to being discovered. Choate might be trying to eliminate everyone who might talk."

"I don't need dead bodies. I need live ones that can tell us where the rest of this group is."

"I know, Margaret," he said. "We're getting very close. There is one problem."

"What?"

"They know it's me after them. Ben Forsberg called me. Threatened me. Said they would smear me and my company with all sorts of allegations if I don't back down. Who knows what he might claim, what he might say? None of it would be true, but I want you to silence the story as much as you can. When you speak to the police chief in Dallas, and I know you will, about this case having implications for Homeland Security, you need to be sure she understands that I'm doing your work and any allegations against me are baseless."

She hesitated, as though he were asking too much. "Sam…"

"Should I call the Homeland secretary? Would that be easier?"

"Of course not, Sam, we'll handle it on this end. Are you coming straight here after you land?"

"No. We have further leads to pursue. But I'll call you when I'm on the ground."

She thanked him and hung up.

Jackie said, "You might have overplayed your hand there."

"Ben and Pilgrim can't hurt us now. Ben fled a murder scene and left behind pictures of his dead wife. No one's going to believe a word either of them say."

"They know about New Orleans. He talked to Delia Moon—"

"She knew no specifics. And they can't get there in time. We move tonight."

Hector pointed the plane southeast toward New Orleans. The hard work was nearly done. Within a day, he knew, his future would be assured.

36

———◦◦◦———

THE PILOT STIRRED AWAKE. Voices jabbered in the kitchen. Two men. Vochek. Talking about...taking the plane. He could smell the tomato soup he'd started to heat and he thought that his nose was the only part of his body working normally. His neck ached, he could barely see, and his hands weighed heavy, as though his flesh had converted to iron. He groped his front pocket for his cell phone—gone. But he remembered the scattering of panic buttons in the safe house. Pressing the button would send a silent alarm to the Homeland office in Dallas and an alert to the Plano Police Department.

He heard whoever was in the kitchen leaving, and he staggered to his feet, fell to his knees, and started to crawl for the alarm button in the bookcase.

The plane was already fueled and loaded, and Pilgrim was going through the flight check when sirens approached.

"Pilgrim." Ben pointed over Pilgrim's shoulder. "We got to go. Now."

At the front entrance of the air park a police car screeched past the gate, sirens flashing.

"Let me explain to them." Vochek reached for the door.

"Ben, don't let her." Pilgrim kicked in the engines, hurried the plane onto the runway. "We can't risk that you might not be persuasive."

The police car wheeled onto the grass around the runway as the jet coursed down the concrete.

"He's going to pull onto the runway," Vochek yelled.

"He's not suicidal." Pilgrim gunned the plane.

The plane hurtled toward the police car. A second patrol car followed the first, both onto the runway.

"He's a little suicidal," Ben said.

The jet powered forward. Straight toward the cars, which both lurched out of the jet's way as time ran thin. The plane's wheels rose; the cars fell away beneath them.

"The officers didn't get out of the cars, so I knew they wouldn't stay parked. Common sense," Pilgrim said.

"Your common sense gave me a heart attack," Ben said.

The plane's radio began to squawk.

"They're going to order us to land," Ben said.

"Explain that we're on a Homeland Security emergency. Your boss got juice?" Pilgrim asked.

Vochek nodded. "She can clear our path. She can also stop us cold."

"Then she gets us cleared all the way to New Orleans. Otherwise, consider the possibility we'll be shot down."

She reached for the radio and asked air traffic for an emergency patch to Homeland Security. Three minutes later Margaret Pritchard was on the line.

"Agent Vochek?"

"I'm aboard the plane. With Mr. Choate and Mr. Forsberg."

"Please repeat."

"Mr. Choate and Mr. Forsberg have surrendered and are in my protective custody."

"Understood."

"We want to deal, Ms. Pritchard," Pilgrim said. "We can give your office everything it needs on the biggest covert group in the government. But we get to fly to New Orleans, no problems. That's what Vochek wants and what we want."

"I'll make sure your way to New Orleans is cleared," Pritchard said, resignation in her tone.

"Thank you, Margaret," Vochek said.

"One thing," Ben said quickly. "Part of the deal. You tell Sam Hector that we've surrendered to Homeland Security and are being questioned by you in a secure location. The media and the Dallas police don't know."

The silence went on so long they thought she'd disconnected the line. "Why do I need to feed him a lie?" Pritchard asked.

Ben gave Vochek a pleading look. "We have some serious evidence against Hector," Vochek said. "It would be best for now if he believes these two pose no threat to him."

"I understand." The line to Pritchard clicked off, and the only noise from the radio was traffic chatter, directions for Pilgrim to rise to a certain altitude. "Will she lie to him?" Ben asked.

"I don't like that she didn't give us an assurance," Vochek said. Ben and Vochek, sitting in the back of the plane, leaned back in their seats. Texas slowly unfolded beneath them as the sunlight began to die. Exhaustion claimed Ben—he hurt all over his body—and he closed his eyes.

He heard Vochek say, "Why?"

"Why what?" Pilgrim asked.

"Why the Cellar? Why was it created?"

"I don't know."

"You joined it and you never asked?"

"Ignorance has its advantages. They didn't hire me for my brains."

"Don't," she said. "You killed for the CIA. And then for the Cellar."

"Actually, more stole and spied than killed."

She went quiet and the hum of the engines became like a blanket. Ben thought of Emily; she hated flying, never would have set foot in a small plane.

"Killed, stole, spied. Which did you do the most?" she asked.

"Does it matter?" Pilgrim said.

"You only killed the bad," she said. Ben could feel the tension coming off her in waves. One did not normally banter with a man who murdered.

"I killed," Pilgrim said, "and it's all bad. I had to train myself not to vomit after I killed. But I won't feel one second of regret for killing Hector."

"If Hector is guilty," Vochek said, "and I'm not saying he is, by any means—you can't kill him. We need him alive."

"I'm not terribly interested in what you need. I'm telling you what's going to happen."

"You're not working for this Cellar anymore."

"I don't work for you, either."

She poked Ben with her finger. "Open your eyes. Tell me why Hector would risk this takeover of a covert group."

Ben considered. "A man like Hector only risks his business to save his business. So whatever he's doing, it has to be something that helps him maintain his bottom line. He's had a lot of deals lost, a lot of contracts shuttled away from him. He told me a few days ago he's in the business of making fear go away. So maybe he needs fear to be back in a big way."

They fell silent as Texas passed beneath them and Louisiana appeared. Ben closed his eyes, exhausted, dozed. He dreamed of Emily, of the soft pressure of her hand in his. Peaceful and quiet. He awoke with a jerk at Pilgrim's words: "There's another plane coming up fast on us."

37

BEN PRESSED HIS FACE TO THE WINDOW. "It's not a fighter jet," he said. "It's a private jet, but bigger than ours."

Vochek said, "They're too close."

"Wait a sec," Pilgrim said, and he pulled the earphone plug so the radio could be heard in the cabin.

"This is Pritchard. The plane will escort you to New Orleans Lakefront Airport. Upon arrival, you will toss out any weapons, leave the plane, hands on head, and then you will lie flat on the tarmac. Do you understand?"

"Understood," Pilgrim said. "Thanks for the escort." He clicked off the line.

"It's just a precaution," Vochek said. "You've been rogue for ten years. They just want to make sure you behave."

"Or make sure they control us," Ben said.

"After they kill me," Pilgrim said, "they'll either promote you as a reward, or kill you because you know too much." Vochek started to shake her head and Pilgrim held up a hand. "Watch your back. At least until the ink's dry on your promotion."

"You're paranoid."

"Tell me," Ben said, "what was going to be the end result of finding all the illicit groups like the Cellar?"

"Shut them down. They're not accountable."

"Right. And then what? Trials for all the participants and those who gave them their orders, a public spectacle, the dirtiest laundry of our government aired for the world to see? Or was the shutdown going to be discreet? You'd have to find a way to shut everyone up."

"We certainly weren't going to eliminate people."

"But you weren't going to give them passes or pardons," Ben said.

"No, I suppose not."

"Forgive me for not wanting to step in front of a firing squad," Pilgrim said.

The gleam of New Orleans, dimmed since the storm, began to unfold beneath them. The radio sounded, the Lakefront Airport—where jets such as theirs would normally land—gave Pilgrim approach instructions.

Now they arrowed across the width of Lake Pontchartrain, the huge lake to the north of New Orleans, one source of the deadly tidal surge that flooded the city. Coming up fast on the city proper.

The radio repeated landing instructions.

Pilgrim scanned the controls. He listened to the reported positions of the planes around him, gauging distance and speed, measuring their own distance from Lakefront and Louis Armstrong New Orleans International.

"This'll work," he said, half to himself, then he dove the plane toward the waters of the lake in a steep dive.

Ben pressed his face to the window; the Homeland plane veered downward as they shot toward earth, trying to stay close to them.

"He's crazy, Ben!" Vochek grabbed at Pilgrim and one-handed he shoved her back in her seat.

"Ben, give me the gun, now," she said.

"No." He didn't point the gun at her but he kept it close. "He knows what he's doing."

"You're as crazy as he is," she said.

Air Traffic Control for Lakefront Airport was not happy, calmly warning Pilgrim that he did not have clearance for the approach he was taking. He raced low over the long cup of Lake Pontchartrain, but he had slowed his descent, flying a bare two hundred feet above the surface, and he came in low over the city. In the puddles of lamplight Ben could see people on the street, watching the plane in surprise and fear, perhaps sure the plane was verging on a crash, before it went past in an instant.

The Homeland plane was the only other aircraft close to them. Pilgrim zoomed over the Superdome, rising to skirt its top, took a turn over the French Quarter, going low again, driving hard along the Mississippi River toward the Lower Ninth Ward. Below in the bright glow of the moon lay a ghostly web of roads, highways, and devastation left over from Katrina, now taking on its own sad permanence. Ben peered at wide swatches of land where nothing had been rebuilt; many homes still lay on limp and broken deathbeds. FEMA trailers dotted yards. He watched the altimeter dip: he was at two hundred feet, soaring fast over the broken city. The engines' roar made a booming echo against the ground.

He took a hard, screaming turn, downward toward the ruins.

He was actually going to land the plane. In the streets. Vochek could see below that it was madness: power lines, still-tilted poles, front yards jagged with fencing, ruined houses, trying to crawl back from death.

The gun. Ben still held it, not pointed at anyone, and his own mouth was a thin line of worry.

"Ben. Talk him out of this."

"He knows what he's doing."

Doubtful. She grabbed at the gun and slammed her elbow hard into Ben's chest. She got both hands on the gun and tried to wrench it from his grasp.

Pilgrim turned the plane hard again, banking, slowing, searching for enough street.

The force of the sudden turn threw Vochek off Ben. He put the gun on the side away from her. Then a small but pile-driving fist hit Ben in the back of the head, smacked his face against the window. His lip split, blood smeared his teeth.

He folded himself over the pistol. He could not let her get the gun; she'd force them to land at Lakefront. The plane took another wrench to port, Pilgrim trying to slow before he ran out of road to land. As the windows dipped, Ben saw the headlights of a car on a deserted street, close enough almost to touch.

Vochek landed on his back, one arm closing around his throat, the other hand's fingers digging for his eyes, and she said, "Please, Ben, give it to me before he kills us."

Pilgrim needed asphalt. In the moon's gleam and the spill of light from cars and houses, he saw five threads of pavement, one a busier cross street on the edge of the neighborhood, where the roads and the lots had been swept clean. The other two choices were less crowded roads. One had fewer houses and FEMA trailers and chain-link fences dotting the yards and was a straight shot. It had the fewest cars parked on the curb. No sign of the Homeland plane close by; they were far above, circling, watching, summoning the local police to intercept Pilgrim. Taking bets if he was actually crazy enough to land.

Well, why wouldn't he be? He had nothing left to lose. Nothing. First time he'd been told to do anything by anyone other than Teach in ten years, and she was dead. He took no more orders. The realization steadied his hands on the controls.

He descended fast, hearing Vochek and Ben struggling behind him. A pickup truck chuffed through an intersection at a crosshatch on the road, going the opposite way, maybe thirty feet below him as they dropped. Doubt— normally a stranger—filled him, and a sour taste broke in his mouth. He could kill someone, and he was supposed to be a Good Guy, eliminating Bad Guys. A minivan, full of kids, or a car, driven by a high school girl, or a motorcycle, with some regular nice guy coming back from a long day's work of rebuilding the nearly lost city—no, he wouldn't let that happen.

He dove the plane down toward the empty blacktop. Had to time it just right, pull up with room to spare, bring it down on three points, with room to slow—

Then the gun erupted.

Vochek knew how to hurt. The eyes, the groin, the bending back of the finger that caused surprised agony. She worked all this brutal magic on Ben, saying, "Ben, let go," again and again. But he wouldn't. She stepped on his wounded foot and he howled. She got a grip on the pistol. He raised the gun and she twisted it, felt his finger depress the trigger. The gun barked. The window shattered; a flick of light hit the wing.

"Stop!" Pilgrim yelled.

Ben kicked back with all his strength, trapped Vochek between himself and her window. He kept her pinned, tried to pry her hands from the gun.

"Nearly there," Pilgrim yelled.

Wheels hit the blacktop. The plane bounced hard, Ben nearly thrown to the ceiling. He kept his iron grip on the gun. He landed back on Vochek, knocking the wind from her. Wings screamed as Pilgrim cut the engines and lifted the flaps. A boom thundered and a shiver rocked the plane, sparks dancing past the window, as a wing clipped metal— a mailbox, a street sign, a chain-link fence—and the plane rumbled forward. Another shriek of protesting metal, a jarring bump, then the plane skidded to a stop.

Pilgrim turned and pulled the gun from both their hands. He put it to Vochek's head.

"The deal is off," Pilgrim said. "Thanks for the lift."

"Pilgrim…" Ben started.

"The police will be here in probably ninety seconds, and we can't trust Homeland. Come on." He opened the door, grabbed Ben, pushed him out onto the pavement.

"Don't do this," Vochek gasped.

"Vochek, don't trust anybody. I don't want to see your lovely face again."

Pilgrim jumped to the asphalt. Behind the plane, a pickup truck and a minivan slammed to a stop. Pilgrim ran toward the truck, his gun out and high to see, and gestured the two women out of the cab. The women stared, agog at the crumpled-winged plane on the road and the crazy man waving a gun. They obeyed, hands up, one crying.

"Very sorry, need the truck. You'll get it back." Pilgrim shoved Ben across to the passenger seat, climbed into the driver's seat. He wheeled the truck hard in a circle, tore around the plane by driving on a grassy edge of the road, and roared away. Through the open window the damp breath of the neighborhood smelled of wet and decay. The sirens rose in their approach: fire truck, police, ambulance.

Above them circled the Homeland plane.

"Ben," Pilgrim said, "I should have given you the choice to stay with her."

"We said we'd stick together." He thought he saw for a moment a flicker of relief on Pilgrim's face. There, then gone. He must have imagined it.

"They're gonna chase us hard. You ready?"

"Yes."

Pilgrim tore along a road of houses of patchwork brick and wood, homes trying to arise from the drowned soil, stripped down and rebuilt.

"I can still hear that plane." Ben leaned out the window. "He's banking, trying to keep us in his sights."

Pilgrim swerved the wheel hard, catching sight of a police car flashing sirens in the rearview, and he wrenched the pickup into a two-wheeling turn toward the thoroughfare of St. Claude Avenue and headed west.

A deputy's car picked them up, followed, lights blazing.

Traffic was light and Pilgrim swerved and accelerated around cars, ducking onto side roads, and then back onto St. Claude. Ben braced himself for the impact that would surely come when Pilgrim miscalculated and rammed into a bumper or a barrier. Pilgrim nearly clipped a construction sign that marked where the street was being repaired, power-turned hard, drove across two yards, and veered down a side street. He was out of sight of the pursuing deputy's car and he stood on the brakes, revved into a grassy parking lot full of cars and trucks, a banner announcing a Saturday night revival meeting, presumably connected to a church that sat back from the street, in redbrick grandeur. Slammed on brakes, nestled in between two large trucks in a loading area for the event. The jet went overhead.

They ducked down and Ben thought, *This is how it ends, me arrested with an ex-spy in a church parking lot.* The jet's whine passed, the deputy's sirens faded, and they eased out of the truck. Pilgrim started feeling along bumpers for key cases, Ben testing for unlocked doors.

More sirens sounded, patrols responding to calls about the downed plane. The energetic strains of modern worship music rose from the tent that stood pitched near the church. Then the sirens faded again. The buzz of a helicopter replaced the churning whine of the Homeland plane.

"I got a winner," Pilgrim said, pulling loose a key box from a bumper. "Come on, before the helicopter spots us. They can fly lower and slower, stick to us like glue."

They pulled away from the revival in a sedate blue Ford sedan.

"I hope this isn't the preacher's car," Ben said. "We're going to hell."

"I'm the only one hell-bound. We'll find you a place to lay low." They could hear the helicopter widening its circles. Pilgrim wheeled the sedan back into traffic, at normal speed.

"Lay low. Forget it. He killed Emily. I'm not sitting on the sidelines."

"Ben. Hector specifically took over the Cellar for this big job. That means I have to fight several people from the Cellar. It'll be like fighting a whole gang of me. You did your part. You don't have to take this on."

"I know I'm not good at shooting and fighting, but I can help you."

"Not now. I promise you, I will kill him for you. For everyone he's hurt." Pilgrim's mouth became a thin slash. "For Teach, and for your wife. You won't have a long wait."

"Good Lord. You know where Hector and the Cellar are at." Of course he knew, and he wasn't going to tell Vochek or the authorities until he knew what kind of reception awaited him and Ben in New Orleans.

"I have an idea where they are," Pilgrim said.

"The Cellar had a safe house here."

"Good guess."

"But if Hector has the Cellar agents believing you turned against Teach—same as Green and De La Pena did—they'll kill you," Ben said.

"Yes, they will. They don't know me from any other jerk on the streets. Hector has all of Teach's pass codes, bank information—he'll seem very legit in their eyes. I will look like the enemy."

"Then let me fight him from another angle. Barker called someone at the Hotel Marquis de Lafayette. Last person he called before he left that house, to betray you and Teach."

"Yeah."

"I want to know who that person is. We know Hector's working for Vochek's boss on security. But maybe he's working for someone else, too."

"Fine," Pilgrim said. "You go get phone records, I'll go fight."

"You better calm down," Ben said, "or you're going to make a mistake and get killed."

Pilgrim pulled the sedan over to the side of the road. "Pardon my anger. I've lost my life, same as you. But I've done it twice now. First I lost my family, my career; and now I've lost Teach and the Cellar. I wanted to retire two days ago. I wanted to leave and be in the real world. He killed my hope." For a moment he was silent, fingers clenching above the steering wheel. "But there's no place out here for me now. As long as I could stay in the Cellar, then I could hope it could be different for me...that I could have a real life. But I can't. Vochek and Homeland, they'd put me in a cell, have me talking for years."

"You offered to do that for Vochek."

"I was desperate, Ben. To get here. Because Hector's not winning. Do you understand me?"

"Yes. I hate him as much as you do. That's why I want you to let me help you—"

"Call me on my cell if you find anything interesting in the phone records. I'll call you when I've killed Hector." He pulled the pilot's stolen cell phone from Ben's hands, activated the screen, memorized the number.

"Assume we succeed, then what?"

"I walk away. You negotiate an immunity, I'll feed you plenty to give Homeland that'll be worth gold to them. It'll buy you your life back."

"Buy your own life back. You'll always be looking over your shoulder."

"No. I won't." Pilgrim drove in silence for several minutes and then turned onto Poydras. On the streets were clumps of tourists, not like in pre-Katrina days, but more than Ben had expected. "Here." Pilgrim pulled a few hundred dollars, hoarded from his storage unit, slid them to Ben. "You won't be able to get the records without bribery. Nothing's cheap. The hotel's a few blocks down that way. Good luck."

"You almost hope I get caught."

"You don't want to be in the cross fire, Ben."

Ben offered his hand. Pilgrim shook it. "Sorry. Not good at good-byes."

"Good-bye, Randall." Ben stepped out of the car. First and only time to use his real name, the one Vochek mentioned.

"Bye, Ben. I'm sorry. For everything."

Ben closed the door, and the car raced off into the night.

38

———◉———

THE CELLAR. They arrived, one at a time, taking rental cars from Louis Armstrong International Airport. The safe house was a two-story family home on the edge of the suburb of Metairie, in a neighborhood spared the Katrina flooding. Hector felt like a magician summoning spirits to do his bidding as each of them arrived, and he greeted each at the door with the pass code that Teach had given him—and with their real name.

Six in all. Two women, four men. The six of them had never been in the same room together, and he could see them glancing at each other, trying not to study each other overmuch. Trying not to be remembered or to remember.

Jackie stood in the back to the room, arms crossed, wearing sunglasses.

"I'm afraid I bear tragic news. Teach is dead," Hector said when they had all gathered. He pushed a button on his laptop, which was hooked to a projector. A slightly grainy photo of Teach lying dead on the carpet. He'd snapped the picture with his cell phone when he'd run back to the apartment, knowing proof of her death might be useful.

One of the men rubbed his eyes as though weary. One of the women gasped. The rest were silent.

"Let me assure you that the Cellar continues as it always has. The transition to my leadership will be as seamless as possible. Like you all, I am ex-CIA. I worked in Special Ops as deep cover. I currently run, in my regular life, a private security firm. But I've worked with Teach in partnership with the Cellar for the past several years." It was best, he thought, to weave truth and lie together.

"Who killed her?" one of the men asked.

He clicked another button. Pilgrim's face appeared on the screen. "She was found dead in an apartment leased to this man. He is a Cellar operative known as Pilgrim. He is also responsible for the deaths of three other Cellar agents." Pilgrim flashed the file photos of Barker, Green, and De La Pena, one by one, and let the growing anger fill the room. "He killed one in Austin, two in Dallas. This is the most grievous attack on the Cellar in its history, especially coming as it did from within."

"Why did he turn on us?" one of the women asked.

"For profit. He got bribed by our target." Hector slicked the words with disdain. "We just came into possession of information about a terrorist group called Blood of Fire being underground here in New Orleans. They are gathered here to launch an attack. We're going to kill them." He moved the screen to a detailed map showing a house near the south shore of Lake Pontchartrain, in the Lakeview neighborhood. "Tonight. We move fast because they leave the house tomorrow. We're not giving them a chance." He handed them copies of files, photos, of the six young men.

"Why isn't Homeland handling this? Why not just arrest them?" the second woman asked.

"We haven't fed the information to Homeland. The terrorists know about us from Pilgrim. We don't want the terrorists captured and talking about us. They go in the ground. All of them."

The phone rang. He glanced at the number display. "Excuse me. Study the maps of the locale and of the house. This is a fairly straightforward operation, but I welcome your suggestions." He displayed tactical maps on the screen, stepped into the other room, shut the door, and answered the phone.

It was Margaret Pritchard. "We have a problem," she said.

He wanted to say, *Then solve it,* but she still believed the only agenda at work here was hers. "Yes, Margaret?"

"Two of the people from the covert group—I'm told they call it the Cellar—took one of my agents and her plane and they're in New Orleans. One of them, Choate, offered a deal to tell everything he knows about the Cellar to us, but he and his partner ran once they got here. They wanted me to tell you they were being held for questioning by Homeland. I'm wondering why they'd make that request, why they'd want you to believe they were out of the loop."

Hector stayed calm. Pilgrim didn't know the location of the safe house; only Teach had. But did he know the target, would he try to interfere? He couldn't know. He couldn't.

"You should know serious allegations about you are being made by one of my agents, Sam. I think you've done a wonderful job in flushing out these people, but we have to find the rest of them and I want to talk to you about your methods."

"Is this Agent Vochek? Is she the one they, um, kidnapped?" He remembered the name of the woman who'd called him in Dallas; he'd never returned her message. She'd been in a plane with Pilgrim and Forsberg. He wondered what had been said, what deal might be struck between them and this Vochek woman. This was a disaster for him.

Useless Nicky Lynch, missing Pilgrim when he had the chance to kill him. If he'd only shot him and Jackie planted the photos—then Pilgrim would be dead, Ben Forsberg would be under suspicion for having ties to a dead rogue CIA agent, with evidence pointing back to his wife's murder planted on the dead agent's body. A millimeter was making a huge difference in his life right now.

"Yes. She's here with me now. I'm not sharing her allegations with anyone, and I've asked her to keep quiet for now. But, Sam, I have serious concerns—"

"Margaret. I know it's late, but I can come over now and we can sort this out. You're at your usual suite?"

"Yes," she said.

"I'll see you shortly."

He walked back into the room; the team was gathered around a map. "New information. They may be rolling earlier than we thought. We need to go now." He explained his basic plan of how they were to approach, kill any sentry, and rip through the house in an orderly fashion, room by room. "This group is not remotely ready for our level of expertise."

"A bit rushed," one of the men said in a tone of doubt.

"It's a two-story house. They're mostly sleeping. You have more guns. They don't. It's not calculus," Hector said. He forced the iron out of his voice, because now they were all watching him. They weren't contractors, he remembered. These were a different breed, ex-Agency like him. "I know Teach's loss is devastating. But these guys have every reason to expose us if Pilgrim gives away our entire organization. So we take them out before they do."

He left them discussing the maps, sharing thoughts on how best to proceed given their skill sets and styles.

He gestured Jackie down the hallway to the den.

Jackie shut the door, crossed his arms. "Quite a bit of fiction you've told."

Hector realized, too late, he'd given Jackie an unwelcome taste of power, letting him attend the meeting, listen to the lies. Jackie could expose him as a fraud.

"Not all of it's fiction," Hector said.

Jackie rolled his eyes.

Hector leaned close to Jackie's ear. "I have a job for you. I need you to kill two people."

"All right."

"Do you know New Orleans?"

"I can find any place if I got a map."

"Use the GPS in the rental car. You'll be killing two women. One in her late fifties, Margaret Pritchard, and the other a younger woman, Joanna Vochek. They're at this hotel, this suite number. I need it done silent and fast. Both may be armed. Pritchard is a fool but Vochek isn't. They're expecting me; they'll be getting you."

Jackie studied the address, put it in his pocket.

"Pilgrim and Forsberg are in New Orleans. We don't know where."

Jackie blew an irritated sigh. "What if Pilgrim and Ben know where your team here is headed?"

The corner of Hector's mouth jerked. "They don't. They couldn't."

"Never say 'couldn't.'"

"Then my new colleagues in the Cellar will be happy to kill them."

Behind them, the clock chimed midnight.

KHALED'S REPORT— NEW ORLEANS

I CAN'T SLEEP. I hear snoring coming from the other rooms, and I cannot settle my thoughts. My mind is too full of worry. Later today I begin my work, and I must do it perfectly. With no room for error, no mistakes. It is strange to think of a job this way.

Tonight I saw on the news more coverage about the attack on the Homeland Security office that had not even officially opened yet in Austin, by a group of Lebanese men. I could feel everyone in the room tonight watch me when it was announced they were Lebanese, as though I brought a contagion of incompetence with me. Perhaps I am imagining it, reading so much into every reaction, because I am aware of the constant lie that my life is about to become.

A lie until I die. It is an odd, discomfiting feeling, one that works into your bones. I feel like tonight is the last night forever of the life I knew. Before I thought my very identity—who I am at heart—changed when I was recruited. That my uselessness ended then, and I became hopeful and useful all at once. But tonight is truly the end of my old life, and the beginning of another for me.

I lay awake, feeling the change in my bones.

39

———◆———

"I REALLY NEED YOUR HELP," Ben said with a tourist's awkward grin. The night clerk at the Hotel Marquis de Lafayette flexed an automatic, customer-centric smile in response. But any murmured request asked past midnight probably meant vice was involved. Ben could see the clerk steel himself against a polite inquiry as to where one might locate the pricier hookers.

"Yes, sir?"

"My wife called someone staying here last Monday. I'd like to know who that someone is."

"Sir, I can't release our phone records."

"I'll pay you two hundred dollars." Ben kept his smile friendly.

The clerk blinked. "Sir. I could lose my job. I'm sorry I can't help you."

"I understand. Five hundred dollars."

"Sir. Please." The clerk reddened with embarrassment.

"Cash," Ben said. "No one will ever know. But I have to have that phone number. My children. My wife wants to take my kids from me. I had an affair. So did she, but she didn't have the guts to confess to it."

"Sir, respectfully, I don't want to know—"

"My kids. I can do shared custody but I can't lose them from my life. Help me level the playing field. Please. Six hundred dollars. If you don't need the money, you must have family here that could use it. I know how hard things have been since Katrina."

"Sir." The clerk wet his lips. "I'm not sure I could even give you enough information to help you . . ."

"She called at 11:09 A.M. Spoke for twelve minutes. You should have a record of the incoming call. Which room it was routed to and who was in that room. That's all I need."

"Sir. Pardon my question. How do I know you don't mean ill to whoever she called?" This question followed a long sigh, low in the throat. Wrestling with the ethics. Calculating how much six hundred cash would buy. The clerk was maybe twenty-two and wore a plain wedding band on his finger.

"I swear I don't."

"I . . . I . . ."

"Six hundred. You're not doing a bad deed. You're helping yourself and you're helping me, and trust me, I deserve a little help right now."

"I'm not sure I can even get the information . . ." The clerk glanced over his shoulder. "My manager . . ."

Ben slid three hundred-dollar bills to the clerk. "Here's half. The rest when you get me the records."

The clerk didn't look at the bills. Then he picked them up and tucked them into his pocket. He went into the back of the lobby office, was gone for thirty seconds, returned, and said, "Twenty minutes."

Ben nodded and went into the bar. A few people drank and chatted in hushed tones—it wasn't a loud, conventioneer crowd. He had the sense he'd walked into a room of bureaucrats, here for the reconstruction, persuading themselves it was okay to relax with a beer. The TV above the bar showed the news of the emergency landing—as it was being described—on Marais Street in the still-devastated Lower Ninth Ward.

He ordered a club soda, drank half, and leaned against the bar. Then quickly turned away from the door.

Walking across the lobby he saw Joanna Vochek and a navy-suited, ash-blond woman wearing large eyeglasses, moving toward the elevators, deep in conversation.

Good Lord. What were the odds? All the hotels in town...but then he thought. A constant stream of people with federal agencies came and went from New Orleans with the reconstruction. They might keep rooms on permanent reserve, and hotels made deals with agencies to keep their business. That he knew from his consulting work.

Barker's contact here might be someone inside the government.

Ben waited for the two women to vanish inside the elevator and then stepped back into the lobby.

The clerk stood at the desk, frowning at the computer screen and looking guilty of several felonies.

"Sir," he said in a low whisper. "I can't get the information. The manager's on the computer and I can't access the phone database records, I can't, here's your money back..."

"Please, keep trying. But can you tell me this—is there a suite or set of rooms often used by the federal authorities who come here?"

"Yes, sir. From several different agencies. FEMA, Commerce, Homeland Security, of course FEMA's part of Homeland—"

"I need the names of every government-connected guest

who stayed here last Monday and their phone calls. Can you do that for an extra hundred?"

The clerk frowned, as though asking questions about government workers made him uneasy. "I'll try."

"Yes. But please, hurry." Ben returned to the bar, stayed near the door, avoiding eye contact with anyone.

Ten minutes later the clerk jerked his head toward the back of the lobby. The man's forehead glistened like he might sweat to death, a sheen on his face that showed nerves on edge.

Ben walked past the counter, kept going toward a stairway. He glanced back and the clerk gave a short, savage nod. He went up the stairs toward a mezzanine that held conference areas and ballrooms. The landing was deserted and the clerk jogged past him, as if intent on another errand, not looking at him.

Ben followed the clerk to a closed ballroom. The clerk stepped inside and Ben followed him. The ballroom stood dark, empty; the floral aroma of carpet shampoo reeked like cheap perfume.

The clerk said: "The money, please."

Ben handed him the rest of the cash and the clerk thumbed through the bills. Then he pushed an envelope into Ben's chest. He opened it, unfolded the pages; the list of people with government ties at the hotel last Monday was at least fifteen names long. Each list included incoming and outgoing calls.

"We're done. We never saw each other."

"Thank you," Ben said, but the clerk was already gone.

He stood in the deserted ballroom and ran a finger down the names. They meant nothing to him and there was no indication of which agency they were with...except at the end.

Margaret Pritchard in suite 1201. The clerk had penciled in, in block letters: "RECEIVED CALL ON MONDAY AT THE TIME YOU SAID."

The name of Vochek's boss, who had called them on the plane.

Why had Barker called her? Barker worked for Teach; he betrayed Teach and Pilgrim to Hector; how did he connect to Vochek's boss?

Ben leaned against the wall. He scanned the printout under the calls. The next number called from Pritchard's room was an Austin area code: 512-555-3998. He'd heard the number before, but he couldn't remember how he knew it. He racked his memory. Then he remembered a nasal stranger's voice on his answering machine, damning him in front of Kidwell and Vochek: 555-3998 had been the number at Adam Reynolds's office.

Margaret Pritchard had been in direct contact with Adam Reynolds. Which meant she might know about his search software that had unearthed a few of the Cellar's members. So who had Reynolds and Barker been working for—Hector or Pritchard? If Hector hired the Lynch brothers to kill Adam, and Pritchard worked with Hector—did she view Reynolds as an ally or a threat? At the least she'd been in contact with Barker, who was hiring death squads.

Hector had given someone their own private CIA. Maybe Pritchard hadn't been used by Hector; maybe she was fully aware of his brutal actions.

Ben had been a deal maker a few days ago; the smart thing now would be to cut a deal with Vochek. Show her this evidence, implicating her boss. Get her to help him find the truth.

He knew the odds of victory were not in Pilgrim's favor.

He was exhausted, hurt, and outnumbered. So if Hector escaped Pilgrim's fury, he could not escape Ben's. Ben would expose his conspiracy, strip him of his company, destroy his fortune. The idea gave him a cold shiver of pleasure.

The wounds in his arm and his foot throbbed. He opened the pilot's stolen cell phone. He found Vochek's number listed in it. He dialed.

40

You and I are at cross-purposes," Vochek said. "We can't be."

Pritchard crossed her arms, paced the hotel suite, face frowning in thought.

Vochek touched her boss's shoulder and Pritchard stopped walking. "I'm telling you, we need to find Pilgrim and Ben, get them talking."

"They've already talked plenty to you," Pritchard said. "You're calling Choate by that asinine code name."

"We've gotten in too deep with Hector. Take him and his people off this project until we're sure he's not hijacking what we're trying to do. At least until we can find out if he's really connected to Emily Forsberg's murder."

Pritchard pressed a hand to her stomach. "I'm starving. Have you eaten?"

"No."

Pritchard picked up the phone, called room service, ordered a pot of decaf, two omelets, and potatoes O'Brien. She hung up. "You want me to take the word of a CIA fugitive and a man who is tied to an assassin. Over that of one of the most respected government contractors in the country."

"How exactly is Hector helping us?"

"I told you, providing infrastructure to help us ID the off-the-books agents."

"And when you find these agents?"

"Then they'll be arrested. You act like this is news. Are you doubting my word?"

"No. I'm doubting his. Has he given you a single name other than that of Pilgrim?"

"No."

"Yet Adam Reynolds is dead. His girlfriend is dead."

"Because the Cellar's trying to silence them." She said this as though stating the obvious.

"Adam Reynolds found them, didn't he? He gave the names to Hector. But Hector's not giving them to you."

"That's ridiculous."

"You didn't even tell me about Reynolds's software to find aliases through financial trails. At least Pilgrim and Ben told me. Why didn't you?"

Pritchard waved a dismissive hand. "We didn't know if the software would even work."

"That's not the reason. The reason is that for it to identify likely false identities, it had to work across a huge range of databases that Adam Reynolds had no access to. But you got him the access. Illegally."

No noise but the hum of the air conditioner. "I told you we have leeway to find these people." She practically spat the words at Vochek.

The disappointment Vochek felt toward Pritchard welled up in her chest. "If we break every law to find these people, Margaret, we're no better than they are. We're turning into them."

"Spare me the lecture on civil liberties."

And I wished my mom was more like you? More poised, more perfect? "We need to see Hector's service record at the CIA. Pilgrim claimed he's an assassin."

"So what if he was?" Pritchard said. "It has nothing to do with his current work."

"His clients might feel differently," Vochek said. Her cell phone rang. "Yes?"

"Vochek? It's Ben Forsberg."

"Where are you?"

"Nearby. Sorry we ran."

"I'm not sure I blame you," she said quietly.

"Are you with your boss?"

"Yes." She glanced at Pritchard, who stood with crossed arms.

"I have evidence tying your boss to Barker, the guy who betrayed the Cellar, and to Adam Reynolds. I believe she might be able to clarify this situation, how the pieces fit together."

Vochek didn't look at Pritchard but she could sense the other woman tensing, standing close to her. Vochek turned and walked to the window. She glanced down to the darkened sidewalks as though she expected to see Ben watching her window. "I think you're right."

"Are the two of you alone?"

"Yes."

"I want to talk to you both. Together. Because if she wants to save her career, she better help bring Hector to justice. I want a deal, hashed out between us."

Evidence. It would either damn Margaret or it could be explained, but either way, Ben would be in her custody. "Suite 1201," she said.

He hung up. She thought, suddenly, of the lost Afghan

kids and wondered if she'd gone to work for a woman who was not the cure but part of the problem.

"Who was that?" Pritchard asked.

Vochek spoke to her boss with cool authority: "Sit down, Margaret, we're going to have a talk."

Vochek said nothing to Ben when she opened the door and he came into the room. He handed her the list of phone numbers and the gun he'd had on the plane, the one they'd fought for. "Vote of confidence in you standing by me," he said.

Vochek took the gun and carried it into the bedroom.

Margaret Pritchard watched and then she got up from the couch and moved toward the phone.

Ben stepped between her and the phone and picked it up, pulled the cord from the wall.

"You've already been on the phone quite enough," he said.

"You have some nerve."

"I've gotten a lot more recently. You hired Hector to help you find these clandestine groups. He's gone off the books himself."

She looked past his shoulder to Vochek. "If you want to keep your job, Joanna, you'll arrest this man."

Vochek didn't move. "I think we've become too much like the people we're hunting, Margaret. Let's get all the facts out."

"The Cellar agent Barker called you in this room. If you didn't know about the Cellar, how did you know Barker?" Ben asked. "He's a computer hacker who went underground rather than serve time. You've been consorting with a fugitive criminal. Terrible at congressional review time."

"The phone record is wrong."

"Fine. One of my clients does a lot of consulting work for the Department of Justice and has great connections there. I'll be glad to call the attorney general at home tonight and let you explain all this to her."

Margaret Pritchard went back to the couch, stood, arms crossed. "I hear you want a deal. I'm listening." She said it like she was the one doing him a favor.

"Hector goes down. Hard. He's a murderer and he's hired murderers to kill people for him."

"If I give up Hector, it'll be news, and our operation goes public. The whole point of stopping groups like the Cellar this way was to keep it out of the public eye."

"I don't care if the government gets embarrassed. It's not fatal."

"We hardly want our enemies and our allies to know details of our most illicit operations, and if we go public with him, all his work for me goes public, too."

"Then give him to us privately."

"You want me to let you kill him? Forget it."

"You don't care about the numerous people he's killed."

"I don't know that he's killed anyone!" Pritchard yelled.

"He showed me proof that he killed my wife." Ben put his hands on Pritchard's shoulders and pushed her into the chair. She didn't resist. "You protect him, you're protecting a murderer. How did you know Barker?"

Pritchard's mouth worked as if she were unsure that she could form the words. Finally she said: "Barker came to Homeland and got steered to me. He wanted to betray the Cellar, for payment and for a pardon."

"And you steered him to Hector."

Pritchard nodded. "Barker was our foot in the door.

He only knew of Teach, but not her specific location; he couldn't hand us any of the rest of the Cellar. But he gave us a couple of identities the Cellar had used—that he had set up for agents—and they let us test Reynolds's software to find more of the IDs used by the Cellar. Barker called me Monday to let me know the operation was starting to draw out Pilgrim and the rest of the Cellar, that they had gotten wind of Adam Reynolds trying to track down their accounts and their identities. But I had no idea Hector was working any other angle, such as targeting Pilgrim. Or you."

"Except Barker betrayed you, too, Ms. Pritchard. He fed you limited information while giving everything to Hector. He hired the sniper who killed Reynolds and tried to kill Pilgrim. He hired the gunmen who killed Kidwell and kidnapped Teach—and Hector never gave Teach to you, which would have handed you the entire Cellar immediately. He killed her right in front of my eyes. Not what you wanted, is it?"

Pritchard put a hand to her mouth.

"Why would he kill Reynolds?" Ben leaned down and yelled in Pritchard's face. "Tell me!"

"I don't know," she said.

"I thought..." Ben stopped. "Adam Reynolds originally designed this software to find terrorists. Did he call you Monday because he found, not the Cellar, but actual terrorists?"

Pritchard rubbed her temples, as if fending off a migraine.

"Answer him, Margaret," Vochek said.

"He made a mistake," she said. "He found suspicious activity centering on a group of men using suspect IDs traveling to New Orleans. But they're not terrorists."

"Who are they?"

Pritchard seemed not to hear him. "I came to New Orleans to check it out. That's why I was here. It's not a problem."

"Who is Hector targeting?" Ben asked. "Because whatever's here, it's why he's taken over the Cellar."

"He couldn't be after them," Pritchard said in a whisper. "No reason to go after them."

Ben grabbed her shoulders. "Tell us."

"Reynolds's search queries...they found a group of Arabic men traveling under a pattern that suggested assumed names, coming into the country a few weeks ago, all ending up in New Orleans. But these men aren't terrorists. They're training at a CIA safe house." Pritchard swallowed.

"Oh, no," Ben said.

"They're Arabs preparing to infiltrate and spy on terrorist groups overseas. To be the native eyes and ears we haven't been able to have in places like Beirut and Baghdad and Damascus. We've never had true, trained spies working deep cover inside Hezbollah or al-Qaeda or any of the other networks. Our best hope of destroying terrorist networks from inside."

Ben let her go. "Where is this safe house?"

"I don't have the location...that's classified..."

"But Adam gave Hector the same information he gave you," Vochek said. "Hector's going to use the Cellar to kill a CIA team. Why would he—"

"Because Hector needs the war on terror to keep going for a good long time," Ben said. "It's fueling his bottom line." He thought of Pilgrim's Indonesian story; the Dragon aka Hector framing Pilgrim in exchange for a security contract for his new company, profiting from fear and chaos.

Hector was repeating his own history, but now on a much wider and more dangerous scale.

The knock on the door came, a man announcing room service.

The waiter, a gentle, hardworking man who had been with the hotel for twenty years and had been one of the first employees to return in the wake of Katrina, knocked on the door, announced, "Room service." He was tired, his feet ached, and he was ready to go off duty. He nodded at the young man ambling down the hallway, turned back toward the door, and felt the cool metal touch his temple. He froze.

"You're going to walk in and leave the door propped open. Do it and you won't get hurt. Argue and you're dead. I don't want to hurt you. Nod if you understand." The voice was a lightly accented whisper.

The waiter, stiff with fear, nodded. The young man stepped back against the wall, where he wouldn't be seen.

The door opened.

41

———◆◉◆———

PILGRIM WATCHED THE CARS LEAVE—two of them. One was a van holding the Cellar agents, the other a sedan with just Hector. Jackie had taken off five minutes earlier in a third car, and Pilgrim let him go. He had to stay with Hector.

The two vehicles pulled onto Veterans Boulevard, headed east, then headed north toward Lake Pontchartrain. Traffic was heavier than normal—Saturday night in New Orleans—and he hung back, keeping an eye on Hector's car. They weren't wasting any time; whatever this job was, they were moving now.

He did not want to kill anyone in the Cellar. They had made the same choice he had, to take a broken life and rebuild it into meaningful work. Perhaps they hadn't chosen entirely for virtuous reasons; he himself had no desire to rot in an Indonesian prison. They had all done work that would offer no acclaim and few rewards, other than Teach's assurance they had done a Good Thing.

What could be in New Orleans that interested Hector so that he needed the Cellar? Hector Global could command a thousand trained men for action anywhere in the world. But those men wouldn't kill at will, especially outside a war zone.

This had to be a job that his normal security forces would refuse to do. Because there would be questions. Repercussions. Hector needed deniability.

If he could take Hector out with a shot—then the rest of the group would come after him, perhaps abandon the target if they lost the element of surprise.

He stayed close as they began to head into the patchwork of rebuilt and devastated neighborhoods close to the massive lake.

And if he missed Hector, and the Cellar caught him… well. His beginning in this life had been messy, at Hector's hands, and his exit would cost Hector dearly. He would make sure the price was high.

42

⸺◉⸺

THE WAITER, MOUTH A THIN LINE, pushed the room service cart into the room. Ben saw the coffee and carafe and the covered dishes. His stomach rumbled. But the waiter said nothing, no hello, how are you, kept his head bowed as if expecting a blow.

Pritchard stepped forward to sign the ticket. Two sharp bleats, the waiter falling over the tray, Pritchard reeling, collapsing onto her back. Jackie Lynch stood in the doorway, suppressor-capped gun raised, his eyes seeking his next target, closing the suite's door behind him.

Vochek stumbled backward toward the coffee table. Jackie raised the gun.

"No!" Ben yelled. "No!"

Jackie saw Ben. A twisted smile touched his battered lips and he shifted the gun's aim from Vochek toward Ben.

But in the second it took for the gun to point toward Ben, Vochek rushed Jackie and kicked him in the solar plexus. He staggered back and she threw herself against him so that the gun pointed only at the floor.

Ben ran and slammed Jackie against the wall, leveraging all his weight into the younger man's shoulder, pinning the gun between them, closing his hands around the weapon.

Fury fueled his muscles. He got hold of Jackie's pinky and snapped hard.

Jackie screeched and fired, the bullet popping into the carpet.

Vochek tangled fingers in Jackie's long hair, knocked his head against the wall. Once, twice, and he roared in anger. Ben twisted the gun around, toward Jackie; he tried to fire but Jackie's broken, bent finger jammed the trigger.

Jackie head-butted Ben's face, hammering into his cheek, but even with the bolt of pain, Ben did not let go. Jackie wrenched free of Vochek's grip. With Ben pinning his hands, he landed a kick hard in Vochek's chest, and she fell to the floor.

"It ends now!" Jackie screamed. He knocked Ben loose; Ben fell against the cart. The heat of the coffee decanter touched his arm. He grabbed the carafe and swung it hard—no time to unscrew the top, Jackie was lifting the gun to put a bullet between Ben's eyes. Ben caught the gun hard but couldn't knock it free of Jackie's grip. Ben swung the carafe back, trying to connect with Jackie's head, but missed. Jackie leveled the gun to fire again and Ben caught his hand, raised the gun toward the ceiling.

"I'm going to kill you—" Ben shouted.

Vochek got up and ran toward the bedroom.

Jackie grunted in fury, started to wrench his hand from Ben's grip.

With the other hand, frantic, Ben thumbed the pour control on the hot carafe and dumped coffee on Jackie's groin. Jackie shrieked and tried to jump back through the wall. Ben slammed the carafe into Jackie's face. Hot coffee splashed Ben's hand. He didn't feel pain.

Jackie's face contorted in rage. He bent and Ben grabbed

the gun, but Jackie kept his grip. Screaming with fury, he slapped the gun into Ben's face, once, twice, as Ben fought to keep a grip on the pistol.

Don't let go don't let go, he thought.

Ben fell to his knees, his forehead bleeding, his cheek cut. Jackie wrenched the pistol from Ben's hold and swung it toward him.

The sound of the shot boomed and a hole appeared in Jackie's hand, a nickel-sized coin of gore, and then Vochek shot him again, in the stomach, and Jackie folded, dropping the gun.

Vochek stood over Pritchard, the gun Ben had surrendered to her in her hands. "Get his gun," she yelled.

Jackie lunged for the gun as Ben grabbed it and Vochek shot him again, in the chest. He shrieked and curled into a ball. Ben locked the gun on Jackie's head.

"Where is Hector? Where's his target?"

"Ah, please," Jackie moaned. "Hurts, hurts."

"We'll get you a doctor, but tell us where's the target," Ben said.

"Nicky, Nicky," Jackie sobbed. Spit and snot flew from his face and he gagged, writhing on the carpet. "No, no, no…" and then a broken hum. His eyes widened in pain, then he went still.

Ben stood. His mind felt wiped clean, blank, his body shivering with adrenaline. No. This wasn't over. He reached into Jackie's pocket. He found car keys, a pass card, and a scrap of paper with the hotel's address. No cell phone. He took the keys.

Vochek knelt by Pritchard, touched her throat. "Ben… call the front desk."

Ben checked the poor waiter, slumped by the cart. He

was dead as well. "This is Hector cleaning house," Ben said. "Shutting up Pritchard and you before you became a bigger threat to him, before you started questioning his tactics and results. He doesn't need you anymore. We have to find him. Now. Call the CIA. Tell them their safe house is in danger. Or the police."

"We don't even know where to tell the police to go. And calling the CIA, they'll have to confirm my identity. That's a lot of bureaucracy to navigate."

"Check her cell phone. Check the page of phone records I got on her. Someone at the CIA told her about the operation so she wouldn't interfere. There has to be a record."

Vochek nodded.

"I have another idea." He closed his hand around Jackie's car keys. He stood and hurried down the hallway, past a couple of frightened guests who'd heard the fight. "I'll be right back," he lied.

"Ben!" Vochek yelled at his back. "Stop! Where are you going?"

The breeze outside the hotel was damp and cool. Ben took in a bracing breath as he exited via the hotel's fire exit into a narrow brick alley. Sirens flashed, the police already pulling into the front of the Hotel Marquis de Lafayette, blue and red light painting the bricks bright as a child's room.

Ben put Jackie's gun in his pocket. He went down the bricked alleyway by the hotel, toward the closest parking lot. He thumbed the remote on the keys, kept at it until he hit the third row and a rental Chevrolet winked its lights.

He searched the seat, the glove compartment. Jackie was from Belfast; presumably he didn't know New Orleans well. There should be a page of directions, maybe, that Ben could backtrack, follow to where Jackie came from.

Nothing. The scrap in his pocket carried only the address of the hotel, no directions.

Then he noticed the GPS monitor. He touched the screen and the GPS purred to life. He studied the controls, tapped a button that displayed the last search. Which was for the Hotel Marquis de Lafayette. He went to the previous address. It was in Metairie.

Okay, then off to Metairie.

But caution made him pause. *Think like Jackie.* Where would Jackie have been before coming to execute the hit? Perhaps at wherever the Cellar group convened, with Hector, and they wouldn't be there now. He checked again. Up another address, to a warehouse near Louis Armstrong International. Then the next address, as he retraced the list, was that of the car rental company.

He had to choose where to go. He tried to think like Hector. If things went bad, or the Cellar people didn't accept Hector or believe his story, then Hector would need a place to hide. Maybe it was the warehouse.

Or maybe these were directions summoned by the last customer to rent the car. He could waste precious time on a pointless drive.

Warehouse. Hector Global had deployed a security force here in the chaotic, sad aftermath of Katrina. Near the airport. He remembered contracts signed and negotiated, the difficulty of tracking down the owners of the property in the exodus after the storm, when Hector Global wanted to rent the space.

It was all he had to go on.

He clicked back to the warehouse map, studied it, and pulled out of the lot. He switched on the cell phone he'd stolen from the pilot. The battery showed the phone's charge was nearly at its end. He had no recharger. He called Pilgrim.

43

MUCH OF THE LAKEVIEW neighborhood remained a ghost town—very few homes newly rebuilt, others razed, far more abandoned. The shells had taken on the look of abstract monuments. It had been a myth that only the poor neighborhoods of New Orleans drowned in Katrina; this was a district of what had been nice middle- and upper-middle-class homes. Pilgrim thought if he blinked in the moonlight—now fading behind heavy clouds—he could see how pretty the yards and the homes had once been. Statues remained in a few backyards of the ruins, arms and legs broken, bodies slanted and bowed as though praying for mercy to their own stone-faced deity. Suffocated oaks and Japanese maples stood, dead, ignored, tottering like nature's own memorial to her fury.

As they approached the lakefront on West End Boulevard, Pilgrim had to back off from the cars, turn into a lot, hold position, then hurry to keep their taillights in sight, then fall back again. Finally they turned onto a street. He drove past, then turned right onto Robert E. Lee and circled back and turned into the neighborhood, a few streets south of the road they had taken.

His cell phone chirped.

"The Cellar is attacking a CIA safe house." Ben sounded frantic. "It's a training place for a group of Arab recruits being infiltrated as spies back into terrorist networks."

That traitor, Pilgrim thought. He felt hatred lick through his heart. *No, stay cool,* he told himself.

"But I don't know where the house is…"

Pilgrim said, "No worries. I'm there. Ben, you did awesome."

"Listen. I think I know where Hector's based here. A warehouse, by the airport." He gave Pilgrim the address. "Vochek's trying to warn the CIA. I'm going to this warehouse to see if I can find evidence against him. Or do you want me to come help you?"

"I'll take care of it."

"Pilgrim—"

Pilgrim hung up. Nothing more to say and no time to waste. *Ben, you scored a big one.* He remembered when he had told Ben, with a hard ugliness in his words, *You don't have what it takes.* He had been wrong.

He thought: *Me saving the CIA, that's a definition of irony. I get to go fight for the CIA when they wouldn't lift a finger to spring me out of an Indonesian jail unless I joined their dirty secret group.*

Full circle. This was the end result of his life. So different from what he'd thought it would be. He remembered the joy in his stepdad's face when he'd graduated from school, the pride he felt when he joined the Agency, the mix of shock and awe at his daughter's birth, the warmth of new life being held in his unworthy arms. Everything then brimmed with promise. If he had just not gone after Gumalar in an attempt to protect his family—if he had not

missed with his shot on the Dragon through that window—
if he hadn't gotten caught by the police.

If. If. If.

No more ifs. There was only what was, his beginning
fading as though it belonged to a different man, what was
his likely end at hand. He was on a collision course with
the man who had undone his life. He had no illusions about
getting out of this mess alive.

Pilgrim parked in an empty lot and slipped out of the
car. He cut through two yards between houses under construction and saw a street of mostly razed lots. The grass
grew high on two of the lots, and he darted low through the
growth.

Half a block ahead, he heard a plink. A streetlight, probably installed after the storm, died. Before the light vanished, he saw a large home, ample grounds surrounding
it, a newly built stone wall, set a bit away from the other
homes and lots.

The target.

The Cellar team would be fast. The safe house probably
had reinforced doors and windows, but they would deactivate the alarm systems and they would be in and murdering and out in sixty seconds. In the house, one dim light
gleamed on a second floor, someone unable to sleep or
standing guard.

He'd never slept well while on training; too eager to
learn, to soak up data and techniques and analysis. He felt
an instant kindred spirit with the night owl in the target
house.

He hurried back to the van. Shot out the lock, yanked
open the door. A man inside, headphones on, turned toward
him. He went for his gun and Pilgrim stopped him with a

kick in the gut. The guy collapsed, airless. Pilgrim care-fully deactivated the headphones and wrapped the cable around the guy's neck. He tightened it hard into the throat's flesh, then loosened it a bit for a display of mercy, tightened it again while he asked his question.

"How many of them on the attack?"

The guy struggled and Pilgrim yanked the cable tighter. Turning purple, the guy held up six fingers. Hector and five more Cellar agents, not counting this one.

"Guns? Explosives?"

"Guns, knives. Nothing heavier." The guy choked.

"What's your call sign? Don't lie to me. If I give the wrong sign and I have to run, I'll kill you on my way out. Right now you're getting to live." He eased up enough on the cable and the guy said, "Strict numbers. I'm Seven."

"By the way, I didn't kill Teach. You get out of this alive and I don't, kill Hector for me." He slammed the guy's head against the corner of the equipment table, twice, and the guy slumped unconscious.

Pilgrim's own clothes were not night stalker ready—he wore khakis and a pale shirt. The unconscious man wore a black turtleneck and black pants. Pilgrim relieved him of his dark clothes; they were tight on Pilgrim's big frame but they fit well enough.

Pilgrim took the guy's gun and knife, fished an earpiece from the curl of his ear, and tucked it into his own. He activated it and listened to the Cellar chatter as the team deployed. One and Two had deactivated the perimeter secu-rity system and were approaching the house, to deal with its alarm box. Which meant two of them should be close to the low stone wall, holding back to watch the group's rear, ready to join the others when the alarm system was cut.

For an instant Pilgrim considered revving the van, laying on the horn, creating a disturbance to awaken everyone in the house. But that would trigger a retreat, all of them heading straight for him. He'd be outnumbered and outgunned. And if he went live on the com network and informed them that Hector killed Teach—there was the chance they might not believe him. He had killed two other Cellar agents in self-defense, but when it was dark and tense, one could not always have rational discussions with heavily armed people.

So he'd have to do this the hard way.

He slipped out of the van.

You're going to die. He was fairly sure of the outcome. Six now against one, and if anyone inside the CIA safe house was armed—and no doubt they were—they were just as likely to shoot him.

Do what's necessary. He had done it for ten years, and Ben kept telling him that it was fine, it was understandable. Ben was one of those people who thought dirty jobs had their place in the cogs of society; as long as his own hands didn't get bloodied, it was okay. Lots of people thought that way. But now Pilgrim faced killing his own colleagues to keep them from doing a serious and harmful wrong to the country, and it wasn't their fault.

Do what you have to do.

His heart weighed like a stone.

He listened to the silence. No one saying anything, which meant they were waiting for the alarm system to go down. He crept from the van—every streetlight had been doused. The road was dark, the moon hiding its face.

He studied the length of the wall. Five feet high, a foot wide. He got close to the house's main driveway. A spot along here was a likely station for whoever was ordered to hold back—enough to cover a retreat for those at the alarm box, far back enough to see any encroaching danger.

He stopped ten feet shy of the driveway, listened. After a minute he heard, four feet to his left, the faintest rustle of a heel shifting weight in grass.

He moved back, heard a whispered "Copy" as someone announced they were nearly through the decode sequence for the alarm, and went over the wall.

Pilgrim practically landed on one of them, a woman, his feet knocking into her back, nailing her to the grass. The other was a man, short and powerfully built. Pilgrim grabbed his head, slammed it against the stone with three brutal blows, breaking the man's nose, savaging his cheek. The man went down; Pilgrim dropped him. He knelt by the woman; she was semiconscious and he struck the flat of his palm against her neck, knocking her out.

He scooped their earpieces from their ears. Three down, four to go.

"Five, Four, report." Hector's baritone in his earpiece. The noise of the takedown drew his attention.

"This is Seven," Pilgrim whispered. "I see them, they are heading back to the van. Four is tapping at ear. I'll check their pieces."

A pause, as though his whisper was being judged. "Tell them to get back here."

"Copy." Pilgrim ran low and hard, moving toward a small stone outbuilding where a driveway dead-ended. He had to neutralize the team: three more agents, two of them working on the alarm.

And where was Hector?

"We're found," he heard a woman say, both in his

earpiece and in his ear, and a kick hammered into his chest. She'd been behind the outbuilding and he'd been careless. Her blow staggered him. A flash of silver danced in the spare moonlight; she had a knife, trying to avoid the noise of a gun that would rouse the house. She slashed at him with the blade, slicing through the borrowed black turtleneck and scoring across his chest. But she overshot on the blow, tried to recover by launching another powerhouse kick at his face. He caught her leg high and shoved her hard into the brick building she'd hidden behind. Hushed and sudden chatter from the others filled his ear.

They knew he was there.

"Alarm down," a man announced.

"Hit now," Hector ordered.

Pilgrim fractured his attacker's arm with the next blow, but better than killing her, he thought. She dropped the knife and contained her scream—brave and well trained, trying not to alarm the target. He hit her twice, hard, with respect and regret, and she went down, maybe not knocked out but hurt enough to be out of the fight.

Two more Cellar agents and Hector remained. Pilgrim was at the house's side porch and he figured the assault would open at the back, away from the street.

He heard the muted sound of a shot hitting steel, a reinforced door. The opportunity for stealth had passed; he was too late. He spoke into the earpiece. "Hector killed Teach. Not me. Shoot him. Shoot *him*."

No answer. No acknowledgment. Two more shots.

"You're not killing terrorists. You're attacking a CIA safe house. He's a traitor," Pilgrim said. He broke into a hard run. "Four are down, none are dead. I'm not the liar. Stand down."

Nothing. They were ignoring him, or Hector had silenced the communications network. He could see movement inside the windows.

Hector and the Cellar were already inside.

They knew he was here; one would be watching the door for him while the others began the kills. The door was a trap. So he fired rounds at a back window, bullets slamming into the reinforced glass. He vaulted up the porch steps. Those inside would think he was stupid and heading for the nearly unbreakable glass he was trying to shatter with his gunfire. He kept firing at the pane but at the last moment he leapt through the doorway.

The feint worked. He hit the floor, rolled out of the back hallway into the dining room, his gun spitting, and he caught one Cellar agent waiting for him close to the window, in the knees, the agent firing back, a bullet needling into the meat of Pilgrim's shoulder. He rolled hard, under a table, fired again, screaming without thinking, "CIA! CIA!"

He was once, and always would be, and now he was again.

A bullet smacked into the table he was under, fired from his left. He could see one body, in T-shirt and pajama pants, on the kitchen floor. They'd already killed one. He shot the agent closest to the window again in the leg, and the wounded agent staggered into the kitchen.

A hallway phone began to ring. *Thanks, Vochek, you got their attention. Too late.*

A second Cellar agent had also made a retreat into the kitchen, firing at Pilgrim from an awkward angle, pinning him down. Bullets cracked into the back of the pine chairs at the dinner table.

"Abort!" Pilgrim yelled in the pause between the shots. "Hector killed Teach!"

Silence. The pause lengthened and he risked bolting from the table down the hallway.

As he ran toward the end of the hall, the lights came on.

Pilgrim could see on the stairwell a young man no more than twenty-three: black-haired, wearing eyeglasses, mouth twisted in fright, holding a Glock with trembling hands.

Hector crouched at the bottom of the stairs, aiming at the kid.

Pilgrim fired and the bullet sizzled hard into Hector's gun, the impact powering the weapon from his hand. Hector ran into a room beyond the stairs, Pilgrim firing, the back of Hector's jacket tearing as a bullet hit him between neck and arm. But Hector kept going, out the front.

The young Arab swiveled his gun toward Pilgrim, firing blindly in panic.

Pilgrim retreated back down the hallway and out the back door. The remaining two Cellar agents had fled the kitchen and were running across the yard, the uninjured one carrying the man Pilgrim had shot.

Pilgrim hit the grass, ran around the house toward the stone wall.

A blast of gunfire erupted from the house's upper windows. The CIA trainees were awake and responding. Bullets churned the lawn by his feet. They were shooting at him in the darkness, thinking he was the enemy.

In the sudden gleam of the van's headlights on the street, Pilgrim saw Hector hauling himself over the stone wall.

Lights flickered on at the safe house. Upstairs, downstairs.

Pilgrim hit the stone wall, vaulted over it. Agony flamed his shoulder. The Cellar van kicked to life, and in the rising glow of lights from the safe house he saw the van tech, not Hector, at the wheel, slowing long enough for the woman with the broken arm to stagger inside.

Where was Hector?

The van surged at him, pedal to the floor, closing on him, and he dodged the impact, jumping into high weeds, a bullet snipping off the tops of the grasses by his head. He went low and ran and the van accelerated past him, took off.

Four lots further down, a car started on a cracked driveway that lacked a house. No lights.

Hector. Pilgrim turned and dashed through the yards, the empty lots, hauled himself over a newly built fence, reached his own car.

He revved back onto West End, saw Hector's car in the distance. Hector turned onto Veterans Boulevard heading west, his car's headlights coming alive. Pilgrim followed long enough to believe that Hector was not heading back to the Cellar safe house in Metairie but further west, toward the airport.

Toward where Ben thought Hector had a hiding hole.

Run home, Pilgrim thought. His arm ached. He steered with his elbow, did a one-handed click through the call log to the stolen cell phone Ben had, dialed.

No answer.

Run home, he thought, *so Ben and I can kill you.*

44

Bᴇɴ ᴛᴜʀɴᴇᴅ ᴏɴᴛᴏ ᴀ darkened street near Louis Armstrong International. Warehousing and storage facilities lined the road. He saw signs for FEMA and a bevy of government contractors, some of whom had once been clients of his.

The address he had was for an entire complex of warehouses, with a darkened, empty guard station. But the wooden arm was down. He noticed there was a passkey reader. He tried the passkey he'd taken from Jackie and the arm lifted and he drove into the complex.

A scattering of cars sat in the parking lot slots near the various warehouses—there were at least four large warehouses. The one he wanted, B, lay dark, no cars close by. He parked Jackie's rental near the door—let Hector see Jackie was back, safe and sound. The sign on the door indicated this was "MLS Limited." The name of one of the shell companies used by Hector; he must have rented the space in this name, not Hector Global. Ben tried the two keys on Jackie's ring that didn't have the rental car company tag on it. The second one worked. With his heart in his throat, he eased open the door.

Darkness. He locked the door behind him; it closed with

a soft click. He held the gun in one hand. Even if he died now, Vochek would have enough to put pressure on Hector.

But he was not going to wait on juries and lawyers and trials to avenge Emily.

Ben took a shambling step forward in the darkness, hand out. He touched wall, found the hinge and frame of the door. He slid fingers along cool steel and closed them around a doorknob. He stepped into a darkened hallway, where a gleam of light lined the frame of a big set of double doors. He headed for them, his heart pounding loud enough, he thought, to echo against the walls.

He found a light switch, flicked it on. He tried the pilot's cell phone again—the battery was completely drained. Useless. He began to explore.

Half the warehouse space was a maze of cubicles, thrown up in apparent haste; the other half held nothing. Most of the cubicles were empty, bare of computer or chair. He went to the largest office, guessing it belonged to a senior manager. He broke the door open with a fire extinguisher.

The laptop inside wasn't passworded. He began to search the network's file hierarchy.

Most of MLS's business seemed tied to contracts for rebuilding government offices in New Orleans and the Mississippi Gulf Coast. Nothing of interest.

He searched for the name "Reynolds." Found payment spreadsheets financing months of software development. He picked up the desk phone, called the Hotel Marquis de Lafayette, asked to be connected to suite 1201.

"Vochek?"

"Ben, where are you?" She sounded furious.

He gave her the address. "I found Hector's records of underwriting Reynolds's research. He funded a lot of stuff through one of these shell companies. You should get over here." He gave her the address and she hung up.

What else was here? He thought of what he'd found about MLS when he hunted through the business databases back in the Blarney's bar. Its founding had been a few months before Emily's death, along with the maze of other shell companies that were seemingly connected to it. He opened the e-mail database, hunted for messages from Hector from the time that the company was founded. He found several, searched through them. One included a spreadsheet from Hector with a note: *Here are payments we need made, please do electronically only.* He clicked on the file. It opened.

It listed financial transactions for services rendered and services received, for a period of two weeks. One was a transaction marked one day after Emily's death. Notes read on the transaction were a mishmash: *retainer, travel (two connections, DFW), Agency handling bonus, completion bonus.*

He blinked. *Completion bonus.* No. He clicked to see who the payment had been made to.

Bile rose in his throat.

The door opened, slammed. He heard footsteps stumbling across the concrete. "Jackie! Jackie, I'm shot...we have to get out of here."

Ben stood. Hector leaned against the far wall. Easing out of a black leather jacket, his back wet with blood, gasping.

"Jackie's not here." Ben aimed Jackie's gun at Hector. His voice didn't sound like his own anymore. Cool. Quiet. As though rage had reached a level that did not demand anger or screaming or confusion as to why a tragedy had destroyed his life.

Now there was only what had to be done.

"Ben." Hector raised his gun and pulled the trigger. Clicked on empty. Hector closed his eyes. "It's damaged, anyway." He dropped the gun with a clatter. And with a black smile, like he didn't need the gun. It made Ben's skin prickle.

"Even I know to count my bullets now," Ben said. And he had two left. He'd checked the clip on the drive over to the warehouse.

"Ben. We're both in trouble. But we don't have to be..."

"You were never the negotiator, I was. You can't sweet-talk me, Sam, just tell me what I want to know."

Even with a gun aimed at him, Sam Hector did not care for orders. He couldn't keep the frown of disdain from his face. "Ben, you listen to me—"

"No. Just tell me where Pilgrim is."

Hector stayed on the wall. "Full of CIA bullets. Dead. But you don't have to be. The CIA will want you dead, too, Ben. I can save you. We can come to a deal..."

"No, we can't. I'm turning you over to Homeland Security, and Agent Vochek is going to make her career by bringing you down."

"Don't be so sure—"

"Jackie missed. Vochek put him down."

Ben could almost hear the mental gears shift in Hector's brain. "Listen, Ben, how many laws have you broken in this insane pursuit? Dozens. You're going to need serious help, I can help you." He slowed his speech as though he could double the persuasive power of each word. "We can help each other..."

On the other side of the warehouse a window shattered.

"You never told me why you killed Emily," Ben said. "She

must have found out about the multiple companies you were setting up, that you wanted to have no trace back to Hector Global. The expansion of your dirty work." He heard footsteps behind him. "You explain something to me. I found a payment to the Cellar's financial front, Sparta Consulting, from one of your sham companies the day after she died..."

"Ben?" Pilgrim. His shoulder bloodied, he staggered into the warehouse holding a gun. He came close to Ben, less than five feet away. He aimed his gun at Hector.

"Did you stop the attack?" Ben's voice rang hard as iron.

"Yes. Would you please shoot him? Then maybe you can patch me up again." Pilgrim stumbled.

"I will. When you tell me who killed Emily."

"Hector did..." Pilgrim said.

"No." Ben shook his head. "Hector's buddies in the CIA wanted her dead because the sham companies Hector set up were for them and she found out. They gave the dirty job to Sparta Consulting, which means they gave it to Teach. I found the payment. I have to know who inside the Cellar killed her."

"Maui," Hector said, a helpful tone. "Two years ago. A single shot through a kitchen window. I have pictures a friend in the CIA gave me."

Pilgrim's face, pale from loss of blood, went the color of bone. "What?"

"Who killed her, Pilgrim?" Ben said.

"Ben, I don't know..."

"I think you do know." Hector's voice was iron. "Flight through Dallas on the payment schedule, Ben. I think you know who likes to fly through Dallas, see his kid whenever he can."

Ben's eyes went wide, the gun shook in his hand. The

silence in the warehouse pressed like the dead air inside a sealed coffin.

"Ben..." Pilgrim tried to say. "Maui?"

"Did you kill a woman in Maui two years ago?" Ben whispered. "Answer me."

Pilgrim opened and shut his mouth.

"Teach wrote up a list of all the jobs for me. That's when I knew Emily was a Cellar job," Hector said. "I didn't order her death, Ben, my friends at the CIA did. They sent their best to do the worst."

In the Dallas apartment, Hector had started to speak of Emily, and he'd said, *You mean who?* and raised the gun to shoot Ben, and Teach had launched herself at him... before he could finish.

Ben closed his eyes, for just a half second, then turned the gun toward Pilgrim. "Drop your gun. Get over by the wall. With him. Right now!"

"Ben, I...I..." Pilgrim stopped. He dropped the gun, put a hand to his forehead.

Hector spoke in a low voice, and to Ben it sounded like bones cracking. "Teach was told by one of her taskmasters that Emily was selling secrets to China. That she was meeting a Chinese agent in Maui to pass Agency secrets she'd learned through my contracts with the Agency. She had to be taken out."

"Is this true?" Ben yelled. He remembered Pilgrim's litany of sins: *A couple of times I killed people selling secrets to the Chinese.*

Pilgrim looked up from the concrete and met his stare. "Yes, Ben. I...yes. I killed her."

Ben thought his head would explode from the wave of pain. "You...you..."

"I had no idea," Pilgrim said. "They gave me an address and her description. Nothing else about her."

Ben thought: *He didn't even know her name.*

"He pulled the trigger, Ben, that's all that matters," Hector said.

Pilgrim swallowed, tried to speak, failed, then managed. "I...I was told to wait for a phone call. It would mean to make it look random, shoot out some nearby windows, then go ahead."

You have to kill him. What Ben had thought in the fury of the fight with Jackie, the thoughts crowded into his head like a cancer.

"Ben," Hector said, "your only hope is to make a deal with me. What do you want in compensation? I'll give it to you. Bringing me down won't bring Emily back. Your career's over now, you know that. You may be facing prison time. My contacts in the government can pardon you. I have the power to save you, Ben; he has nothing. You just have to stay quiet."

"You stay quiet," Ben said. He kept his stare locked on Pilgrim.

"My hands are clean, his are bloodied."

"You do what's necessary, Ben," Pilgrim said quietly.

The word *necessary* burned Ben's brain like a hot iron against flesh. *You do the necessary work,* he'd reassured Pilgrim, more than once, during the past few days. His chest ached.

Ben steadied the gun on Pilgrim. "You shot my wife to death." Every word was ice in Ben's throat.

Pilgrim nodded, as though a noose already decorated his neck. Slowly. He closed his eyes, his mouth worked.

"Ben, shoot him," Hector said. "Nothing can bring back

Emily. But you don't have to let him live. Shoot him, you're a hero. You've killed a rogue CIA agent. The government will exonerate you from all charges."

Pilgrim made a square with fingers over his heart. "Your aim sucks. Hit inside here and it's done."

Ben fired. The bullet caught the chest perfectly, and Hector jerked and whimpered at the spreading crimson blossom on his shirt.

"Pilgrim killed her," Ben said, "but you gave the order."

Hector sagged to the floor, expression blanking, a gurgle and then he was done, the bullet perfect in the chest.

Ben raised the gun again at Pilgrim. He still held the square for vengeance over his heart.

One bullet left. Ben's grip tightened on the gun. Decide.

"Put your hands down," Ben said, "I'm not going to kill you. They lied to you about her."

Pilgrim lowered his hands. He took a step toward Ben. "I'm so sorry. Because you are my friend."

"God help you." The gun trembled in Ben's hand. Then he lowered it and turned away from Pilgrim.

"Ben…"

"Get the hell away from me. Please. Just go."

The door busted inward. Vochek and four men in Homeland Security windbreakers rushed the room, guns out and ready.

Ben and Pilgrim froze, five feet apart. The guns swiveled on Ben, the only one obviously armed.

"Ben, drop your weapon," Vochek ordered.

Ben obeyed. The pistol clattered to the concrete.

"Move away from the gun," one of the men ordered and Ben took a step back.

"Pilgrim, on the ground, now," Vochek said. She softened her tone. "Please."

Pilgrim didn't move. He ignored the men and Vochek. "I thought we won. I thought we finally won... How many bullets left, Ben?"

"One," Ben said. "But don't."

"Shut up and get on the ground!" one of the agents yelled.

Pilgrim looked straight into Ben's eyes. "Necessary," he said, then jumped for Ben's gun. His fingers closed around it, lifted it from the floor. The shots cannoned and echoed, an awful salute. Pilgrim staggered against the wall, sliding down while blood smeared the gray concrete behind him.

Ben grabbed Pilgrim and caught him before he sprawled on the floor. Held him through the rattle of his final breaths. Then lowered him to the ground.

KHALED'S REPORT— VIRGINIA

I HAVE NOT BEEN ASKED to write my thoughts for a report for four months, since the attack on the house in New Orleans. Perhaps it is time again for another analysis of my handwriting by the folks in Langley, to see if I have lost my nerve to stay with my job.

At first, when I realized the house was being breached— I thought it was yet another test. We have been tested so thoroughly, without the proverbial safety nets. Then the gunfire simply sounded far too real. I hurried down the steps and I saw an older man, he raised a gun at me and stupidly I froze. I will never make that mistake again. Then a second man shot the gun from the older man's hand, and I shot at the second man because I was scared to death.

The man who saved me—I will never forget his face. Determined, courageous, but hard. Unyielding, like stone. It is the face I try to wear as I do my job.

I wasn't sure that we would be permitted to begin our work—there was of course fear that we had been compromised, our names found, to be fed back to the terrorist networks we seek to destroy. But then we were assured that everyone who had found out about our names was dead. The people who attacked us were misled. I do not know what happened to our attackers who escaped; we were all moved that morning to another house, this one in Atlanta. There we waited to know our fates.

Now I am back for a short visit. The terrorist rivals to Blood of Fire, the scum who paid Khaled Murad to kill my brothers with a bomb, have cells across Europe. I have infiltrated such a cell in Paris—with a certain amount of ease, as they believe that I think my brothers were cut down by the Israelis and Americans and that I am a highly motivated convert to their cause. The cell believes I am doing their filthy work by scouring bombing locations: they want to start a wave of terror attacks against banks and stock brokerages in America, Saudi Arabia, Jordan, and France, to weaken the economies, to fray the strength of alliances. I expect to have the details soon, and if I do my job right, the attacks will never happen and an interconnection of cells, from Paris to New York and beyond, will be compromised and destroyed.

And no other innocent families will have to suffer. That drives me, keeps me sharp, keeps me alive until the work is done.

They tell me if my cover and my name are blown, they will give me a new life, protect me. Perhaps. They might just send me to work somewhere else. Which is fine, as once the taste of deception gets in your blood—it is nearly unimaginable to live without it.

I have to go back to work. I remember the man's face, and I hope I wear a similar mask of strength and resolve.

45

A MONTH AFTER NEW ORLEANS, Ben Forsberg sat on a park bench under the shade of a pine tree in Tyler, Texas. He was waiting for the girl and her mother to walk by; he had shadowed them for a few days, carefully, so that they didn't notice him watching them. Picking the right moment to say hello.

The east Texas summer was in full, brutal bloom, and the humidity and heat beat like a whip. But a temperamental wind, rising and fading, offered a touch of relief. The park was full. Dogs walked beside their masters, boys sliced the sky with Frisbees, picnickers lounged in the shade, couples strolled under the pines.

Then here came the mother and daughter, holding a kite. Laughing.

He walked and then stopped in front of them. "Mrs. Choate?"

The woman froze and it took her a good five seconds to break her silence. "Well, I once was. I'm Kimberly Dawson now."

The girl gaped at him.

Ben flicked an awkward smile. "My name is Ben Forsberg. I knew your husband Randall in Indonesia."

"Oh, " the woman said.

"What was said about him wasn't true. He wasn't a drug smuggler. He was framed. I thought you should know the truth."

The two were silent. The teenager trembled, as if she might turn and run.

"Is this a sick joke?" Mrs. Dawson said. "It's not at all funny…"

"No joke. Please, just give me a minute. Tamara, you look like your dad."

"I know," Tamara said. "I've seen pictures."

Mrs. Dawson stepped closer to the girl. "Did you want something, Mr. Forsberg?" She put a protective arm around the girl, unhappy with the past reaching out toward them, in the sunlight of a perfect summer day.

"I thought Tamara might like to have a keepsake of her father's." He handed the girl a sketchbook, small and black. A hole marred the lower right corner. "I'm sorry it's damaged."

Tamara opened the book and gasped at the sketches of herself, from babyhood onward, her face captured in perfect details. She put a hand over her mouth.

"How did he know what I would look like?" Tamara flipped through the pages. "Mom, these drawings, they're amazing…" She stopped at the drawing of herself sitting on a park bench, in the cooling shade of the pines. Stared at the paper, and then up at the park around her, as if it could not be. Realizing what the picture meant, looking up the hill to see where the man must have stood and watched.

"Good imagination," Mrs. Dawson said in a voice tinged with frost. "Do you work for my late husband's company, Mr. Forsberg?"

He sensed she knew something of Randall's work for the CIA. "No—I was just his friend." He leaned down to the girl. "Tamara, I didn't know your father for very long, but I know that he loved you very much. You can see it in the sketches, his love for you. And I know he always wanted to do the right thing. I know...he would have loved to have his life with you. I really wish he could have. Everything would have been different." Everything. Pilgrim's life. Ben's life.

Tamara closed the book, folded her fingers around it. She seemed too stunned to smile or cry. "Thank you."

"You're welcome," Ben said to them both and walked away, out of the shadow of the pines, into the bright sunlight, into his beginning.

ACKNOWLEDGMENTS

Many thanks to Mitch Hoffman, Lindsey Rose, Ben Sevier, Brian Tart, Lisa Johnson, Erika Imranyi, David Shelley, Ursula Mackenzie, Jenny Fry, Thalia Proctor, Nathalie Morse, Kara Welsh, Kristen Weber, Peter Ginsberg, Shirley Stewart, Holly Frederick, Dave Barbor, Nathan Bransford, Joyce and Al Preisser, Phil Hunt, MD, and Charlyne Cooper.

Special thanks to Christine Wiltz, a wonderful writer and guide to New Orleans, and to my mother, Elizabeth Norrid, my guide to the Dallas suburbs.

And always, heartfelt thanks to Leslie, Charles, and William.

When a beautiful woman asks for his
help, ex-CIA agent Sam Capra becomes
caught in a battle with the most dangerous
enemy ever—a man who owns the people
who run the world...

Please turn this page
for a sneak peek at

DOWNFALL

1

———◦⟨◉⟩◦———

Wednesday, November 3, afternoon

San Francisco, California

The simplest beginnings can unravel a life. A family. A world.

In this case, chewing gum.

Diana Keene reached into her mom's ugly new purse in the middle of their argument to snatch a slice of spearmint. She saw three cell phones hidden at the bottom of the purse.

One pink, one blue, one green. Cheap models she'd never seen before, not like the smartphone Mom kept glued to her side at all times, befitting a public relations executive.

"And since you'll be running the company while I'm gone," Mom was saying, her back to her daughter while she stuffed a sweater into her luggage, "no sauntering into the office at nine, Diana. Be there by seven thirty. Give yourself time to scan the news feeds from the East Coast."

Diana grabbed the gum, stepped away from the purse, and considered whether or not to confront her mother in her little white lie. She decided to dance around the edges.

"I don't think it's healthy to go without a cell phone for

two weeks." Diana crossed her arms, staring at her mother's back. She unwrapped the gum, slid the stick into her mouth. "What if I need you?"

"You'll survive." Her mother, Janice, zipped up her small suitcase, turned to face her daughter with a smile.

"What if a client throws a fit? Or I do something wrong?"

"Deal with it. You'll survive." Janice straightened up and smiled at her daughter.

"Mom—what if I need—" and then Diana broke off, ashamed. She stared past her mother's shoulder, out at the stunning view of San Francisco Bay, the hump of Alcatraz, the distant stretch of the Golden Gate. It was a cloudless day, the early haze burned away, the blue of the sky bright. *Need what? Need you to keep running my life for me?*

"Need money?" Mom, as she often did, finished the sentence for her but misinterpreted what she meant. "Diana, you're a grown woman with a good job. You can survive for two weeks without any"—and here Mom did her air quotes, bending her fingers—"emergency loans."

"You're right." *Why are you lying to me, Mom?* she thought. "Where is this no-contact retreat again?"

"New Mexico."

"And I have no way to contact you—none at all?" *Like on these three cheap phones?*

"Cell phones are forbidden. You could call the lodge and leave a message, I suppose," Janice said, but in a tone that made it clear that she didn't want her Bikram yoga or her bird-watching or her organic lunch interrupted. "The whole point is to get away from the world, sweetheart."

Mom stuck with the lie, and Diana felt her stomach twist. "This just isn't like you, withdrawing so completely from the world. And from your work. And from me."

"Yes, I'm a workaholic, sweetheart, and it's made me tired and sick. I'm ready for a break, and I'm ready for you to be fine with it."

Diana thought, *Confront her with the lie. And then she knows you snooped in her purse like a kid would, and you're twenty-three, not thirteen, and...maybe Mom has a good reason.* She thought of the hours her mother had worked, everything she'd done for Diana. In the car. She'd ask her about the phones in the car.

"I'm ready."

Diana jingled her keys. "Fine, let's go."

Mom's town house was the entire top floor of the building. They took the elevator down and walked across the building's small lawn (a rarity in San Francisco), through the heavy metal gate to Green Street. Diana put her mother's bag in the back of the Jaguar that Janice had bought her for her last birthday. Diana drove out of the lovely neighborhood of Russian Hill. Janice talked about what needed to be done at work while she was gone: account reviews, pitching stories on clients to the leading business publications, preparing for client product launches in January. Diana kept waiting for her mom to stop lying.

They were ten minutes from the airport and Diana said, "Why are you taking three, yes three, cell phones to a place that forbids them?"

Her mother looked straight ahead and said, "So when they confiscate one, I'll have extras hidden away."

Diana laughed. "You troublemaker. Give me the numbers and I'll call you or text you."

"No. Don't call me." She looked out the window. "Just let me go do what I need to do and don't call me."

Her tone was far too serious. "Mom..."

"Do not call me, Diana, and frankly, I don't appreciate you rooting around in my purse. Stay out of my business."

The words were like knives, sharp, and to Diana's ears not like Mom.

The drive turned into a painful silence as Diana took the exit for the airport.

"I don't want this to be our good-bye, honey," Janice said.

"Are you really going on this retreat?" Diana pulled up to the curbside drop-off.

"Of course I am." Steel returned to Mom's voice. "I'll see you in two weeks. Maybe sooner if I get bored." Janice leaned over and gave Diana a kiss on the cheek, an awkward sideways hug.

You're still lying to me, Diana thought. *I don't believe you.*

"Love you, honey," Mom said. "More than you can know."

"Love you, too, Mom. I hope you have a great time at your *retreat.*"

Mom glanced at her. "Two weeks will let you make a splash at the office while I'm gone. Be smart, show everyone you deserve to be my successor. You'll be running it when I'm dead and gone." Janice's voice nearly broke on the last words, like she needed to clear her throat. She squeezed Diana's hand.

Diana didn't care for talk like that—for any suggestion of a Mom-free world. "I'll keep everything running smoothly."

Then Mom stepped out of the car, grabbed her small suitcase, and walked toward the terminal entrance.

Diana thought of jumping out of the car, running to her for one more hug, and thought, *No, I won't, because you're clearly lying to me and I want to know why.*

Her mother had never lied to her. The reason had to be big. Two weeks where Mom didn't want anyone to know where she was. She headed back toward the city. But not to her own apartment. Back to Russian Hill, back to Mom's.

Diana felt a cold tapping of terror down her spine, her imagination dancing with the possibilities behind her mother's lie.

Janice Keene watched her daughter, the only true good thing she had done in her life, drive away until Diana was gone from sight in the eddying swarm of cars, cabs, and limos.

Inside her purse the pink phone rang. She answered it.

A voice of a man, with a soft mixed accent of an American who'd spent much time in London, said, "You'll be traveling under the name Marian Atkins. Inside the lining of your purse is an appropriate ID. There'll be a package for you at your hotel when you arrive with what you need. Call me on this phone when the first job is done, and then destroy the phone. I'll call you then on the green phone. The blue phone for the last job."

"I understand."

"Remember you're doing it all for your daughter, Janice. And then you can rest easy."

"I know."

The man hung up. Janice Keene went to the ladies' room and tore open the lining of the purse and yes, there was a California driver's license and a credit card in the name of Marian Atkins. Attached was a sticky note with an airline and a confirmation number and a hotel name with another confirmation number. The purse had been delivered to her house yesterday via an overnight courier, from an address in New York.

Janice walked to one of the airline's self-service kiosks and tapped in the first number. The screen brought up an itinerary that informed her she was booked on a flight to Portland, Oregon. It spat out a boarding pass for Marian Atkins.

She collected the pass and walked with resolve toward the security lines.

Janice Keene was going to do what she must to ensure the world—that uncertain, awful, wonderful place—could never hurt her Diana. To be sure her daughter had a perfect life, just as perfect as the last seven years had been for her mother.

No matter who had to die.

2

Wednesday, November 3, afternoon

"Sam! I want to get married here!"

"Of course you do, darling," I said. I smiled at the venue's event planner as we walked through the large marble atrium of the Conover House, one of the grander spots to host a wedding or conference in San Francisco. The romantic grin on my face was the kind I'd worn when I got married for the first time. Mila's hand was clenched in mine, and her smile was dazzling. Pure bridal joy.

"Well, let me give you a tour," the planner said. She was a tall woman, fortyish, in a smart gray suit. She'd sized us up the moment we arrived—sans appointment with that hurried disregard of the truly moneyed—and we were dressed to kill. No pun intended.

"One thing first," I said.

"She will show us a cost estimate later, darling," Mila said, ever the impatient bride. She leaned in close to me, her hair smelling of lavender, her eyes dancing with mischief. "Whatever it is, I'm sure it will be worth it."

"My question isn't cost. It's security," I said. "You have security here, yes, during events?"

"Yes, of course, if that is a concern."

"It is." I didn't elaborate on a reason. I just kept my fake smile in place.

"We have a contract with a topflight security firm here. And a system of monitors and cameras throughout the building." She gestured up at a small camera in the top corner of the atrium. I flexed the smile for the camera's benefit.

"He is such the worrywart." Mila looked stunning in her dark, snug dress, every inch the giddy bride. She wore a ring on her hand, a lovely diamond, that sparkled grandly on her finger. "Now the building."

"One more question," I said. "You have cameras monitored, yes?"

"Yes. Our on-site team can respond. Or they're happy to work with your own security team, if you should have one."

"That's very reassuring," I said, and off we went on the tour of the beautiful old building, which had once been a very grand bank, the planner pointing out the venue's features and facilities.

"I am thinking," Mila exclaimed as we walked along the marble floors, "of a 1920s theme for the wedding. Sam, is that not brilliant?"

"Brilliant," I said. The architecture and decor certainly fit her idea. We were on the second floor by now, and I spotted a men's room as we headed toward a grand staircase leading to the third floor. "I'm feeling a bit unwell, please excuse me. You all go on, I'll catch up."

"He is so nervous to marry me," Mila said to the planner as I went through the men's room doors. "We have been through so much together, you see."

That was true. The door shut behind me. No cameras in here. I went into a stall, counted to sixty, and then I walked out and headed downstairs. The planner had already told us that most of the food service and administrative offices were on the first floor.

I assumed security was there as well. There might be a guard on duty, but there were no events being hosted right now, one conference having ended at noon. I tested the door marked SECURITY, lockpick at the ready.

But the door was unlocked.

I stepped inside. A small chamber, because they needed the real estate for food and rentals. Nine monitors set up to show various rooms and entrances of the Conover House. But no guard. Bathroom break?

One monitor was tuned to a cable news channel. The vice president of the United States had died last week from a sudden stroke, and conjecture about who the president would appoint as his successor was rampant. To me it sounded like a festival of endless talking heads. On the security monitors I saw Mila and the planner strolling on the third floor, and Mila pantomimed excitement to keep the planner focused on her, not on wondering where I was at or why I was taking so long in the bathroom.

A stack of DVDs stood on the rack, each in a jewel box, with a date and time range written on it, tied to a particular camera. The dates went back for a week. Liability issues, I thought. The venue wanted to protect itself. Because even among a well-heeled crowd, fights break out, people get drunk, tumbles happen down the stairs.

Or someone tries to commit a murder and fails.

I pulled one disc out of its jewel box for an evening three nights ago, from 8:00 P.M. to 10:00 P.M., for the main ballroom. I replaced it with a similar disc. The discs got reused, I figured, at the end of the week. I slid the jewel box home and slipped the original video disc into the small of my back, against my belt. My jacket hid it.

On the screen, Mila bounced on the tiptoes of her elegantly shod feet, enraptured with the thoughts of the perfect wedding reception.

The door opened. A guard, midtwenties, about my age, stepped in. He looked annoyed but not angry to see me. "Sir, you're not supposed to be in here."

"Sorry. I was getting a tour with my fiancée"—I pointed toward Mila on the screen—"and I had a security question that I didn't wish to ask in front of her while we're getting the tour for our wedding reception. The door was unlocked."

"Yes, sir?"

"Are your people armed?"

The guard blinked. "No. We've never needed to be."

"Thank you." I didn't explain my question. I knew my intrusion would be mentioned to the planner, and they'd wonder why I was so obsessed with security. I didn't need to give an answer since Mila and I wouldn't return here. I nodded and I walked past him, and I was entirely sure that as I went up the two flights of stairs he watched me on the screen. I rejoined Mila and the planner and made sure to give Mila a convincing kiss for the benefit of the security guard. Her mouth was tight under mine, firm and warm.

We finished the tour, discussed possible booking dates eight months from now, and promised to call back soon.

Then we headed out into the busy Financial District, walked to the car, and drove back toward my bar in the Haight. I told Mila what I'd found, handed her the stolen disc.

"You asked if their guards were armed? I suspect

every date I mention to the planner now, the venue will be booked," Mila said. "I am so disappointed."

"I could kill you," I said.

"What, the wedding is off?" she said in mock surprise.

"I got caught. I had to talk my way out."

"You have gotten lazy and sloppy," she said. She slipped off the diamond engagement ring—I had no idea where she'd gotten it—and put it in her pocket.

"I told you I didn't want to do...*this* anymore."

"Do what?"

"Be your spy, your thief, your hired gun." I kept my hands steady on the wheel. "I have a son now."

"And the reason you have him back is me," she said. "I've given you much and asked for little."

"Mila..."

"Fine. Let's go see your son. And"—she held up the disc I'd stolen—"let's see who our would-be killer is."

My bar in San Francisco—one of thirty plus I own around the world—was called The Select and it wasn't open yet; I'd decided while my son Daniel was here not to open until five in the afternoon. It gave me more time with him. I parked behind the bar in a shared lot and opened the door with a key. The bar itself was silent. Upstairs, I could hear laughter and music and my heart melted a bit. Call me sentimental. I'd fought far too hard to get my son back to ever feel embarrassed by emotion.

Upstairs, in the office/apartment above The Select, my son Daniel, ten months old, was on a blanket, crawling and laughing, while Leonie played with him. I'd been lucky. Leonie hadn't enrolled yet in art school, so she had the time to travel with me, bring Daniel along as I went to several of my bars over the past two weeks: New York, Austin, Boston. We'd flown down from my bar in Vancouver yesterday, at Mila's insistence, because there was a problem.

Mila knelt to tickle Daniel's nose, earned a giggle from him, and then she completely ignored Leonie. Leonie ignored her back. They don't like each other and I'm not entirely sure why. Leonie is not Daniel's mother; she is, well, a nanny of sorts, an art student-turned-forger. She'd lost a lot in her life, and I'd saved Leonie from a criminal syndicate called the Nine Suns. The same syndicate that kidnapped Daniel and his mother, even before he was born, and destroyed my CIA career. Leonie had been good to Daniel and taken care of him when no one else would. She was deeply attached to my son, and so I'd asked her to stay in his life. We'd had a brief fling—under highly stressful circumstances—and were back to being just friends. Leonie had been nothing but perfect with Daniel, but I knew Mila thought I'd made a mistake, asking a former criminal to watch over my son.

I hoped Mila was wrong.

Mila slid the disc into a laptop on the desk.

"Here he is." She pointed. "Dalton Monroe." She clicked with the mouse and a red dot appeared on Monroe, a tall, rangy man in his sixties. He wore a suit and seemed determined to meet and greet everyone in the room, which was at least two hundred people.

In his right hand was a glass of bourbon.

"It's no easy thing to poison a man in front of two hundred witnesses," Mila said. "I admire the nerve."

I picked up Daniel and sat next to her. He squirmed a little on my lap, eager to watch the red dot, like it was a game. Leonie stretched out on Daniel's blanket and began to sketch in a pad aimlessly.

"Two hundred people, but it gets pared down pretty fast," I said. "Look. He has a bodyguard near him. Maybe five admirers in a knot around him. Beyond that, a few people watching him directly, angling for their chance to talk to him. Maybe fifteen, at any given second, looking at him. And looking at that same moment at the poisoner."

She accelerated the feed; forty minutes into the video, Dalton Monroe stumbled badly, clearly ill. He dropped the bourbon glass. The bodyguard hurried him out, Monroe smiling, waving off concerns from the other guests. He had then been taken to a private medical clinic, where it was diagnosed that he'd ingested a nonfatal dose of digitalis. The press were told he'd simply become ill at the party and had to leave. Dalton Monroe was worth a billion dollars and did not care to have it known that someone tried to poison him at a reception celebrating his latest business acquisition, a local software company he'd bought to fold into his empire.

"He's Round Table, right?" I asked Mila. The Round Table. My secret benefactors. A network of resource-rich and powerful people who want to be a force for good in the world, behind the scenes. They have Mila as their face to me; they gave me the bars to run, a web of safe houses around the world.

They helped me get back my son. I know little about them, except that they started off as a CIA experiment that finally broke free to pursue their own agenda.

"Yes," Mila said. "Someone tried to kill a Round Table member. I want you to find out who."

"I said I'd run the bars for you all. Nothing more." I settled Daniel on my knee.

"Sam, perhaps Leonie wouldn't mind taking Daniel for a walk," Mila said. "The day is so lovely."

"I don't mind." Leonie was normally chatty with me, but always quiet around Mila.

"No, would you leave him, please?" I got down on the blanket with him, wriggled fingers at him. I felt like I never got to see him enough, even when he was traveling with me.

"Fine," Leonie said. "I'll go get an iced coffee." I thought she already had the ice in her voice. She left. Mila stood at the window while I played and made bubbling noises at Daniel, and I figured she waited until she saw Leonie on the street below.

"You need to be nicer to her," I said. "You can trust her to keep her mouth shut about the Round Table." And I knew we could—we'd given Leonie a far safer, brighter new life.

"I will never trust her."

"I do, end of discussion."

"I understand you want to be with your son," Mila said. "I do. But the bars, a very good livelihood for you, were not free. There was a price attached."

"I'm not ungrateful. But I'm also not a police detective."

"The Round Table never wants the police involved. If this poisoning attempt on Monroe was because he is a member of the Table, then we must know without involving the police. Felix will help you." Felix was the manager of The Select. The senior managers of my bars know about the Round Table and were recruited to help with their work.

"What about you?"

Daniel grabbed my wiggling fingers and laughed. Sweetest sound ever.

"I have to return to Los Angeles tomorrow on other business. I'm sure you can handle this."

"And what do I do when I find out who tried to poison Monroe?"

"Give me their name. Then the Round Table will decide how to proceed." She got up from the laptop, gave me a smile dimmer than her fake bridal one. "Don't pretend you're not itching for some action. A man like you doesn't like to sit and play with a baby on a blanket for long."

"Actually, I like nothing better." I made a face at Daniel. "Don't we? Don't we like playing on the blanket?" Daniel concurred with laughter but then gave me a rather serious frown, as though a more detailed answer required thought.

Mila didn't smile. "I know you love Daniel. But I also know you, Sam. You cannot sit at a desk; you cannot play on a floor. You need something more."

I looked up at her. "No, I don't."

"Sam. Send Leonie and Daniel home to New Orleans. They've been traveling with you for two weeks; a baby needs routine and order, not bars and airplanes. I'll even give Leonie and Daniel a ride to the airport, get them their tickets. Then you go home when you've cleared up this little case for me, yes?"

I was a former undercover CIA agent, not a detective, but I nodded. Anything to get her to go. If I found Monroe's poisoner, fine. If I didn't, then maybe I could make a new deal with the Round Table. One that kept me out of trouble. One that let me play on blankets. Then I could go home to New Orleans for a while. I had to find a way to make this balance work.

"That planner will be so disappointed that we're not getting married there," I said. I don't even know why I mentioned it. The words felt odd in my mouth, and I was glad Leonie wasn't there, even though we were just friends now.

Mila crooked a smile at me. "Maybe if you find our poisoner," she said, "I'll throw you a big party."

ABOUT THE AUTHOR

Jeff Abbott is the *New York Times*–bestselling, award-winning author of thirteen novels. His books include the Sam Capra thrillers *Adrenaline* and *The Last Minute*, as well as the standalone novels *Panic, Fear,* and *Collision. The Last Minute* won an International Thriller Writers award, and Jeff is also a three-time nominee for the Edgar award. He lives in Austin with his family. You can visit his website at www.jeffabbott.com.